# THE PARKERS AT SALTRAM

£3

# The Parkers at SALTRAM

## 1769–89

*Everyday Life in an Eighteenth-century House*

Ronald Fletcher

British Broadcasting Corporation

SALTRAM HOUSE is the property of The National Trust. Thanks are due to the Trust and the Curator of Saltram, Patrick Dawes, for the co-operation and assistance given to the BBC throughout the time when the story of the Parkers was recreated for television and this book.

Saltram is open to the public April to October (full information from The National Trust). It lies on the east bank of the River Plym, 2 miles west of Plympton and $3\frac{1}{2}$ miles east of Plymouth City Centre, between the A38 and A379 main roads.

The television programmes *The Parkers at Saltram* were originally shown in 1969, and repeated on BBC-1, October to December 1970.

The colour photographs are by Roy Smith A.I.I.P. of Tom Molland Ltd, Plymouth, assisted by David Huntley. Those opposite pages 72 and 152 are reproduced by permission of The National Trust, the others were specially taken for the BBC. The black and white photographs taken at Saltram at the time of the television programmes are also by Roy Smith.

Acknowledgment for permission to reproduce illustrations is also due to Robert Chapman, The Courtauld Institute of Art, The General Post Office (Crown Copyright), History Today, The Henry E. Huntington Library and Art Gallery, The Mansell Collection, The National Gallery, The National Portrait Gallery, Radio Times Hulton Picture Library, The Royal Society of Arts, The Trustees of the British Museum and The Trustees of Sir John Soane's Museum.

First published 1970
© Ronald Fletcher 1970

Published by the British Broadcasting Corporation
35 Marylebone High Street, London W1M 4AA

SBN 563 10207 1

Printed in England by
Jolly and Barber Limited, Rugby, Warwickshire

# CONTENTS

|  |  |
|---|---|
| PREFACE | 7 |
| 1 LOVE AND INHERITANCE | 11 |
| ...to this Delightful Place | |
| 2 MASTER BEDROOM AND MORNING ROOM | 27 |
| the New Master | |
| 3 KITCHEN AND EATING ROOM | 43 |
| High Society above and below stairs | |
| 4 THE LIBRARY | 59 |
| every Distance and Dimension of the World... | |
| 5 THE GREAT ROOM | 73 |
| the Great Age of Candlelight | |
| 6 THE STABLE BLOCK | 90 |
| 'Saltram': a name on the Turf | |
| 7 CHINESE CHIPPENDALE BEDROOM | 106 |
| take what you want, says God: take it – and Pay for it | |
| 8 NURSERY AND SCHOOLROOM | 123 |
| the young Parkers | |

9 THE RED VELVET    145
DRAWING ROOM
*times of Contentment ... perhaps the happiest times of all*

10 LEAVE-TAKING    167
*the lead coffin trundling over the West Country road ...*

EPILOGUE    187
*a New World ... the momentous events of War and Peace*

NOTES    195

BOOKS FOR FURTHER    210
READING
*with details of museums and eighteenth-century houses*

INDEX
    215

*The end-papers of this book are reproductions of the Chinese wallpapers which still decorate Theresa's rooms. The paper at the front of the book is from her Dressing Room; that at the back is from the connected Chippendale Bedroom. (see Chapter 7)*

# Preface

*The Parkers at Saltram* was originally a television essay in social history. This book has grown out of it.

The basic idea for the programmes, which originated with the producer Victor Poole, was to create a picture of English society in the late eighteenth century not by undertaking a formal sociological analysis, or by adopting a general panoramic view, but by telling the story of one family and its day-to-day life: dwelling, in turn, on the activities which took place in each room of their home – kitchen, library, bedrooms, drawing room – so that through these could be seen the conditions and characteristics of society at large. Saltram was the house which captivated us, and so 'The Parkers at Saltram' became the centre of our story.

Many contributions went into the making of the series. Every effort was made to ensure the authenticity of the materials used. All the prints, for example, were of the period, and were carefully researched by Barry Bright. The same was true of the actual objects: coaches, fans, snuff-boxes, dolls, surgical instruments – for which Iris Furlong combed the country and its museums. Costumes were exquisitely reproduced by Olive Harris. Family letters and account books were indefatigably sought out by Giles Oakley. Even the actual Marriage Settlement of John and Theresa Parker was unearthed: a real prize. The production itself involved an unusual array of skills. It was realised with the aid of an Outside Broadcast Unit headed by Jack Belasco and directed by Ray Colley. All the members of the team – floor managers, camera-men, lighting and sound technicians, electricians and riggers – worked with a care and enthusiasm impossible adequately to describe, despite the many difficulties of moving from room to room in the house.

There was, however, a wider aspect of our work. In the present debate as to the quality of television and the directions in which it might go, it is important to see that television offers qualities of excellence in education which no other medium can provide. The social life of a period can be recreated in a many-dimensioned way which is simply not possible in school room or lecture theatre. A richness of historical detail can be presented in an intellectually exact – yet in a living – way. And this, in quite a distinctive manner, can be productive of original knowledge. The people who comment in these following chapters on the life of their times were, until this series began, dead pieces of paper in long-forgotten files. Television has brought them to life again. A short time ago, such a selection of letters might have become a little-known volume in a reference library. Now – they are living voices for all to hear. The curiously entrenched distinction between education and entertainment needs, clearly, to be killed stone dead. In the re-creation and re-juvenation of education in our time, television is no poor relation to schools, colleges and universities, but a medium which can produce a new richness for all.

When writing the scripts for the series, I had to build them about the available visual material, and they were arranged in relation to the over-all treatment of the producer. The order of the programmes also had a viewing audience in mind. In writing the book, I have kept as closely as possible to this original form, but the flow of the story and the sequence of family events have dictated a slightly different ordering of the chapters. Also, in view of the many letters asking for further information, I have added more details about the family and the period, and also some notes on the chapters. These indicate other dimensions of the historical context within which our relatively simple story of the Parkers was couched.

A word must be said about the illustrations which include actors. The series was not in any sense a dramatization. Actors were introduced only to give a living impression that the rooms and the things in them were being used, to establish an identity and continuity of the characters, and, quite literally, to exhibit the costumes. In the book, it is the same.

It is pleasing, finally, to say that the letters of the Parkers appear with the consent of the Earl of Morley, the present head of the family. Clearly, this is not purely a history of the Parkers. Even so, though we began it as an essay in social history, our feelings were soon engaged by the Parkers as people. As we read their letters, their characters seemed to emerge and take over the story from us.

John Parker – who could never resist his cards and horses, and who, despite his Oxford education and life in London as a Member of Parliament, still loved nothing more than to mess about at home and roam on horseback through the fields and woods of Devon, and who never lost his broad Devonshire dialect; Theresa – his wife – a charming, delicate, sensitive woman, artistically and socially accomplished, but most deeply attached to her family and children; Nanny – her sister – placed by circumstances so firmly at the very heart of the family . . . and the colourful friends who surrounded them: Georgiana, the Duchess of Devonshire, Sir Joshua Reynolds . . . Soon, they themselves were telling their own story.

We left Saltram with a warm appreciation of what the Parkers had been, and of what – in the full glow of the Enlightenment, and on the brink of our own mechanical age – they had made. Like all worthwhile creative ventures, the making of *The Parkers at Saltram* brought more to life in us, and in itself, than we were at all aware of when we began it. This book is a grateful record.

*Ronald Fletcher*
*Suffolk, May 1970*

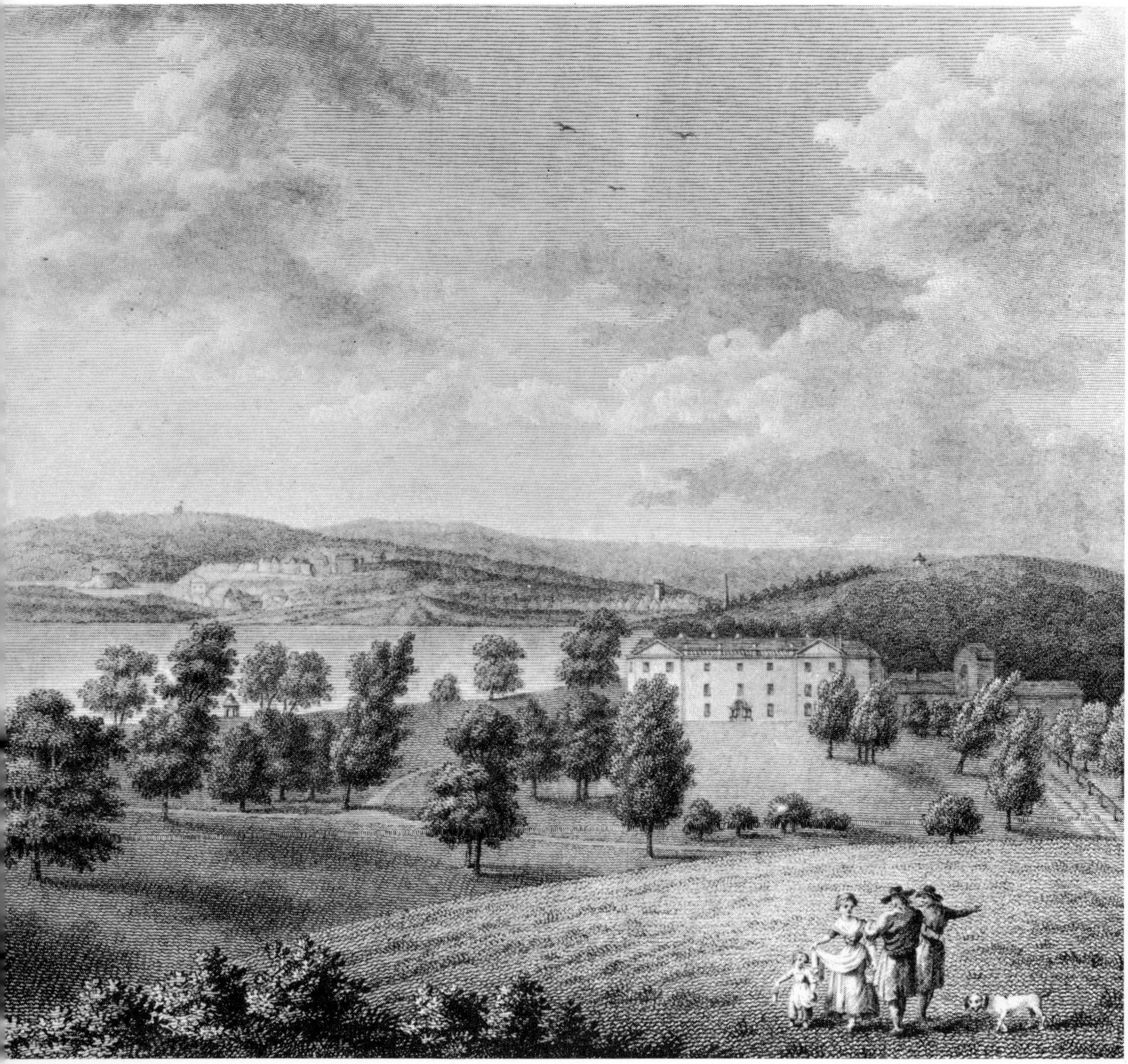

# I LOVE AND INHERITANCE

## ... *to this Delightful Place*

It was here, to Saltram: standing simply, gracefully, on the banks of the River Plym in Devonshire, that Theresa Parker came as a young bride, just three life-times ago. Her first letters to her father – who was old now, and frail, and was to die only a year later – and to her brothers Thomas and 'Fritz', were full of the sheer pleasure which she found in the house itself and in the graciousness and attention with which Mr Parker (her husband) and everyone else received her:

... On Monday came thro' charming country to this delightful place. I could not help thinking how happy you would all have been to have seen the manner in which I was entertained, French Horns playing all dinner time and again in the wood in the evening when the guns were fired, but I will not say any more about it, how much I was pleased, as Mr Parker will very likely see this letter and may fancy I am complimenting him.[1]

Only two hundred years ago, Theresa was expressing her delight; yet this was before the American Revolution had startled all the crowned and aristocratic heads throughout Europe, and before the French Revolution had, quite literally, chopped some of them off. It was two months before Napoleon was born – let alone before he pressed his way round Spain, Egypt, Austria, Moscow – blowing ancient authority to bits and having the old rulers dancing pathetically at the end of his own strings.

It was before the smoke was rising too thickly from factory chimneys, before the country was filled with pit-wheels and steam, black polluted streets and the clanking of engines: those dark satanic mills which Blake saw rising to suffocate the human spirit. It was before all this, in 1769, that Theresa came as a young wife to a west country summer and the 'golden age' of English agrarian society.

\*

People sometimes say, rather jokingly, about a rural community: 'The only culture they possess is *agri-*

culture'. But they could well save their condescension – for agriculture is one of the greatest elements of culture that men have created, a combination of arts by which they have re-shaped nature as well as earned their bread, and most other things have stemmed from it.

When Theresa came to her new home, agriculture was actively changing. 'Landscape plotted and pieced; fold, fallow and plough . . .' the shape of the English countryside as we have all come to know and love it, was then in the making. New methods, new patterns of crops, new implements, were vitalising husbandry. Estates were growing larger and were more thoughtfully worked. Wastes – of heather, furze, moors, forests, marshes – were being enclosed and cultivated. Theresa was soon writing to her elder brother:

We are in the midst of our Harvest, and amongst the many improvements you will find at this place those in farming are none of the least. The whole Down that you may remember between Boringdon and Cann Quarry, besides two hundred acres of the same sort of furze Brake, is now covered with all sorts of corn, and affords a prospect of Plenty that is really very striking.[2]

The joy of seeing fields of corn and barley waving, shining in the wind; of herds and flocks in rich pastures; of tree-shaded meadows and streams; the joy of quiet fishing in pond and river, of coursing hares on a long summer evening; the country habit still had England by the heart – and a deeply satisfying and comely habit it was in many ways. But not by any means entirely.

The making of the new agriculture also had its anguished side. The land was filled not only with new crops and implements, but with a growing number of paupers, beggars and vagrants. The country habit had them by the heart, too. It fastened on their hearts with a cruel, hungry, diseased, and – all too often – a fatal grasp.

But Theresa, on that first homecoming, saw only the Devonshire summer, and the great house – which captivated her at once, as it did all who came to see it; and she was taken, in fact, on various pleasure trips: on a 'pretty boat' on the Plymouth waters, and on long drives through the countryside.

\*

The man who brought her here – the man who lies right at the heart of our story – was John Parker, master of

Saltram. He was much involved in politics, a Member of Parliament for the County, and had a wide experience of life in London. But Sir Joshua Reynolds[3], who was a close friend and lived nearby, placed him in his portrait where, it seems, he most liked to be: with his feet in the leafmould, his back against a five-barred gate, and his gun in the crook of his arm; with the comfortable feeling of outdoor clothes about him, and his hair not bewigged and powdered beyond all sanity*.

Whatever the complexities into which society led him, he seems always to have remained pungent, ironical, his feet still firmly down to earth on his native heath. The Duchess of Devonshire – the lovely, lively Georgiana – who was herself something of a 'card': provoking, likeable and notorious throughout society for her readiness to cock a snook at too much sophistication – had a decided liking for him.

We went this evening to Mr Parker's. Lady Elizabeth was, as I expected, enchanted with the beauty of the place. We walked ourselves tired, and I had the pleasure of finding Parker as dirty, as comical and talking as bad English as ever. There is certainly a degree of humour about him that makes one laugh, he is so short, and always talking in a strain of irony.[4]

He could also behave . . . unusually; according to his inclination! Theresa once wrote to the younger of her brothers, Frederick, who had the family nick-name of 'Fritz':

We have here incessant violent rains which confines us all to the House except Mr Parker – who rides in the midst of it from Morning till Night.

A gun, a horse, fields and woods to ride in – day or night, rain or shine – these were the things for Mr Parker. There was something wayward as well as definite and decided about him. Still, there must have been other things too. Theresa – whose God-Mother was Maria Theresa of Austria, wife of the Holy Roman Emperor (amongst other things) – was a cultured, sensitive woman, with delicacy of perception as well as thoughtfulness in judgment. She took marriage seriously; especially the personal aspects of it; and looked for qualities of character, and even sensibility to beauty, in such a match. When, for

*see portrait facing p.33.

*Thomas, Lord Grantham: Theresa's elder brother. This portrait hangs in the Library at Saltram.*

example, she was later asked by Thomas – now Lord Grantham and head of the family – about the marriage expectations of Fritz, she was as realistic as anyone else of her day, but quite emphatic in laying importance upon qualities other than those of property and income:

> I will endeavour to execute Fritz's Commission as well as I can, but at present do not know whom to recommend. There is a little Miss Crop with a large fortune that is very pretty, but no further. There is a Miss Duncombe to spare (one of Lady Radnor's daughters) there is a dismal Miss Griesly, Miss Ellarways and many more that I should be sorry to see Mrs Frederick Robinson. I should advise him not to think of so much as £60,000 and to study nothing but his happiness; he says nothing of Beauty – which I don't understand; indeed I must talk to him fully upon the whole subject before I allow him to think of a wife.[5]

Sisterly concern, indeed! Clearly, Mr Parker must have passed tests other than those of hunting, shooting and fishing, before Theresa had decided to marry him, and, in fact, the two of them were to work closely and happily together in many ways.

As always, however, the circumstances within which they were to live had been shaped largely by others, and a long time ago. Saltram, the house – and John Parker its master – had had eventful lives before Theresa arrived on the scene.

\*

Saltram was bought originally by John's grandfather, George Parker, who was Member of Parliament for Plymouth for a short time, and in whose hands the building up of the family estate – which had gone on over many generations – was brought to a certain substantial culmination. But before he died in 1743, he had time to do little more than enclose the house within 220 acres of deerpark; with a licence from the Crown which secured '... for himself and his heirs the said closes for ever ...' and which protected it from all unwanted intruders from the surrounding countryside. Penalties were prescribed for those:

> ... who shall presume to enter the said Park or warren for the purpose of driving, hunting, fowling or therein taking, chasing or disturbing stags does or game or other wild animals or birds etc. without the will and licence of the said G. Parker etc.[6]

Only in 1743, when John's father inherited the estate, was it occupied by the family. John's mother, Lady Catherine, was daughter of the Earl of Poulett: a woman of judgement, taste, and energy; indeed, to judge by the letters written about her – 'proud and wilful'. Saltram was really her creation. It was she who began the alterations to the house at a time when her husband was seriously ill; planning to make it her home after his death. But he recovered, and decided to make the house the seat of the family. They moved in together – from Boringdon, their previous home – in 1743.

In those days, Saltram was only an old Tudor Manor House and it was this that Lady Catherine transformed.

*Lady Catherine – still looking down from the panels of the Staircase Hall – as 'proud and wilful' as some had described her.*

The Tudor kitchen with its great, roomy fireplace, the small sheltered quadrangle of Tudor brick, and the old staircase tower, were left at the heart of the house, and it was about them that the new south, east and west wings were added. Some parts of the house were especially marked by all the qualities of Lady Catherine's work and judgment. In the Entrance Hall the stucco ceiling and the detailed panels over the doorways were Italian and of very fine quality; and the fireplace was given a carved stone chimney-piece – probably at the hands of Thomas Carter the elder, who was working from about 1735 to 1766. Decorative designs were carried through from the Entrance Hall into the large, imposing Staircase Hall, and there the quality of the woodwork, especially, had to be seen and touched to be believed. Proud and wilful? Perhaps. What is certain is that Lady Catherine insisted upon the highest excellence in all the materials, the art, the craftsmanship, which went into the work done for her.

Already by the 1750s the beautiful decorations, the new proportions, had turned Saltram into a well-known country house.

\*

It was a fit setting for the story of John and Theresa: a story of personal love and arranged inheritance.

Marriage and controlled inheritance – the passing on of the estate, intact, from father to elder son – were, in those days, the essential institutions by which great estates were built up and continued. They had become so complex as to be the professional business of lawyers. Marriage, far from being a small matter of personal affection in society, was – on the contrary – an institution right at the heart of property, power and politics. By the building up of fortunes and the making of marriage settlements, nothing less than a reconstitution of the English ruling classes was taking place. The great landlords were still the ruling power of England, but, by the avenues of wealth and marriage, they were becoming an 'open' ruling class.

Eminent men who built up fortunes in politics, the professions, trade, manufacture, were all, by the mechanisms of marriage and inheritance, able to merge with the ranks of the landed aristocracy. English society in the eighteenth century was not merely one of landowners and peasants. In all the complexities of social actuality, it became very finely graded. Blackstone, the lawyer, for example, distinguished forty grades of status[7].

This system of family settlements – which fixed the portions of the younger children, any annual income (pin-money) of the wife, and her jointure (the provision for her widowhood) – had, however, its troubles. It doomed younger sons to a feckless career-adventuring: seeking a place in Church, or army, or political office. It doomed many daughters to ill-provided spinsterdom. It also enabled, perhaps even encouraged, an elder son to borrow lavishly with full certainty of inheriting later. His estate, when inherited, might well be encumbered with jointure-provisions, portions, mortgages and heavy personal debts from the start.

The marriage of John and Theresa was no exception. Theresa was the daughter of the first Lord Grantham, born whilst he was ambassador to Maria Theresa and negotiating with no less a person than Frederick the Great. She brought wealth and titled connection into an already substantial and well-connected estate; one which could give her the station and security to which she was accustomed.

Their marriage settlement, dated 13th May 1769, was a large document of many pages, painstakingly inscribed by quill-pen on thick serviceable parchment, and the signatures of John Parker, Theresa Robinson, her father (Grantham), and Thomas Robinson (her elder brother) were set against the heavy seals. The language was the involved language of the law – but it made provisions for the payment of Theresa's dowry, and for any children of their marriage. With the settlement was also a marriage bond which had the advantage of being written in language which all could understand:

Whereas a marriage is agreed upon and intended with the

*Dated the 13th May 1769*

*John Parker Esqr*
*with*
*The Honourable Miss*
*Theresa Robinson*

*Marriage Settlement*

*The very large marriage settlement was folded as small as possible (the folds can be seen in the flat document opposite) leaving only the title and date showing. The date: 13th May 1769 can be seen quite clearly. Theresa wrote her first letter from Saltram thirteen days later. John Parker – Grantham (Theresa's father) – Theresa Robinson – Thomas Robinson (her elder brother): the signatures over the heavy seals are quite plain. The document is approximately two feet square.*

permission of Almighty God soon to be had and solemnised between the said John Parker and the Honourable Theresa Robinson, spinster . . .[8]

So the simpler wording went on until it came to the direct statement of the marriage portion – £6,000 payable on completion of the marriage, and, in addition:

. . . six thousand pounds to be paid to the said John Parker by the said Thomas Lord Grantham one year *after his decease* with interest for the same at the rate of four per cent per annum, to be computed *from* his decease, and that for the more effectual receiving the payment of the said sum of six thousand pounds – they should enter into a bond or obligation to the said John Parker to the agreed sum of twelve thousand pounds.[8]

Mr Parker did, in fact, begin to keep a small notebook in which he entered records of the payments received in accordance with the terms of the settlement. These were sometimes regular, sometimes irregular. On 5th February, 1774, he recorded the receipt of £240 – one year's interest; on 10th October, 1776, £480 – two year's interest; and on 17th August, 1780, he entered the receipt of £3,040. John Parker, however, was not the most regular of men in financial matters. Money was for use and spending, not for too much exercise in the accounting of it, and there were many blank pages in his book.

He too, of course, had much to offer Theresa in return. When his father died in 1768, he inherited Saltram and other estates, and even the way of this was rather dramatic. It was no simple matter of a cheque from an Executor. On his death, his father left, besides the estate, 135 bags of cash amounting to some £30,000, together with £2,000 in Bankers' notes and bills, but this was distributed all over the house, in the strangest places, all of which were indicated in a carefully written note which he left.

For example: cash 'in the bags from number 1, to number 68' were 'placed in the closet in Lady Cath[es] Room: £9,500 14 0'. . . . . . . . .

18

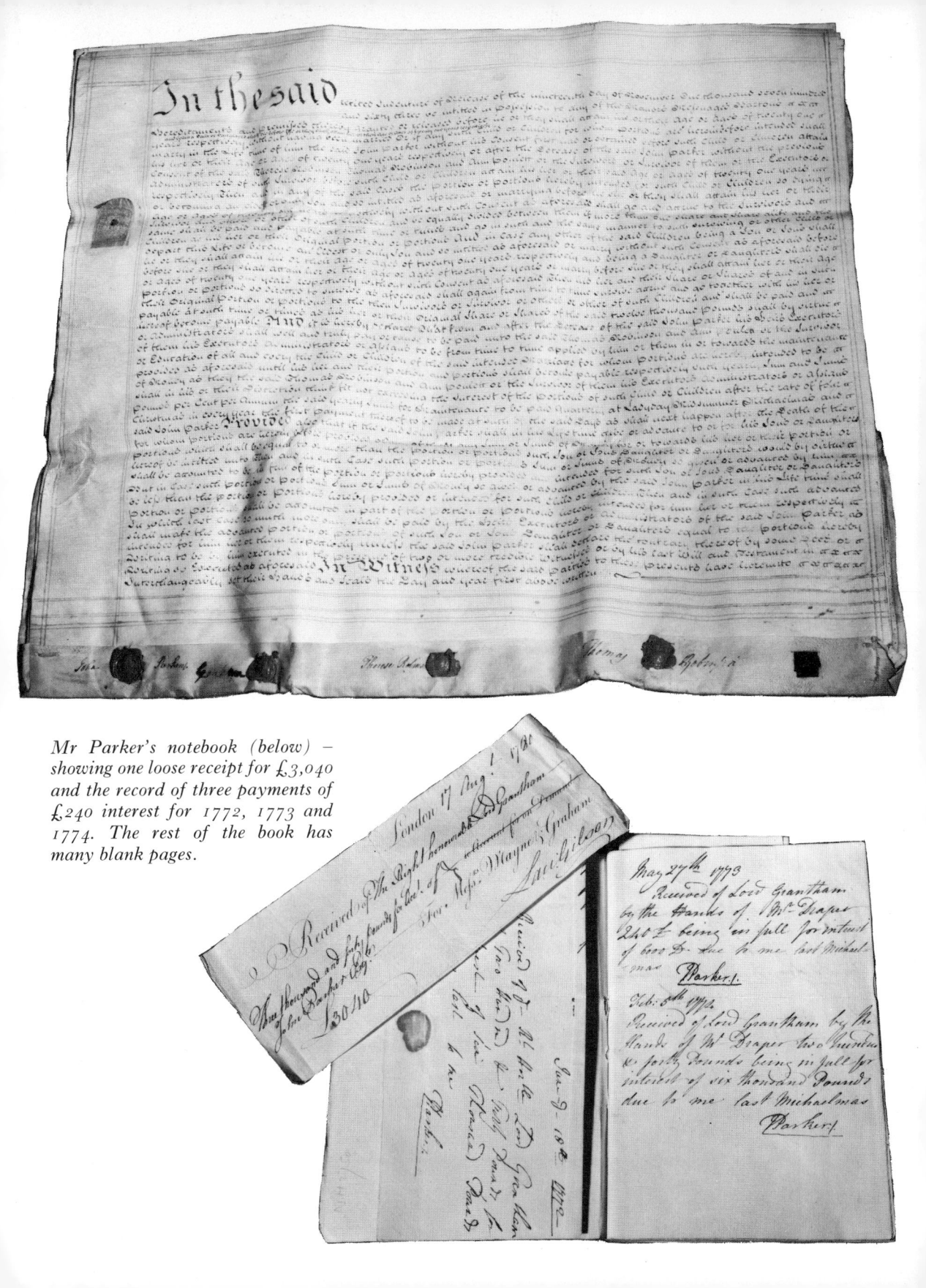

*Mr Parker's notebook (below) – showing one loose receipt for £3,040 and the record of three payments of £240 interest for 1772, 1773 and 1774. The rest of the book has many blank pages.*

Some was left in a mahogany bookcase, and bags number 115 to 135 were '. . . placed in the Wainscott Toilet,' and contained £3,928 16 6.

Though left in bags, and in cash, the records of the sums in each place of storage were remarkably precise – even to a sixpence.

The size of this inheritance might be roughly estimated by comparing it with the average workman's wage in Devon at the time – which was about 7 shillings a week; £18 a year.

\*

Much had happened to Mr Parker himself, however, before he inherited Saltram. He had been up at Oxford, where he was particularly friendly with Lord Shelburne, and it was through Shelburne's influence that he became a Member of Parliament – at first for Bodmin, for a year (in 1761), and afterwards for the County of Devonshire. During the sixties he enjoyed a wide experience of life in London, and politically, he was associated with the Duke of Newcastle and Lord Bute who, after the accession of George III, thought of him as a likely supporter of the King. Politics aside, he enjoyed a varied social life. He was, for example, a close friend of Sir Joshua Reynolds. They shot together in the country and dined frequently in London, and, with Shelburne, they mingled with those people who were beginning to patronise Robert Adam for the decoration of their houses. They knew many of the colourful characters who enlivened London society at the time. Even Dr Johnson – that great, scarred, snuff-coated, large-wigged, black-stockinged lump of bad manners and learning with his dirty fists and a laugh like a rhinoceros – visited Saltram during these years[9]. London had much to offer, then as always. Whether good, bad, trivial, profound – it was, at least, a colourful city: varying between extravagance and ennui. Horace Walpole, one of the great spectators of the age – if seeming, sometimes, rather self-consciously so – described the typical year in this way:

The Parliament opens; everybody is bribed and the new establishment is conceived to be composed of adamant. November passes with two or three self-murders and a new play. Christmas arrives; everybody goes out of town; and a riot happens in one of the theatres. The Parliament meets again; taxes are warmly

*Mr Parker knew London well. This is John Adam Street showing the house of the Royal Society of Arts. Its members then included Sir Joshua Reynolds, Boswell, Goldsmith, Pitt, and even Mr Chippendale – maker of mahogany furniture.*

opposed; and some citizen makes his fortune by a subscription. The Opposition languishes; balls and assemblies begin; some master and miss begin to get together; and talked of, and give occasion for forty more matches being invented; an unexpected debate starts up at the end of the session that makes more noise than anything that was designed to make a noise, and subsides again in a new peerage or two. Ranelagh opens and Vauxhall; one produces a scandal, and t'other a drunken quarrel. People separate, some to Tunbridge, and some to all the other horse races in England; and so the year comes again to October.[10]

The yearly round, the common task – or so it sounded; but some saw other sides of the great city. One innocent Scots clergyman – who had come on horse-back all the way from Clunie, in Perthshire, just out of interest – saw Mammon in the shining lights of Vauxhall Gardens and the streets round about:

Curious attachments formed here. Vast numbers of ladies of pleasure. Good Heavens! What prostitution and corruption prevail in this city! What a contrast this to the Lakes of Cumberland, and the Caves of Yorkshire! Do not many of these strumpets seem modest? and are not many of them even of an angelic form? But alas! It is plainly nothing else but outward semblance; within all is vice and rottenness. And these beautiful female *children*, what have they to do here at this time of the night, or rather of the morning, when they ought to sleep in their beds at home . . . How exceedingly contemptible are the lights of Vauxhall! Enough of it. Let us quit this scene![11]

Adultery and gambling, [said another,] were the rage of the day; they were the chivalry of fashionable life, in which there was the same emulation among the great as in the jousts and tournaments of the medieval period.

Though from the depths of the west country, John Parker was a man of Metropolitan experience; a member of those propertied classes – relatively small in number, and relatively well known to each other – who were drawn together from all over the country into the centre of the London season. He was far from being the kind of country gentleman caricatured by Mr Addison as the 'Fox-hunter'[12] – who thought there had been no good weather since the Revolution; who loved his dog dearly because it had once bitten a Dissenter; and was strongly inclined to the view that witches were really Presbyterians in another guise. He had a wide experience of fashionable life in both country and town.

*The Orangery at Saltram. An orangery was a common, fashionable feature of the great houses of the time.*

He had also been previously married. When he was thirty, he had married Frances Hort – the daughter of an Archbishop and the cousin of his friend Shelburne. Together, they had set out on the Grand Tour of Europe; but whilst abroad, tragically, she had died.

When, a few years afterwards, he inherited Saltram, and he and Theresa were married, John Parker was already, therefore, a man of mature experience, of substantial property and responsibility, and established in politics. He was thirty-five. Theresa was ten years younger – but, despite her relative youthfulness, a woman of mature judgement. Together, with a shared enjoyment and enthusiasm, they gave their minds to the reshaping of Saltram; to continuing the improvements to the house which Lady Catherine had so substantially begun.

Their own interest lay chiefly in certain internal alterations: the making of a great Drawing Room, on which they were to spend something like £10,000; the improvement of the Library – which was later changed into an Eating Room; and on internal decorations, and the building up of a good collection of paintings. Even so, there was also a good deal of outside building. The stable block was completed. The 'Castle', a pleasant summer retreat designed (in its interior) by Robert Adam; the delightful Orangery; the greenhouse; and a new Stag entrance and Lodges; were all planned and begun. It was a busy and enjoyable time. Only two years after their marriage, Theresa wrote to Fritz:

The Hot Houses, Kitchen Gardens are just finished. The Castle, the other lodges and a Green House employ the next year, and after that we turn farmer and make such improvements in Land, Estates, and Ploughs that Posterity shall bless the day.... [And, one year later:] All our building draws very near a conclusion ... though a new Eating Room is thought of at a distance.[13]

In all this they had the continual advice of friends in London (like Shelburne), of Theresa's brothers – Grantham and Fritz – and of Sir Joshua Reynolds who quickly came to have a warm affection and admiration for Theresa, and visited the house regularly. Through these friends, they came to employ Robert Adam and the various artists who worked for him. Saltram soon became known as one of the most delightful houses in the country.

\*

During these early years, in all these many activities, Theresa and Mr Parker settled happily into a regular pattern of life among an affectionate and very varied circle of friends. Some aspects of their life were typical of those in their station, many were likeable, and some amusing.

Theresa did not share her husband's enthusiasm for leaf-mould, horses, and riding in the drenching rain, but, nonetheless, she was happiest if 'Company' could be kept within very limited bounds. She did not think much of the County 'Company' either. She wrote, almost with a sigh of resignation:

We expect a good deal of Company this week, Sir Thomas Acland, Sir F. Chichester, and half the County. You may guess how agreeable it will be; how far I shall think so, I may as well keep to myself.[14]

And she confided in Fritz:

The worst of Spring in London is that the whole County of Devonshire come to town. Sir John Chichester just arrived – such a log of wood . . . Don't betray me about the County, but really they are for bad, though to anyone else I must only speak of them as worthy respectable Country Gentlemen.[15]

It was comical, too, how she and her sister Anne, who was affectionately called 'Nanny' by everyone in the family, with whom she was very close, and who stayed at Saltram very frequently, came to form and share the same impressions of particular people. It is obvious, for example, that Montague Parker – John's brother, who lived on the smaller estate of Whiteway nearby – was infinitely more rooted in the earth and its animals than he. He seldom 'shone in conversation', said Theresa, 'but in Woodcock season'. And Nanny wrote to Fritz:

There is nobody here at present except Mr Montague. He is as great a Nimrod as ever, he does nothing but hunt now, he goes out every day. They are very extraordinary hares for they breed after they are killed, for by his account, if he kills a brace by night it is generally two by the morning. But pray don't take any notice of what I say about him for he is really very civil to me.[16]

Montague, in short, was obviously a bare-faced liar when it came to hunting; or perhaps, more kindly, an exaggerator? With him, clearly, it was always the *biggest* – whether it was caught or got away – but he was an amiable man it seems, for all that.

*Montague – John Parker's brother – who could not only tell a tall story, but also insist upon it. This portrait by Sir Joshua Reynolds, hangs in the Morning Room (see opposite p. 152).*

Theresa also fully shared Mr Parker's hectic life, divided between London and Devon, and enjoyed visits to the race-courses, the theatre, and the Pleasure Gardens from time to time. They rented a London house in Sackville Street, and some of Theresa's letters from there pictured the kind of life they led. Members of Parliament, even then, obviously had their late-night sittings. In March of 1772, Theresa wrote:

The Royal Marriage Bill has occasioned two late Days this week, one till three o'clock the other between 1 and 2 in the morning, today it comes over again and is expected to be later than ever, Monday the same.[17]

And Mr Parker obviously continued his card-playing club life in London:

Mr Parker likes to play his game at Whist at Boodles almost every evening so that I have nothing else to do ... the play ... sometimes uses him well, and sometimes ill.[18]

Sometimes, however, there were parties of a different kind, like that given by Lord Stanley:

There were parties dispersed all over the Gardens, some dancing, some singing, some swinging between the trees and in short everything in a Watteau style and had the prettiest effect imaginable. The company danced in a very long and magnificent room prepared for the occasion and when Supper was ready Curtains drew up at each end and in the middle opening other rooms filled with Tables very handsomely furnished for fourteen or twenty people to sit down to each. Festoon of real flowers between the trees . . . and everything you can conceive in Fairy Tables was seen there.[19]

London, clearly, had some charms rather more delicate than those of Vauxhall.

In many other ways, the life of Theresa and John Parker at Saltram and in London quickly deepened into a mutual sensitivity and concern, and an enjoyed partnership in their many activities: in sickness and in health, in private and in social life, in artistic and more material concerns. This was strongly evident in their approach to their children. Three years after coming to Saltram, Theresa was expecting her first child. Grantham had chaffed her in a letter: 'Children are a plague, what say you?' She replied:

I cannot answer that paragraph in your letter by saying your observation is very just . . . I must own I look upon them in the same light that I do every near and tender connection, as a great addition of Pleasure and Happiness affording a proportionable degree of Care and Pain – I think the want of them would be a real evil, and am willing to run the risk, trusting that no particular misfortune will make a larger share of the latter prevail.[20]

Gay, responsive to all the liveliness and fashion of society, Theresa nonetheless took life, and marriage, and close personal ties very seriously, and there was always a certain touch of nobility about her. The birth was, in fact, very difficult, but soon the dangers were over, and Grantham was writing to congratulate her:

I know you suffered, but behaved as you always do. A boy too! It adds to the happiness . . . A blessing in a family it certainly is, a son extends our worldly Views and Prospects, tying thus the Bond of domestic dependence . . . God bless him, and give him the fine Spirit and Temper of his Parents, give him health and manly beauty that results from it, and may we all live to see him happy and studying to make you and us so.[21]

A son and heir.

The small family was established. The continuity of the large family line was secure. Saltram was being transformed into a country house of note: but now not that alone . . . Now, its nature and tradition as a family home was also being deepened.

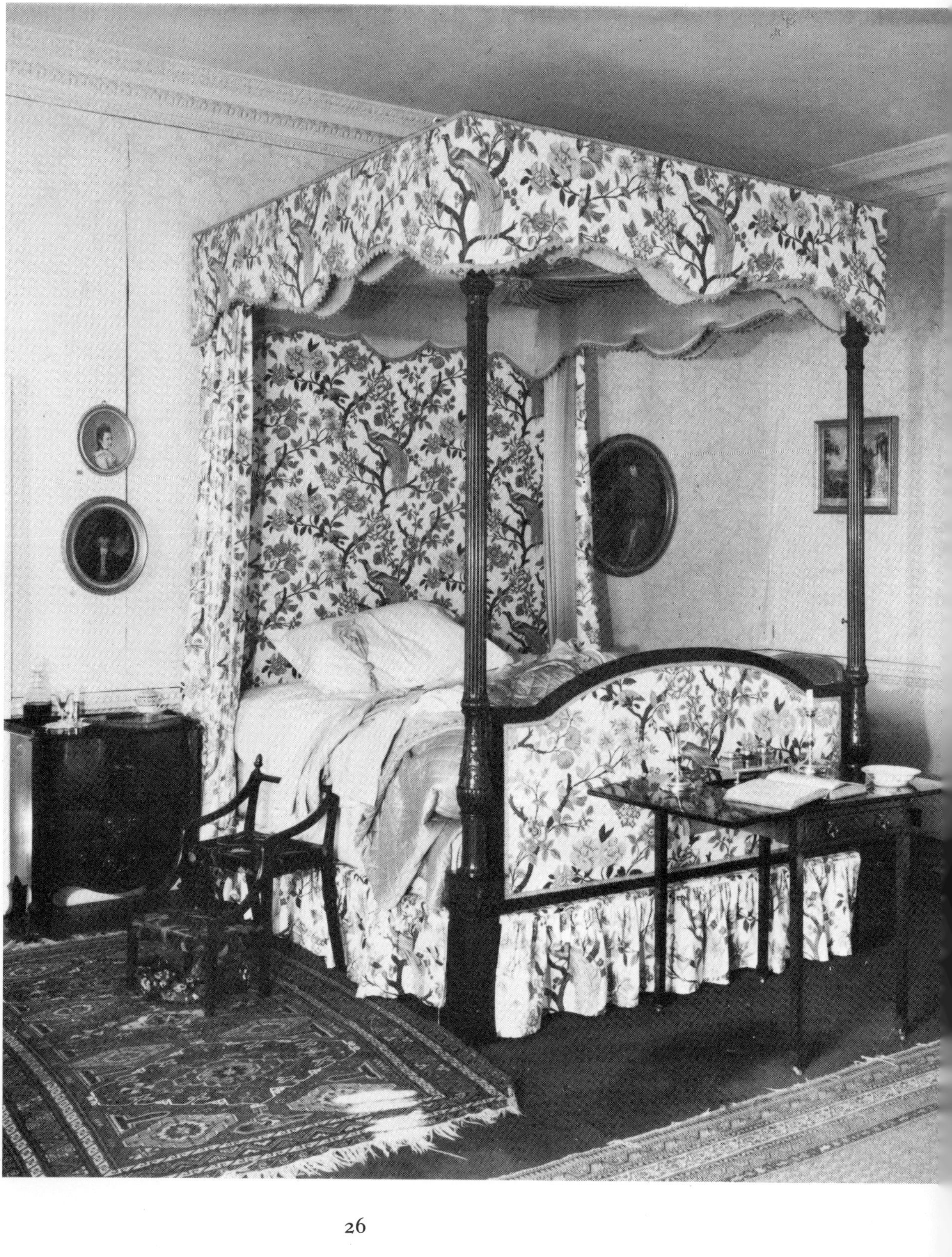

# 2 MASTER BEDROOM AND MORNING ROOM

## *the New Master*

Here, in his bedroom, it was possible to be quiet and alone.

From time to time – he felt a need to be alone.

He enjoyed London. It was busy with friends and social connections. There was the enticement of gambling; cards and the Club; the intrigues of politics . . . the 'Great World' as some liked to call it. But too much of it depressed him. He liked – he needed – to get back to the country; to get out and about, to feel fresh winds round him, to see gray storms driving up from the south-west.

It was good to have a place for privacy: a book or two, a good chair, a slow glass of wine, and silence and solitude with even the candle-flames, tall and graceful, hardly troubling to flicker.

John Parker. The new master of Saltram. . .

For a long time, knowing the happiness of bringing Theresa to his home, he had been unable to free his mind from the death of Frances, his first wife, and that of his father. He had pictures from Italy which reminded him of Frances. And not only Saltram – all around him – but also the very flesh and blood that he was, was the memory of his father. His marriage, his inheritance, were like a personal destiny.

Sometimes the transience of life weighed heavily upon him. His mind turned – though with wariness and timidity – to religion; but what a tangle was there!

Some books had a compelling seriousness. Mr Law's *Serious Call to a Devout and Holy Life*[1] had apparently influenced many; but what a vapour it seemed beside the gambits and innocences of the clergy themselves! The majority of parsons subscribed to the *Thirty-nine Articles* and then took their gentle way through life like winding rivers that had never a thought of getting to the sea: burying their dead – an all too frequent occupation; performing their pastoral duties; making beer; playing cards with modest betting; fishing with nets for tench;

*The elegant bed in the Master Bedroom (see opposite page). The small uppermost picture to the left of the bed is of 'Nanny' (Anne Robinson – see also p. 124), and the larger oval portrait on the right is of young Jack who so loved the uniform of the Devonshire Militia, of which his father was an officer, that a red military coat was specially made for him (see also p. 125).*

coursing hares; watching public hangings – and all with decorum, gentle pleasure, and prevailing good nature[2]. Others, however, were as prink'd and powdered as anything to be seen at Vauxhall Pleasure Gardens. Nanny once said of a Chaplain at one of Lady Pembroke's parties:

... his hair is as well dreped as Lord Carlisle's, and if it is not for 3 very small curls behind you would not know him to be a Parson, he goes by the name of the Marcaroni Parson. I have heard that he wears *weepers*, but cannot say that I have seen them ...[3]

And there were the 'Hunting Parsons'[4] who would rather be chasing hounds than preaching from a pulpit, and had such lurid reputations that you could fancy a pair of horns under their wigs! Most country parsons were taken for granted, and of little note, but what were you to make of those wild clerics in remote parts who kept hounds to keep their tables well supplied with hares; who 'passed the bottle' with drunkards in their parlours; who threw them out 'by the scruff of the neck' when they began to brawl, so that they could fight out their differences in the churchyard among the tombs; and who would even dig a pit in the road so that their Bishop would flounder into it – carriage, horses, and all? Whether true or not – rare stories passed about them!

By contrast, the riding, walking, swimming, shooting John Wesley was direct and sincere to the bone. He knew what he wanted, and he knew what many men in their miserable plight wanted: salvation! There was no wonder that he took the whole of Cornwall by storm; and no doubt he would take the rest of the country in the same way. Even so ... it was dark stuff. '... very stupid, low, bad stuff ... '[5] as some parsons said. The Duchess of Buckinghamshire was more forthright:

... concerning the Methodist Preachers. Their doctrines are most repulsive, and strongly tinctured with impertinence and disrespect towards their superiors, in perpetually endeavouring to level all ranks and do away with distinctions. It is monstrous to be told that you have a heart as sinful as the common wretches that crawl on the earth ...[6]

Religion was either living like everybody else and wearing gaiters to do it, or a troubled, vicious bag of tricks. Yet, from time to time, when feeling both the

*John Wesley – preaching on his father's grave; his congregation moved by deep emotion.*

miracle and the tragedy of the world, and when seeking to go so much more deeply beyond the emptiness and triviality of society, he felt a need that none of these could fulfil. Bishop Butler, in his sermons, came very close:

There is a capacity in the nature of man, which neither riches nor honours, nor sensual gratifications, nor anything in this world can perfectly fill up, or satisfy; there is a deeper and more essential want, than any of these things can be the supply of . . .[7]

But as Butler also said: 'Words, to be sure, are wanting on this subject'. No. For a layman like him, the nature of the world was too profound; reality was too intricate; to be snared in any triviality of words. The world itself was more compelling than any doctrines about it.

And if religion failed; and if sleep would not come with its natural consolation . . . a glass of wine, a draught of opium: these had consolations of their own. These could bring the falling of the night.

*

Waking was better! To leave cloudy night and sleep, and troubled apprehensiveness, yes – to leave even religion behind – and to wake to a bright morning window! Let the awful shapelessness of the soul be left to the theologians who thought they knew something about it. For him, at least some welcome definiteness was given by a good shirt, coat, breeches, and the expected responsibilities of a man about his work.

John Parker was not like some English gentlemen, who, as one foreign visitor declared in some astonishment:

. . . seem absolutely incapable of motion, till they have been wound up by their valets. They have no more use of their hands for any office about their own persons than if they were paralytic. In the morning, if the valet happens to be out of the way, the master must remain helpless and sprawling in bed, like a turtle on its back upon the kitchen of an alderman.[8]

It was a joke in the family that his brother Montague had not seen his own face for years through having been shaved always by his valet; but John Parker was not *so* bad. Sometimes he shaved himself. Still, no matter how considerable the house, there was the limited sanitation of commode and chamber-pot and no water upstairs except by

*Bishop Butler, who preached sermons of a different kind: deeply sensitive, but calm, balanced and philosophical.*

29

the fetching and carrying of servants. Servants were a necessity: and the freshness of a morning shave by his manservant was a delight.

His wig stood there for powdering, but this, too, was a thing of little appeal to him. Increasingly, he wore his own hair. Indeed, the periwig-makers had petitioned the King, complaining that men, in general, were tending to wear their own hair more. It was as though, said Walpole:

... carpenters were to remonstrate that since the peace their trade decays and there is no more demand for wooden legs.9

Still, there was a foppishness about in the country, an absurdity about clothes and wigs, that almost frizzl'd your hair just to hear about it. The Prince de Kaunitz, for example:

... wore satin stays and passed a portion of every morning in walking up and down a room in which four valets puffed a cloud of scented powder, but each of a different colour, in order that it might fall and amalgamate into the exact nuance that best suited their master's taste.10

And there was a never-ending flow of good stories about wigs – their disadvantages and embarrassments: like that about the old Reverend John Coleridge (father of Samuel Taylor Coleridge, the poet) who lived not far away at Ottery St Mary:

On one occasion, having to breakfast with his Bishop, he went into a barber's shop to have his head shaved. Just as the operation was completed the clock struck nine, the hour at which the Bishop punctually breakfasted. Roused, as from a reverie, he instantly left the barber's shop, and in his haste forgetting the wig, appeared at the breakfast table, where the Bishop and his party had assembled. The Bishop, well acquainted with his absent manners, courteously and playfully requested him to walk into an adjoining room, and give his opinion of a mirror which had arrived from London a few days previously, and which disclosed to his astonished guest the consequence of his haste and forgetfulness.11

There was also the poor lady who lost her wig altogether on Westminster Bridge – and suffered the humiliation of having a shortsighted man come up and address the back of her head in condolence!12

John Parker strongly favoured the trend towards the simple and the natural. He had no patience with satin stays and over-elaborate wigs! Sometimes, the social scene of the world seemed a very trivial veil behind which far more sombre realities moved.

*

In these days, how frail and insignificant men seemed before misfortune and death. The plagues were memories now, but still the smallpox took a tenth of every generation and pitted the faces of the living with its foul signs. Illnesses took a sickening toll; many children died in their earliest years; and women were especially vulnerable in the very act of giving life to others. Why was mankind a prey to such dangers, such fears, such insupportable loss?

Mr Parker was apprehensive for the safety of his family. Like all men of his time, he took for granted such cures as bleeding – often partly as a precaution, but on urgent occasions, from both arms, and several times a day:

I am sorry to say I am writing this in a Sick Room. Mr Parker is just recovering an attack of a Fever, which was pretty violent for the time. He was taken on Sunday night and was bloodied and took other precautions on Monday morning. . . Today he was better all but being very low and weak, by fasting, lazing in bed. But tonight I may fairly say he is much better and hope in a few days all will be right.

To think, however, that Theresa and his small son Jack would have to endure the same harshness of illness and treatment – this was something he found hard to bear. To resign *yourself* to pain was one thing; to resign yourself to the same inevitabilities for those you loved was another.

He could never reconcile himself to the indiscriminate ruthlessness of sickness and untimely death; and indeed, over all the people of the time they cast a continual shadow: a threat which was never very far distant.

From the very beginning he had been troubled that his inheritance and the happiness of his marriage to Theresa had been rooted in the death of others: of Frances, and his father. It was the way of destiny that joy, beauty and the very continuity of life for some, was rooted in the mortality of others.

But this continual presence of illness and death did not lead Mr Parker, or others of his time, to take them lightly. He, in his turn, made provisions for his estate and family, by way of guardians and trustees, within the first two or three years of his son's life.

*A bowl, a few phials, a case of surgical instruments looking as forbidding as a set of carpenter's tools. The enormous syringe-like instrument by the candle is an enema pump.*

*Theresa – elegantly portrayed by Sir Joshua Reynolds – and with the appearance of holding her pulse: the pose on which she and her brothers commented as being characterstic of her. Her relatively simple hair-style may be noted. This portrait now hangs in the Great Room.*

These earlier memories, still very near to him, had made him all the more solicitous for Theresa's welfare, and from her first coming to the house he had left nothing undone in trying to make her feel welcome, and at home. Now – as he became more and more deeply attached to her – he was increasingly afraid of the dangers she would have to face.

She seemed gentle, frail, almost as though inwardly preoccupied about her health. In one portrait which Sir Joshua Reynolds painted of her he captured this very delicate and reflective appearance, and her brothers Grantham and Fritz commented especially on the pose – of holding her wrist, or pulse – which was so characteristic of her. Whether it was foolish of him or not, the vulnerability of women especially was something he could never shake from his mind, and the difficulty of Theresa's first birth had served only to strengthen these feelings. He knew that she dearly wanted other children, particularly a daughter, and he himself would welcome a larger family; but, far more than Theresa herself, he was troubled about the risk it entailed.

Theresa fussed much more over the health of her little boy Jack than over her own – from the slightest cold he caught, to the taking of careful precautions for their long coach journeys between Saltram and London. She and Mr Parker had taken very seriously the new method of inoculating against the smallpox[13], and had decided to try the advantage of it – not only a responsible, but a courageous step for them to take at a time when the process was still controversial and new. When Jack was just over two years old, the cost was recorded in Mr Parker's account book: 'To Mr Hawkins for inoculating the child – £42'. They were worried when Jack sickened with the mild attack of the disease, but, in fact, it cleared away perfectly as the doctor had predicted. In this, at least, Mr Parker felt much indebted to the new practices and researches in medicine. But there was also a sardonic streak in him. Could he take the authority of physicians always without question? What was a man to think of those who physicked their patients with:

Live hog Lice, New gathered Earth Worms, Live Toads, Black tips of Crab Claws, Frog's Livers, and the like . . .?[14]

'... to this delightful place.'

'Saltram from the South-West' by Philip Rogers: a detail of this painting is shown on the jacket.

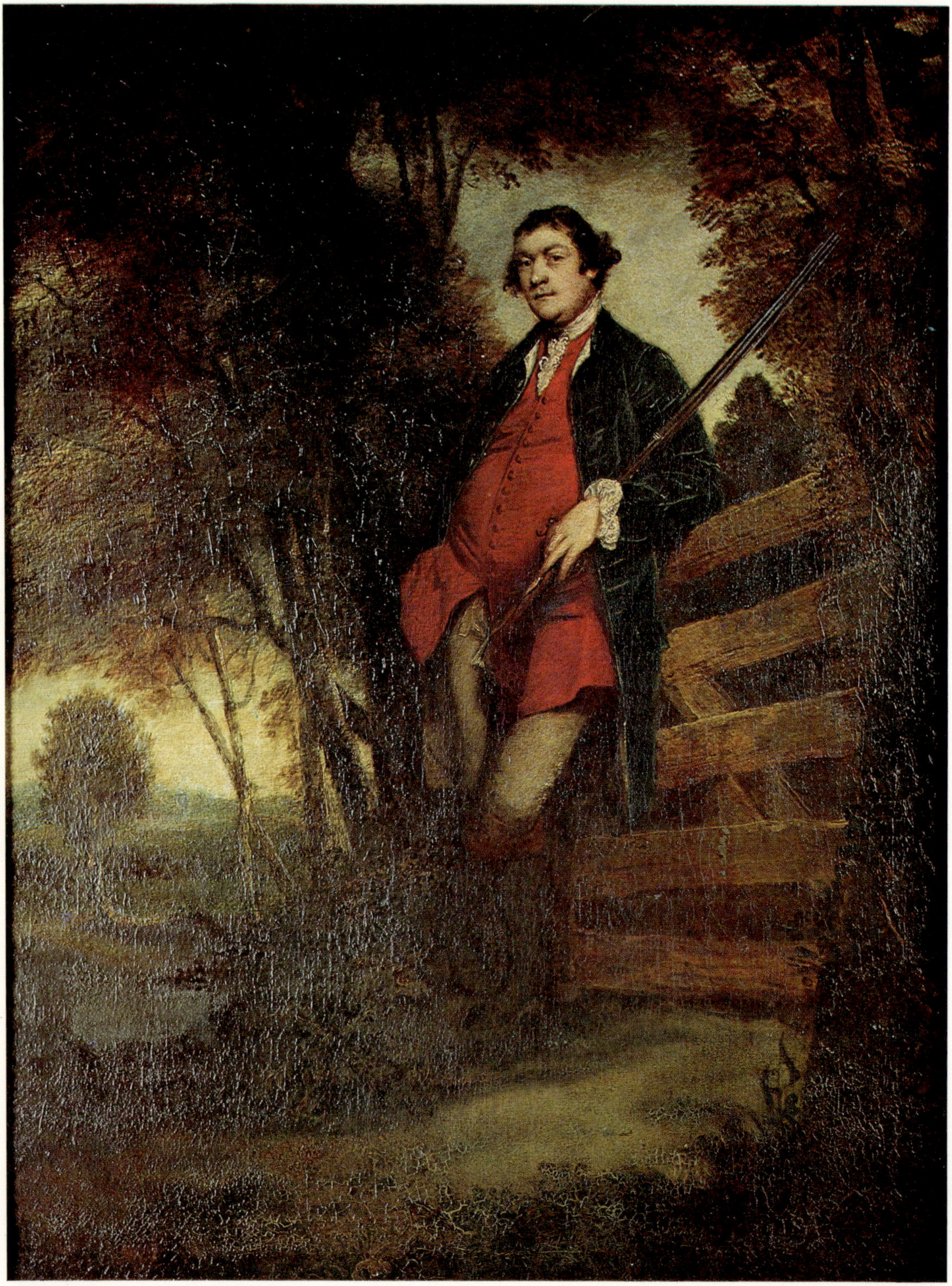

– or with 'The Black Powder' for smallpox:

Take 30 or 40 Live Toads, burn them in a new Pot, to black Cinders or Ashes, and make a fine powder. Dose 3ss, or more in the Small Pox, and is a certain help for such as are ready to die . . .[14]

Lady Wortley Montagu's urge to try inoculation or Dr Jenner's cow-pock vaccination was very persuasive compared with that!

His own humour had more in common with Laurence Sterne – the Tristram Shandy man – who wrote explosively to his friend about his belly-ache and the violent disturbance of his bowels:

Need one go to a physician to be told that all kind of mild opening, saponaceous, dirty-shirt, sud-washing liquors are proper for you; and, consequently, all styptical potations, death and destruction. – If you had not shut up your gall-ducts by these, the glauber salts could not have hurt: – as it was, 'twas much like a match to the gun-powder, by raising a combustion, as all physic does at first; so that you have been let off, – nitre, brimstone, and charcoal all at one blast. – 'Twas well the piece did not burst; for I think it underwent great violence.[15]

To his mind, a physician's prescription of Portuguese snuff, urine and viper's fat for the treatment of ailing eyes, was in no way to be preferred to the farmer's 'excellent receipt to stop purging and vommitting'.

. . . take a large swine and drive it until he dungs. Then take ye dung and putt itt in some new milk, stur itt, and lett it stand a little, or if ye please ye may give it a little boiling. Then strain itt and give ye pashent to drink now and then a spoonfull or two at a time.[16]

It was surely no mystery why ladies made 'Lavender Drops'[17] and why 'The Cordial Balm of Gilead' was advertised for those 'in lowness of spirits'.

When suffering from toothache, too, Mr Parker might have been advised to try herbal washes, a magnet, or soaking the feet in hot water and then rubbing them in bran at bedtime. White teeth were considered a great asset, a sign of beauty, and a practice had arisen of transferring the sound white teeth of the poor into the jaws of the rich; but this expensive and futile transplant cost more than false-teeth, and even these might cost up to five hundred pounds. Sometimes doctors seemed of little use,

*Opposite:*

*'. . . where he most liked to be: with his feet in the leaf-mould, his back against a five-barred gate, and his gun in the crook of his arm.'*

*John Parker: painted by his friend Sir Joshua Reynolds.*

*'Doctor Forceps': a print of 1773 giving a rather macabre impression of the doctor of the times. Crabs' Claws, Live Toads and the Black Powder do not seem far distant from these dark eyes.*

and Mr Parker was sceptical about all but the best of them.

Still . . . transience, and death, and illness, and devious scoundrelly doctors were not everything! There were still positive enjoyments and delights to be had in the world. He needed solitude – but, like the bustle of life in London, he also soon needed to leave it behind. Enough was enough! The night-world of candlelight and thoughtfulness seemed suddenly pale when sunlight came bursting through the window. He liked to rise to the vigour of the country life; its physical effort and ease; to get into out-of-door clothes; to see, through the shining window, the sun steaming the great lawns which his grandfather had enclosed, and to go down to an easy breakfast.

*

Breakfast was the casual meal of the day: about nine o'clock. It was a pleasant thing to sit over toast and chocolate at his leisure; to lounge a little in his clothes for the day; not to have to dress for a meal; to spend an hour over newspapers, or letters, or papers from Westminster; coming round from the night before . . . moving gently into the day.

Travellers from the continent who visited English country houses found the easy-going habits of breakfast

*The breakfast table in the Morning Room at Saltram. Tea, toast and butter, and a leisurely glance through the newspapers . . .*

very attractive, if a little surprising when compared with the strict formality which had to be observed at dinner:

... Breakfast consists of tea and bread and butter in various forms. In the houses of the rich you have coffee, chocolate and so on. The morning newspapers are on the table and those who want to do so, read them during breakfast, so that the conversation is not of a lively nature. At ten o'clock or ten-thirty each member of the party goes off on his own pursuit – hunting, fishing or walking.
In the morning you come down in riding-boots and a shabby coat, you sit where you like, you behave exactly as if you were by yourself, no one takes any notice of you, and it is all extremely comfortable.[18]

John Parker was used to breakfasting alone, and Theresa would still, quite often, stay in her own room until late in the morning. But she was interested in all his plans for the estate, and these hours in the Morning Room were an opportunity for relaxed conversation. Sometimes, with visitors and house-parties, it was not easy; but it was only then that you realised the concoctions that some people were capable of swallowing down at breakfast. There was Mr Poulett, for example, who, as Nanny once said:

... has contrived to find out a nastier breakfast if possible than yellow cucumbers – as he now eats every morning a lemon steeped overnight in small beer.[19]

It was in the quiet of the Morning Room, too, that he could give his mind to possible improvements on the estate – as well as on the house itself – and to those problems connected with them; because problems there were – in plenty!

To 'improve' your estate: to enclose such waste-land as seemed feasible, to use the new implements, to add to your crops and think more carefully about their rotation; these were not only the fashionable ideas – they also seemed profitable. Men in the west country, however, moved slowly. Devon farmers liked proof:

Mr Parker purchased a flock of the Leicester (breed) sheep for his park at Saltram. But from whatever cause, they did not answer the expectations formed of them. They became, notwithstanding every attention that could be paid to them, afflicted with the foot rot. This must have arisen from improper treatment, or perhaps from too much wet in the grass. Notwithstanding the misfortunes attending his experiments,

*'Improvements'* . . . *Like other landowners, Mr Parker had to contemplate the methods of the new agriculture: in this case, the model of a plough.*

*The poor – outside the door of a small, insufficient cottage. Poverty and population were both on the increase.*

and although the breed has not been kept up in its purity, the sheep at Saltram, I was assured by Mr Tricky at Plympton, who is the principal carcass-butcher in that part of the county, are much preferable to any other sheep he can purchase in the county.[20]

Men whose families had been practising husbandry for generations were not convinced until they saw results; but profit was certainly there. Rents were rising all the time. Arthur Young, the most indefatigable man that ever shook his fists at English agriculture, was travelling everywhere, claiming the advantages of the larger estate and the new methods. The decisions of the larger landowners could be very influential.

The freehold property of the county of Devon is also very much divided, perhaps more than in almost any county of England. The large tracts of country granted to the ancient barons, have been subdivided among their descendants, or sold, so that, a few families excepted, there are no very great proprietors, but there are a great number of gentlemen of easy independent fortunes, who pass their time chiefly on their own estates, and live in great harmony with each other, and with the respectable yeomanry in their neighbourhood. In the South Hams in particular, this respectable class of yeomanry is more numerous than in any district of England I have seen. They live in great comfort, and exercise without parade, that old English hospitality which the refinements of modern manners have banished from many other parts of the Kingdom. I observed with much pleasure the attention they paid to their various dependants around them, and their kindness to the poor. Nothing can evince this more strongly than the agreements they have entered into, in the most parts of this district, to supply the labourers and neighbouring poor with grain, at at certain fixed moderate prices, an example well worthy of more general imitation.[21]

Yet, curiously, at the same time, the poor were undoubtedly on the increase.

In Devon, a very rough picture was that 67 families owned a third of the cultivated land; about 600 squires and yeomen another third; and the greatest part of the rest was owned by about 9,000 small proprietors. But 22,000 cottagers owned between them less than *two thousandths* of the whole area[22], and there were many poor besides. Any encroachment on the waste which removed their 'common rights' of running a cow, pigs, geese and fowls on what had been common land, or even getting their firewood from it, brought tragedy for such labouring families, and in the 80 years from 1760 onwards about 7 million acres were enclosed in the country at large. One historian described the fate of some families like this:

On the wild heaths and in the great woods of the southern and midland counties, there abode a race of squatters or 'hutmen' which has since almost retired before advancing civilization. Some few of them may have established by prescription a claim to property in their little tenements and become peasant farmers, but the great majority were ousted as trespassers, with the progress of enclosure, and must have passed into the ranks as mere labourers, if they did not swell those of poachers and other semi-criminal vagrants.[23]

Enclosure was of a limited extent in Devonshire; but the poor rates were tending to rise all over the country[24], and it was not only squatters and vagrants, but labouring families themselves who were poverty-stricken to a point of desperation. The average wage of labourers was about one shilling a day, and their homes reflected this pitiful standard. One lady traveller wrote with surprise and concern about the state of their cottages:

We were surprised in our travels thro' Devonshire to see their cottages of an appearance really meaner than in any county is usual . . . Near Exeter more than twenty were demolished; the poor people were in their beds, and one old woman in hers drowned by the rain being prodigious heavy; it came pouring in such torrents from the hills behind that the houses built only of a composition of clay and straw, call'd cob . . . were instantly overflow'd and tumbling to pieces . . .[25]

How wretched do the miseries of a cottage appear! Want of food, want of fuel, want of clothing! Children perishing of an ague! An unhappy mother unable to relieve their wants, or assuage their pains; nor to allow time sufficient even for the reparation of their rags; whilst the worn-down father, pinch'd by cold, returns at evening close, to a hut devoid of comfort, or the smallest renovation of hope . . .

Some cottages were sound; some landowners improved them; but in some areas cob buildings were almost as numerous as among the earliest, most primitive settlers in Devon. Many were without rough-cast or whitewash, and, at a distance, could not be distinguished from the loam of the fields. Even towards the end of the century, they looked

*Ruined thatch and partly fallen roof . . . Cob-construction could be good and sound, but many cottages were uncared for and derelict.*

like: '... an assemblage of rough and unadorned mud walls, which, frequently in a state of ruin, at once completes the idea of a temporary caravansera, or deserted Tartar village...' and on the moorlands 'three mud walls and a hedge-bank formed the habitations of many of the peasantry'.[26]

The parish workhouse was, of course, provided. Between eighty to ninety per cent of all parish expenditure went on the poor. Poverty began to weigh uncomfortably on the nation's conscience, and even poets were driven to give tongue to what they saw:

> Theirs is yon house that holds the Parish poor,
> Whose walls of mud scarce bear the broken door;
> There, where the putrid vapours, flagging, play,
> And the dull wheel hums doleful through the day; –
> There children dwell who know no parents' care;
> Parents, who know no children's love, dwell there!
> Heart-broken matrons on their joyless bed,
> Forsaken wives, and mothers never wed;
> Dejected widows with unheeded tears,
> And crippled age with more than childhood fears;
> The lame, the blind, and, far the happiest they! –
> The moping idiot, and the madman gay.[27]

Was a poet's vision reliable? Yes, it was. When, later, the Poor Law Commission looked carefully into these parish workhouses, they seemed to do little more than put the poet's lines into an official prose:

In such parishes, when overburdened with poor, we usually find the building called a workhouse occupied by sixty or seventy paupers, made up of a dozen or more neglected children (under the care, perhaps, of a pauper), about twenty or thirty able-bodied adult paupers of both sexes, and probably an equal number of aged and impotent persons. Amidst these the mothers of bastard children and prostitutes live without shame, and associate freely with the youth, who have also the examples and conversation of the frequent inmates of the county jail, the poacher, the vagrant, the decayed beggar, and other characters of the worst description. To these may often be added a solitary blind person, one or two idiots, and not infrequently are heard, from among the rest, the incessant ravings of some neglected lunatic. In such receptacles the sick poor are often immured.[28]

The hard conditions of poor labourers were not only

those of men. Women worked in the south-west for 8d. a day – muck-spreading and weeding. Women could be seen ploughing in Devon. Children were paid 3d. or 4d. a day to pick stones from the fields, and pauper children, boys and girls, were apprenticed to agriculture. A young girl of 9 or 10 years old might be up at five or six o'clock in the morning and to bed at half-past nine at night. She drove cattle to and from the fields, bedded them, washed and boiled potatoes for pigs, milked, scraped yards and loaded dung, drove the horses when loaded with the dung-pots, and dug potatoes and turnips.[29]

The golden age of English agriculture! Was it only a tinsel? The poet's vision was very clear:

> Ye gentle souls who dream of rural ease,
> Whom the smooth stream and smoother sonnet please;
> Go! if the peaceful cot your praises share,
> Go look within, and ask if peace be there;
> If peace be his – that drooping weary sire,
> Or theirs, that offspring round their feeble fire;
> Or hers, that matron pale, whose trembling hand
> Turns on the wretched hearth the expiring brand!
>
> I grant indeed that fields and flocks have charms
> For him that grazes or for him that farms;
> But when amid such pleasing scenes I trace
> The poor laborious natives of the place . . .
> Then shall I dare these real ills to hide
> In tinsel trappings of poetic pride?
> By such examples taught, I paint the cot,
> As *truth* will paint it, and as Bards will *not*![30]

A tinsel – was certainly his answer!

*

Mr Parker had other things to think about – whether people chose to think ill of him or not; and could he, and others like him, help it if, despite such poverty, population continued to increase?

Among the fields and moors of Devon, new developments were afoot. The rural scenes had quarries, mines and places of manufacture in their midst. In Cornwall and Devon, in twenty years, nearly 600,000 tons of copper ore were raised, worth £3½ million[31], and more extensive development was expected. John Parker himself produced slate from Cann Quarry. New methods were coming into the manufacture of cloth. The owners of large estates could not remain blind to such enterprises. They were often asked, and they were sometimes willing, to put capital into them. A Member of Parliament certainly had his attention drawn to these things.

The problems of the poor, of the labourers, were, in fact, entering politics. There were stirrings of a rebellious nature. In the districts of Crediton and Chudleigh there were threats of rioting, and the weavers seemed to be organizing themselves[32]. Trade and manufacture were producing new attitudes among labourers: an independence of mind; an insolence. Henry Fielding – a Justice of the Peace as well as a novelist – had spoken out boldly in the *Public Advertiser*:

... the customs, habits, and manners of the commonalty are greatly changed ... Nothing has wrought such an alteration as the introduction of trade. The narrowness of their fortune is changed into wealth; the simplicity of their manners into craft; their frugality into luxury; their humility into pride; and their subjection into equality ... Now to conceive that so great a change as this in the people should produce no change in the constitution, is to discover, I think, as great ignorance as would appear in the physician who would assert that the whole state of the blood may be entirely altered from poor to rich, from cool to inflamed, without producing any alteration in the constitution of a man.[33]

Fielding was a far-sighted man; but the minds of those in authority hardened against those who dared to organize against their masters.

Transportation was to become a punishment for more offences, and this was far from the 'migration to a milder climate' that some thought it. A convict might be assigned to a settler:

Deprived of liberty, exposed to all the caprice of the family to whose service he may happen to be assigned, and subject to the most summary laws, the condition of a convict in no respect differed from that of a slave ... Idleness and insolence of expression, or even of looks, anything betraying the insurgent's spirit, subjected him to the chain gang, or the triangle, or to hard labour on the roads.[34]

Men like Mr Parker, who bore the responsibilities of large estates and Parliament, also, frequently, served as

*A convict, transported in 1763.*

magistrates, and this could be a great burden. The Devon magistrates – like all others at this time – held a great degree of power, and might meet at their own homes or at local inns. Their duties encompassed not only certain aspects of the criminal law, but also the administration of the County. As always, some were irresponsible and much criticized. Others were public-spirited and responsible for reforms – to the appalling prison conditions, for example. They heard appeals against the rates and they apportioned the money raised from rates to such public works as the building and maintenance of roads and bridges.

Even though much of their work was administrative, however, the magistrates did uphold the law of the land – and this law was harsh. The methods and degrees of punishment were severe.

Hangings were a public spectacle which thousands attended. The bodies of hanged men, left swinging in their chains high on the gallows, were a common sight. As poverty became more severe, and as common rights were being lost, the Game Laws grew increasingly harsh. Men could be imprisoned for six months for killing game on the evidence of only one witness, and, on a second offence, up to twelve months with a public whipping. Public whipping, the public pillory, public branding, were common punishments, and transportation and hanging were becoming punishments for more and more offences. As the number of the poor grew, the penalties became more severe; and in the death sentence, if in nothing else, women shared equality of status with men; as, indeed, did children.

A typical Quarter Sessions list from Devon contained reports of this kind:

Nicholas Cleak convicted of felony let him be transported to some of his Majesty's Colonies and plantations in America for the term of seven years.

Hannah Western an incorrigible rogue let her be whipt four times and imprisoned one year.

A typical Old Bailey list would give notice of the death sentence for such offences as horse-stealing, sheep-stealing (which was common in Devon), forgery, stealing £1. 15s. from a shop, and stealing goods of the value of

41

40s. and upwards in a dwelling house. Stakes were still driven through the bodies of suicides, and the general character of cruelty in punishment was conveyed in the awful words still pronounced on sentencing men for conspiracy:

... that you be taken to the place from whence you came, and from thence you are to be drawn on hurdles to the place of execution, where you are to be hanged by the neck, but not until you are dead; for while you are still living, your bodies are to be taken down, your bowels torn out, and burnt before your faces; your heads are then to be cut off, and your bodies divided each into four quarters, and your heads and quarters to be then at the King's disposal; and may the Almighty God have mercy on your souls.[35]

Justice – and Religion.

*

The master of a great estate had much to think about over his toast and chocolate in the morning room.

The circumstances of history place men in very different situations. The poor were not responsible for having been placed in their hopeless plight. John Parker was not responsible for being placed among a few families who ruled the destinies of hundreds of thousands of their fellows. He was not a cruel man. He could not see – as no man can ever, or will ever, be able to see – the entirety of the social situation in which he lived. The mines of Cornwall, fronting the Atlantic on Pendeen coast; the vagrants by the hedge-banks on the fringes of Dartmoor; the decaying earth-coloured villages to the west; the new weaving establishments at Crediton and Totnes; the smoke beginning to rise more thickly from the slowly accumulating town chimneys throughout the length and breadth of the land; the gradually seething facts of a changing society. He could not see all these beyond these red velvet walls; beyond these portraits of his friends and family; beyond the quiet lawns and the stags roaming outside his window.

# 3 KITCHEN AND EATING ROOM

## *High Society above and below stairs*

An age of great inequality, of poverty, of distress . . .

Yes, indeed – but also an age of great gaiety and sociability! Of cook shops and soup shops and beef shops; of tea and coffee houses; of rabbits smothered with onions; of home-brewed strong beer; of cider by the barrel, rum by the gallon, and wines – whether smuggled or not – to please all the palates that could afford them; of nuts and fruits, and the great convivial art of dining. An age of the most delectable guzzling: when men, perhaps especially men, enjoyed the things of this world, and – with much smacking of lips, spitting, picking of teeth, and swilling and rinsing of mouths – eating and drinking at the heart of it all!

. . . a roasted shoulder of mutton, and a plum pudding, veal cutlets, Frill'd potatoes, cold tongue, Ham, and cold roast beef, and eggs in their shells . . .

or:

. . . a boiled rump beef, a Ham, and half dozen fowls, a roasted saddle of mutton, two very rich puddings, and a good sallet with a fine cucumber . . .

. . . with Punch, Wine, Beer and Cyder for drinking.[1]

These were the meals which a country parson enjoyed! And in the newspaper appeared the kind of casual note that three clergymen, after dinner: 'ate fourteen quarts of nuts, and, during their sitting, drank six bottles of port wine, and NO other liquor!'[2] The golden age, it seems, of the Church of England.

Meals in a great house, for a large company, were of gargantuan proportions.[3]

Mrs Glasse provided menus for each month of the year in her book: *The Art of Cooking made Plain and Easy*. For a dinner in December, for example:

*First Course*
Cods head, Chickens, Stewed Beef, Fricando of Veal, Almond Puddings, Soup Sante, Calves feet pie, small fillet of pork with sharp sauce. Curry, Tongue, Chine of Lamb. And always

observe to send up with your first course all kinds of garden stuff – suitable to your meats.
*Second Course*
Wildfowls, Lambs fry, Orange Puffs, Sturgeon, Salantine, Jellies, Savoury Cake, Prawns, Tancets, Mushrooms, Partridge.
*Third Course*
Rogood Palates, Savoy Cakes, Dutch beef scraped, China oranges, Lamb tails, Half mood, Calves burs, Jargomel peas, Potted larks, Lemon biscuits and fricassie of crawfish.

By and large, the dishes were of meat of all kinds, followed by puddings and rich, elaborate sweets. Peas, beans, cabbage, were grown in the country, but vegetables were not thought much of – to such an extent that the upper classes were probably deficient in certain vitamins. Even so, on occasion, a good piece of beef was salted some days before boiling and then 'besieged with five or six heaps of Cabbage, Carrots, Turnips, and some other herbs and roots – well peppered and salted and swimming in butter . . .' Or a leg of roast or boiled mutton would be 'dished up with the same dainties . . . and with Fowls, Pigs, Ox Trypes, and Tongues, Rabbits and Pigeons, all well moistened with butter without Larding...'[4]

The greater part of the property of a landowner like John Parker was let to tenant farmers, but many foodstuffs were produced on the home farm: milk, eggs, butter, such vegetables as were desired, bacon and meat, and some fruit. 'Specialities', however, were now gaining reputations: Wiltshire Ham, Aylesbury Ducklings, Scotch Beef and fine Turkeys from Norfolk; and fish of all kinds were available: salmon, oysters, lobsters, mackerel, cod, sole, plaice. Highly individual tastes were also indulged – such as 'tench boiled in ale and dressed with lemon and rosemary' – and foreign fruits such as lemons, oranges, melons, dates and figs, were imported.[5] Eating was on a grand and lavish scale!

*Breaking up sugar in the kitchen at Saltram.*

\*

In a large household like Saltram, the management of the kitchen, the instructions for such meals and other domestic matters, were in the hands of a responsible housekeeper and a large staff of servants – the menials: those *intra menia*, as the law had it – 'within walls'! Some wives of country gentlemen, however, though removed if they wished from such mundane tasks, continued to keep a close eye on the affairs of the house. Servants were not to be trusted: If the underservants could be depended on for doing all their business according to the instructions that could be given them, the eye of the Housekeeper would not be necessary to keep everything going on in its proper way, but this is never to be expected and as the Mistress of a large family can neither afford the time, nor even have the power to see what the Servants are about, she must depend on the Housekeeper to see all her orders are enforced and every rule kept up. For rules are not laid down unnecessarily and when neglected the inconvenience is felt in future though perhaps not immediately and when the mischief has crept in it is too late to go back again to a preventive rule.[6]

At Saltram, the servants were sometimes good, sometimes bad, and there were times when even Theresa was moved to impatience. She was as near angry as her nature could be about one coach-trip back from London:

The little boy had a safe journey and he is perfectly well, but many disasters happened from bad management of servants . . . Coachman ill and put into the coach; Postillion upon the Box, stable boy that could not ride postillion, and a very long Elephant Story . . . But as no accident happened we will not repeat it, but so ill contrived at was sufficient to make me rejoice I had not left him behind at Saltram under the sole care of servants.[7]

The menials in a country house formed a society within a society, a hierarchical world of their own: 'High Life Below Stairs' as the theatre presented it.[8] Those with larger responsibilities – the housekeeper, cook, butler and the steward – were likely to come from the families of the lesser gentry or the farmers. Kitchen maids, dairy maids, coachmen, grooms, stable boys and footmen, were the 'lower ranks' and were drawn from the local labouring families. They might even be hired at local fairs (the giglet fairs at Martinmas) in the west country.

They had their own scrupulous 'order' of duties and privileges, regulations and allowances, and even sat at different tables according to their status. They might have had a servants hall, and, on occasion, their own dancing there. Life was far from being always a sober, serious matter. They sometimes aped their superiors, and even addressed each other, and referred to each other, by the name of the masters they served.

*Bread had to be hung up in nets – out of the way of vermin.*

*The Spectator* keeping its observant eye on the habits of the times, once remarked:

Falling in the other day at a Victualling House near the House of Peers, I heard the Maid come down and tell the Landlady at the bar, that my Lord Bishop swore he would throw her out of the window, if she did not bring up more mild beer, and that my Lord Duke would have a double Mug of Purle. My surprize was encreased, in hearing loud and rustick voices speak and answer to each other upon the Public Affairs, by the Names of the most Illustrious of our Nobility; till of a sudden one came running in, and cry'd the House was rising. Down came all the Company together, and away! The Alehouse was immediately filled with Clamour, and scoring one Mug to the Marquis of such a place, Oyl and Vinegar to such an Earl, three quarts to my new Lord for wetting his Title, and so forth . . .

It is a common humour among the retinue of People of Quality, when they are in their revels . . . to assume in a humorous way the Names and Titles of those whose Liveries they wear.[9]

The menials obviously had their moments! There was a good deal of frolicking even within their own pecking order!

\*

*The ceiling and the carpet of the Eating Room (opposite): an excellent example of the intricate detail of Robert Adam's design. The carpet 'reflects' the design of the ceiling.*

Breakfast might be a casual, lounging meal, but dinner was the strictly formal meal of the day, and the Eating Room – designed for Mr Parker by Robert Adam – was an exquisite formal room: with a lofty, airy feeling, quiet egg-shell green walls and pure white lines, and oil paintings blending with their also quiet colours. Mr Parker would as soon feed stags as celebrities, and dogs as Duchesses – though he would make an exception to this for the Duchess of Devonshire! Theresa, too, was no more enamoured than her husband of their dining obligations in the County:

We must spend the next week in returning all our Dining visits which we do not enjoy the thought of much . . . But as we are at home mornings and evenings it is of no great concern.[10]

A thing, clearly, which had to be done! Dinner was, nonetheless, a formal occasion, and Theresa liked people to dress properly for it. She wrote to her brother Grantham once with much impatience:

You may judge of the kind of animal Mr Genneys must be who is just come to his estate and just married and puts on a clean

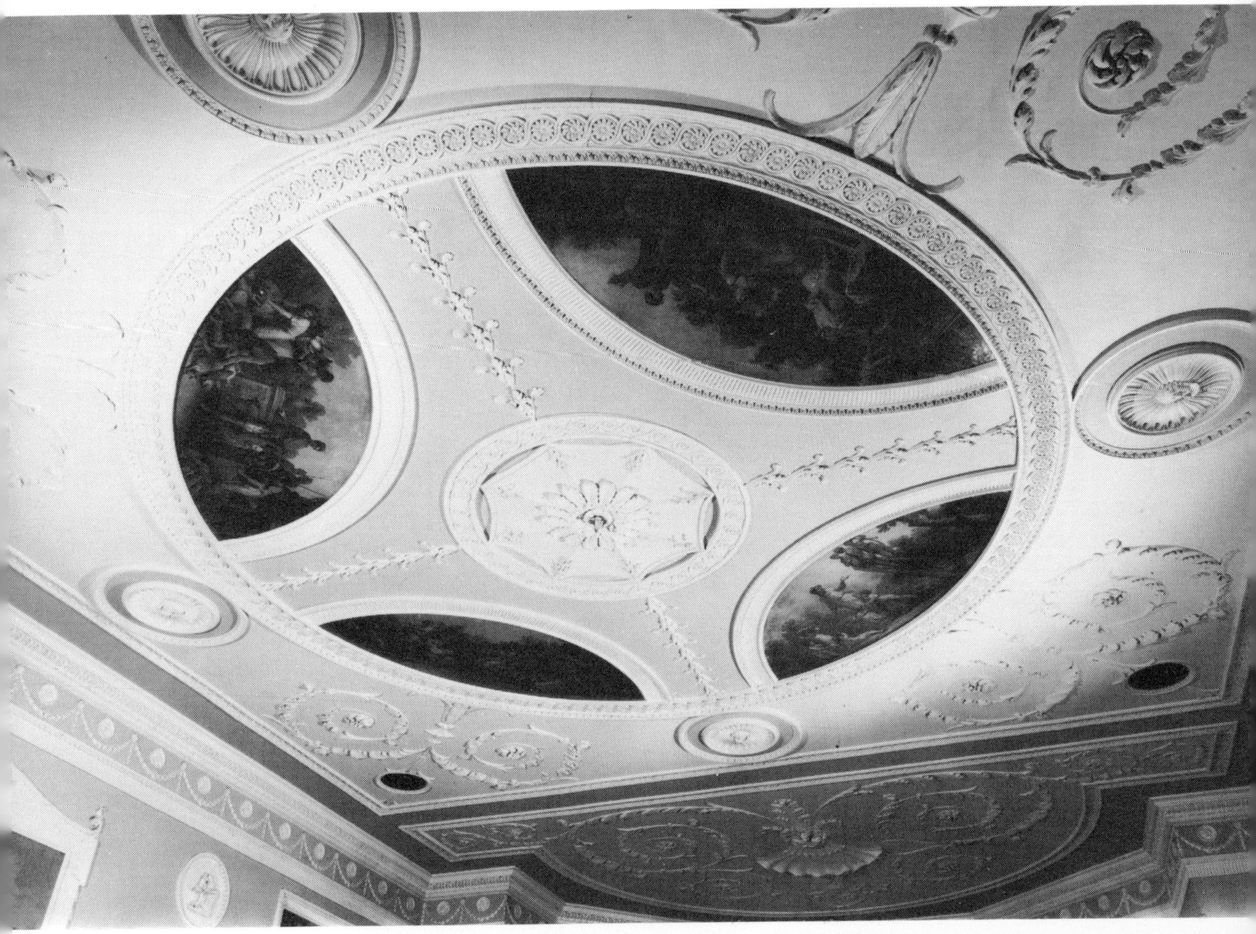

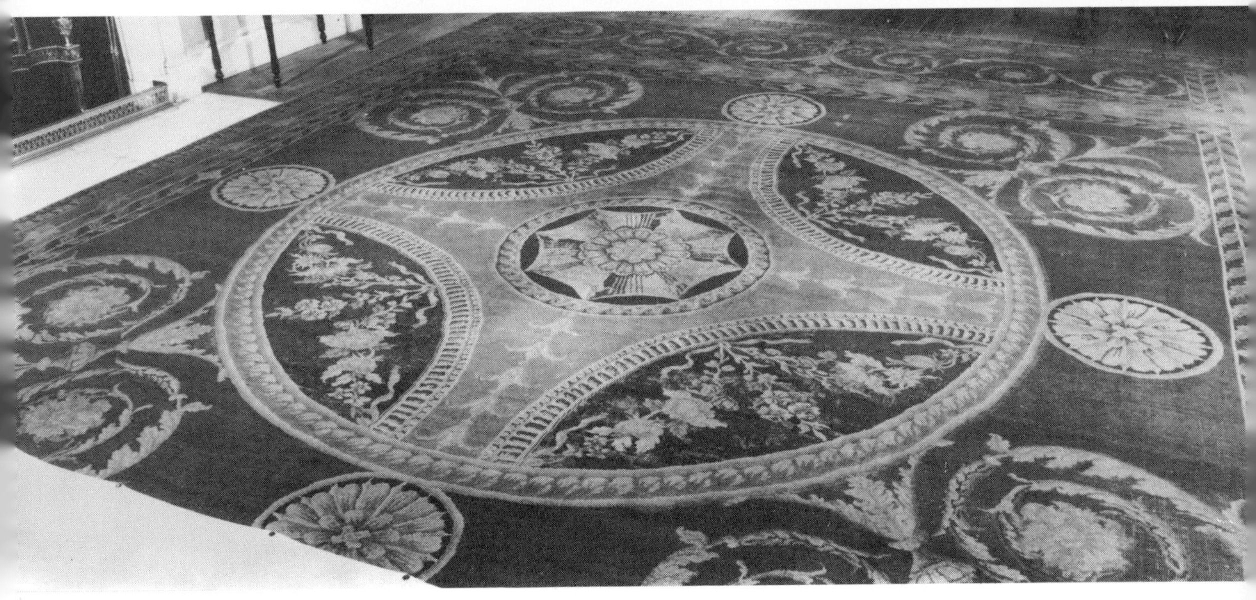

pair of *boots* to come down to dinner! – having never any use for shoes, and not having a pair in the house . . .[11]

Dinner began not earlier than two o'clock in the afternoon, perhaps as late as four.

Montague had married Charity – the daughter of Admiral Ourry at Plympton, and they, and other close friends like Sir Joshua, frequently came. Then there were the County families – the Edgecumbes from across the water, the Chichesters, the Bastards, and others, and officers from the Navy and the Militia. Sometimes, even the local parson might dine with people of 'fortune', if in rather an embarrassed way, and there were sometimes house-parties from London and Yorkshire. Families of very high distinction visited occasionally:

Lord and Lady Chatham who are down upon a wedding visit to Mr J. Pitt have threatened us with their company. I don't love him, but the pleasure of being in company with so remarkable a man would make up for the trouble of receiving them.[12]

The complete change of manners in an English household – from the sheer informality of breakfast, which he found so attractive, to the scrupulous formality of dinner – was astounding to the visiting foreign nobleman. In the morning you came down to breakfast just as you wished; no one seemed to notice you; but, he went on:

. . . in the evening, unless you have just arrived, you must be well-washed and well-groomed. The standard of politeness is uncomfortably high – strangers go first into the dining-room and sit near the hostess and are served in seniority in accordance with a rigid etiquette. For the first few days I was tempted to think that it was done for a joke . . .

When they enter the dining room, each takes his place in the same order; the Mistress of the table sits at the upper end, those of superior rank next to her, right and left, those next in rank following, then the gentlemen, and the master at the lower end; and nothing is considered as a greater mark of ill-breeding, than for a person to interrupt this order, or seat himself higher than he ought. Custom, however, has lately introduced a new mode of seating. A gentlemen and lady sitting alternately round the table, and this, for the better convenience of the ladies' being attended to, and served by the gentlemen next to her. But notwithstanding this promiscuous seating, the ladies, whether above or below, are to be served in order according to their rank or age, and after them the gentlemen, in the same manner.[13]

*Opposite:*

*Theresa and Little Jack painted by Sir Joshua Reynolds.*

'. . . *About two years ago I wished to have the child added to the picture but he made such faces it was impossible to do anything. However, this year he has consented to put him in, and though he sat but an hour you would be astonished to see how strong a likeness it is . . .*'

5 May 1775

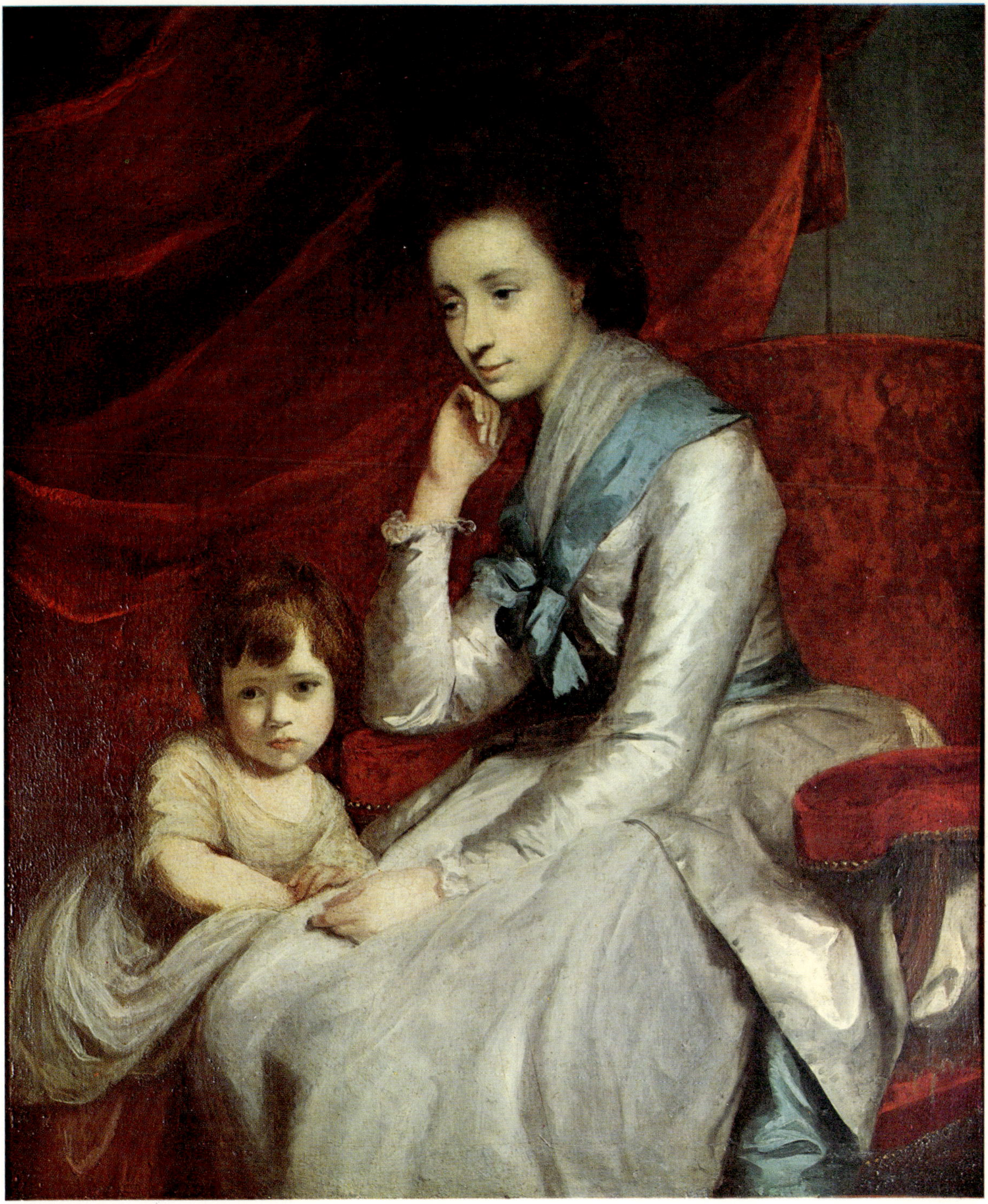

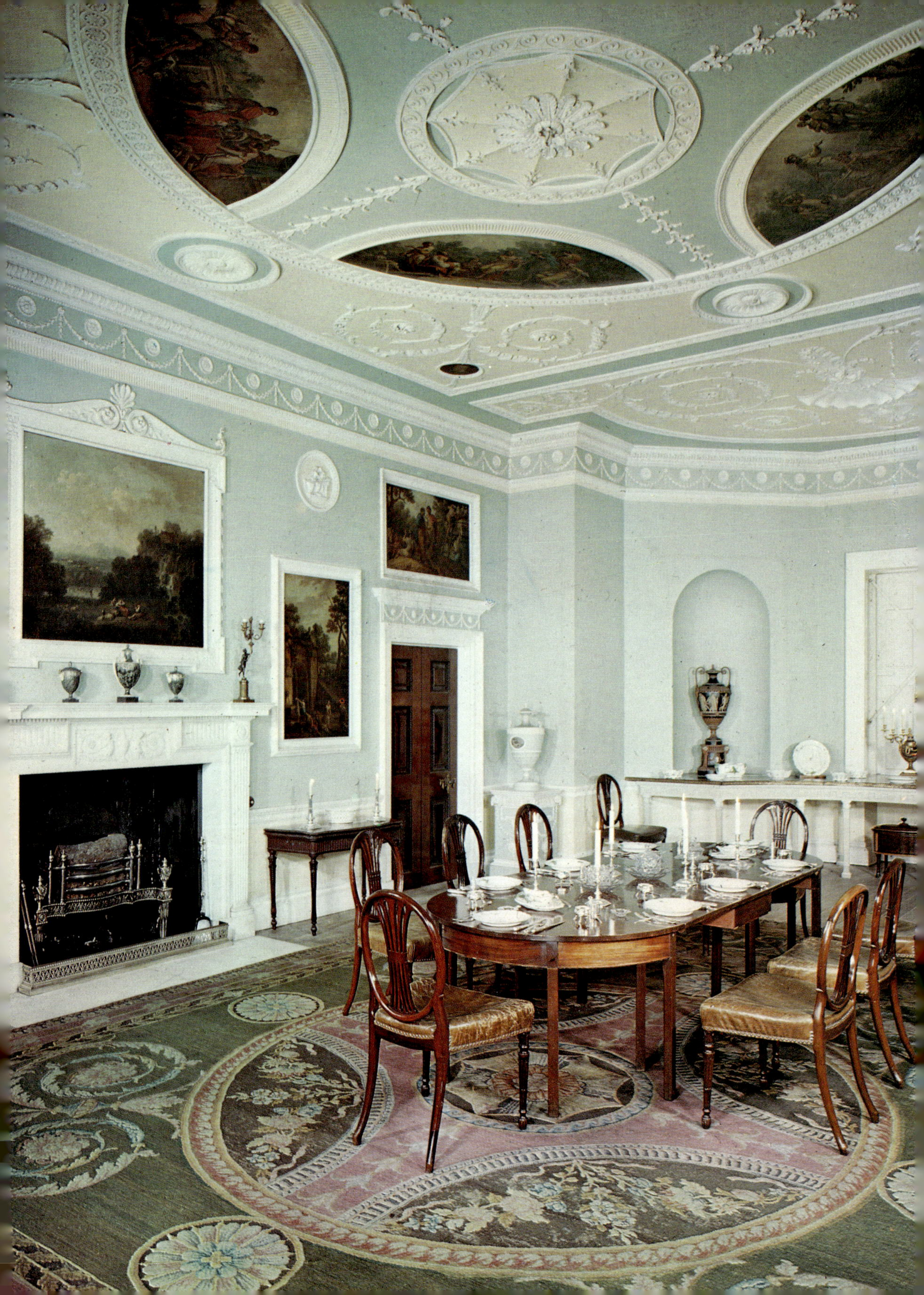

The Eating Room: the chimney-piece was made to Robert Adam's design, as was the curved sideboard at the end of the room. The white urn on a pedestal is a wine-cooler, and in the alcove is an Etruscan urn. Almost all the paintings, on ceiling, walls and furniture, were made by Zucchi and Angelica Kauffman.

'If the underservants could be depended on for doing all their business according to the instructions given them, the eye of the Housekeeper would not be necessary to keep everything going on in its proper way . . .'

The spits turning in Saltram kitchen, the fat dripping into the pan beneath.

'The Floating Island, a pretty dish for the middle of the table... as for the rim of the dish, set it round with fruit or sweetmeats. This looks very pretty in the middle of a table with candles round it and you may make it of as many different colours as you fancy.'

The serious business of eating then lasted for two hours, and this, too, bewildered and distressed the visitor:

You are compelled to extend your stomach to the full in order to please your host. He asks you all the time whether you like the food, and presses you to eat more.

Joints of meat weighed twenty to thirty pounds or more, and there was a wide variety of dishes – roasted meats, poultry, pies, fish, puddings, fruit pies, tarts and jellies:

. . . two fine Codds boiled with Fried Souls round them and oyster sauce, a fine sirloin of beef roasted, some peas soup, and an orange pudding for the first course; for the second, a lease of wild ducks, roasted, a forequarter of lamb and salad and mince pies . . .

. . . a large Cod, a Chine of Mutton, some soup, a Chicken Pye, Puddings and Roots, etc., followed by Pidgeons and Asparagus, a Fillet of Veal with Mushrooms and High Sauce with it, roasted Sweetbreads, hot Lobster, Apricot Tart, and in the middle a Pyramid of Syllabubs and Jellies . . .[14]

These were dishes which repaid attention – but the

*A side-table in the Eating Room, with fruit and the elaborate sweet. Notice the elegant edge of the table with the small painted panel in the centre. It is thought that Angelica Kauffmann painted some of these.*

foreign Duke was only led to think of dinner as 'the most wearisome of English experiences'. Clearly, there must have been something distinctive about the English belly! Even after this, the Duke commented, flabbergasted, and driven to further stresses of dismay:

. . . you are given water in small bowls of very clean glass in order to rinse out your mouth – a custom which strikes me as extremely unfortunate. The more fashionable folk do not rinse out their mouths, but that seems to me even worse; for if you use the water to wash your hands, it becomes dirty and quite disgusting.

\*

To produce this polished performance for the high society above the stairs, the most elaborate work was going on among the menials below.

Continental cookery had its influences upon the English kitchen. Certain elaborations were introduced. Indeed, some of the wealthier households had French as well as English cooks. But the English had decided views about foreigners and their food. The French, they thought, 'boil their meat to rags and there is no porter and very little strong ale' – and Arthur Young (who got about the continent as well as visiting every square inch of the British Isles[15]) thought that their high society was coarse: 'I have seen a gentleman spit so near the cloathes of a Duchess that I have stared at his unconcern'. It was possible, of course, that they had learned such manners from Lord Manchester who, earlier in the century, had been Ambassador in Paris, and about whom there had been the complaint: 'that his Excellency blows his Nose in the Napkins, spitts in the middle of the room, and laughs so loud and like an ordinary body that he was not thought fit for an Ambassador'. This, however, is only conjecture. The Germans 'ate sour crout' and 'spoke High Dutch'. In Italy, the inns were 'miserable' and it was 'too hot'.

The English loved nothing more than to tour the continent – it was so pleasing always to have such overwhelming confirmation of their own superior wealth and quality. To be good, it was, of course, still unquestionable that food had to be *English* food!

Mrs Glasse issued a word of warning to all those who would rather be imposed upon by a 'French booby' than give encouragement to a good English cook:

I have heard of a cook that used six pounds of butter to fry twelve eggs when everybody knows (that understands cooking) that half a pound is full enough or more than need be used: But then it would not be *French*.[16]

Her own recipes given in simple direct language – so that they would interest the 'lower sort' – were sometimes very elaborate:

'The Floating Island, a pretty dish for the middle of the table, at a second course or for Supper.' First take a quart of the thickest cream you can get, make it pretty sweet with fine sugar, pour in a gill of sack, grate the yellow rind of a lemon in and mill the cream till it is all of a thick froth. Then carefully pour the thin from the froth into a dish. Take a French roll, cut it as thin as you can, Lay a layer of roll as light as possible on the cream, then a layer of currant jelly, then a very thin layer or roll, then jelly, then roll, and over that your froth – which you saved from the cream – very well milled up. And lay at top as high as you can heap it. And as for the rim of the dish set it round with fruit or sweetmeats. This looks very pretty in the middle of a table with candles round it and you may make it of as many different colours as you fancy.[16]

The kitchen was a hive of activity – creating the delicacies which appeared on the polished tables above.

\*

There was also one other underground department in every house of consequence. This vaulted, architectured ceiling, with its shadowed quietness, its hushed atmosphere, was not the ceiling of a church or chapel . . . it was the great basement cellar in which the most precious of liquids was stored. Precious... but not too costly for a man of property. Towards the end of the century you could buy a bottle of Superior Old Port for 3s., Prime Old Sherry for 3s. 6d., Prime Madeira for 5s. You could have a gallon of Cognac Brandy for 20s., of Old Jamaica Rum for 15s., and Holland's Geneva Gin for 10s.[17]. The bottles cradled in these dark catacombs were lifted gently and brought back to the light of day in the magnificence of the Eating Room.

Then it was time for dessert and wine, and at this stage the Duke lost all sense of tedium and distaste, and fairly glowed with warm appreciation. Quite obviously, his own aesthetic perceptions were rooted in the eye – not in the gastric juices:

This ceremony over, the cloth is removed and you behold the most beautiful table that it is possible to see. It is indeed remarkable that the English are so much given to the use of mahogany... their tables are made of the most beautiful wood and always have a brilliant polish like that of the finest glass. After the removal of the cloth, the table is covered with all kinds of wine. On the middle of the table there is a small quantity of fruit, a few biscuits (to stimulate thirst) and some butter, for many English people take it at dessert.[18]

At this point, all the servants took their leave, and having taken a glass or two of wine, Theresa and the ladies left the males of the species to their own devices. Then the second major business of the evening began in real earnest. The bottles began to make their seemingly endless circuits of the table. Mr Parker and his friends warmed with a supreme pleasure to their wines. And the spectator Duke looked on with marvelling eyes:

There is not an Englishman who is not completely happy at this moment. They drink in an alarming measure... the bottles make a continuous circuit of the table and the host takes note that everyone is drinking in his turn... When thirst has become an inadequate reason for drinking, a fresh stimulus is supplied by the drinking of 'toasts', that is to say, the host begins by giving the name of a lady; he drinks to her health and everyone is obliged to do likewise. Then each member of the party names some man and the whole ceremony begins again. If more drinking is required, fresh toasts are always ready to hand; politics can supply plenty – one drinks to the health of Mr Pitt or Mr Fox or Lord North... This is the time that I like best: Conversation is as free as it can be, everyone expresses his political opinions with as much frankness as he would employ upon personal subjects...

*'The whores in London and Brighton...' A detail from 'The Rake's Progress' by Hogarth.*

Freedom of speech was the serious, ebullient, belly-flowing, sagacious, witty, weeping-with-tears-of-laughter practice of every society dinner table – perhaps more so than on the benches of the House of Commons. The dinner table... not so much the cornerstone as the drunken inner circle of the English Constitution! The dinner table... the great institution of English politics – cognac and confidentiality! Here, visibly embodied, was the curious mixture of the age (it is differently mixed in every age) of dirt and powder, of belly and beauty, of high culture and bawdiness. Here, surrounded by the highest achievements of art and craftsmanship, 'with all that beauty, all that wealth e'er gave', salacious skeletons came out of cupboards, rumours were dredged up and roared over, the dirty linen of those in high office was lasciviously washed:

*Elegance in the Eating Room: decorative and utilitarian.*

Sometimes conversation becomes extremely free upon highly indecent topics – complete licence is allowed and I have come to the conclusion that the English do not associate the same ideas with certain words that we do. Very often I have heard things mentioned in good society which would be in the grossest taste in France. The sideboard too is furnished with a number of chamber pots and it is a common practice to relieve oneself whilst the rest are drinking; one has no kind of concealment and the practice strikes me as most indecent.

Still... the chamber-pots were most exquisitely wrought in pewter. An English gentleman could admire art in the most unexpected moments; even when the warm fires of the spirit were pulsing through all his members!

What was spoken of at this table?

Perhaps the absurdity of new ideas about land reform; all this damned talk of 'rights'. Perhaps Mr Parker's good fortune in selling a horse at Newmarket (and to the Prince of Wales!) for 200 guineas[19]. Perhaps the Admiral's continual gifts of good turtles for the table – one about 30 lbs for twelve moderate turtle eaters was an ideal size[20]. Perhaps the fact that the Duke of so-and-so had just spent £150 on repairs to his 'ruins' only to have some fool mistake it for an antique relic of King Arthur![21] Perhaps Lord so-and-so's place in Kent which put you in good reach of the whores in both London and Brighton; and old Sterne's little bits about the 'Fille de Chambre' in Paris... it was true, by God![22] And somebody must surely have toasted the Duchess of Devonshire! And differently (in

*Alexander Pope, the poet*

part with good-natured respect, and in part with a great gale of laughter) the Bluestockings![23] Holy Hannah! Lady Wortley Montagu and her cow-pock; and whether that blackguard Pope had succeeded, or whether he was just a poor monster puffing his impotence out in pompous poetry. There would surely, too, be toasts to Farmer George III *and* to Mr Wilkes *and* to the fight between them; also to a favourite courtesan or two: perhaps the superb Miss Kitty Fisher. Perhaps, too, roaring denunciations of the young: of 'youth' – who would 'hum under their breath, whistle, sit down in a large arm-chair and put their feet on another, and sit on any table in the room' – and who were wearing muffs and frills like any powder-puff from France!

After two or three hours of this delightful tippling and cultured conversation . . . a servant would announce that tea was ready, and off they would troop to the drawing room where the ladies and the card tables were awaiting them.

\*

The menials underground had only to clear up the debris.

In Devonshire, there was a known openness and mildness

of character among servants, a good-natured disposition in the service of their masters. Maids and footmen were paid roughly from about £4 to £8 a year, but there were wage entries in Mr Parker's account books of between £6 and £15.

Grace Knight, a scullery maid, worked 18 weeks and received £1.14s.8d. Jennifer Pearse, a housemaid, was paid 7 guineas a year. And Thomas Jennings, a footman, was paid 15 guineas for a full years work.

The attitudes generally expected of servants were those so charmingly portrayed in 'Sir Roger de Coverley':[24]

In a loyal and reliable servant, orders from the Master are received as Favours rather than Duties; and the distinction of approaching him is Part of the Reward for executing what is commanded by him.

Ever since the Plague Years, however, there had been complaints, all over the country, that servants were tending to think themselves above their station. There were still those who thought – if their wage went up to £10 a year – that they were 'grown rich', and that: 'For certain, Sir, my work wasn't worth more' . . . but there were others who seemed to want more than their station properly required. Daniel Defoe once had to protest indignantly that:

. . . he was once so misled by the finery of a Chambermaid as to kiss her for the mistress of the house . . .[25]

A disgraceful situation – and a letter in the newspaper had the same view:

I look upon their exhorbitant increase of wages as chiefly conducive to their impertinence; for when they had five or six pounds a year, a month being out of place was severely felt. And what is this increase of wages for? Not to lay by a little in case of sickness, but to squander in dress. No young woman now can bear a strong pair of leather shoes, but they must wear Spanish leather, and so on in every article of dress . . .[26]

It was also disgraceful, thought Arthur Young, that the families of these menials should have started drinking tea. It was true that labouring families were not so squalidly drunk on the cheap gin and spirits which had kept the grain production good during the earlier half of the century, but the drinking of tea, he insisted, was an abomination that would keep them poor:

If the men come to lose as much of their time at tea as the women, and injure their health by so bad a beverage, the poor . . . will find themselves far more distressed than ever.[27]

They should not drink tea, but spend their money on bread. The price of wheat, no doubt, would then remain good!

It was true that the diet of their own parents might be dry barley bread and potatoes and some cheese, though they had the variety of wheat-broth seasoned with a small piece of meat and pot-herbs, and pies made of bacon and potatoes, and sometimes pilchards, and even sometimes Whitepot (so much liked by Devonshire people) which was a dish of cream, sugar, rice, currants, cinnamon – or made with barley or whole wheat . . .[28]. But they themselves, in the big house, would have better food and drink than most.

It was true, too, that schools were being set up by Hannah More and others – Holy Hannah as Horace Walpole called her – to educate and train servants – despite the fact that some thought it disastrous to educate the poor. ('The peasant's mind should never be inspired with a desire to amend his circumstances by the quitting of his cast . . .'[29]) Even so – whatever the cause – there was certainly an independence of mind about some of them; a pride; even a libidinousness!

Mr Smollett's 'Winifred' in *Humphrey Clinker* came very close to the mark:

Oh Molly, the servants at Bath are the devil incarnate. They light the candle at both ends. Here's nothing but wasting, and tricking, and thieving, and then they are never content . . . I ketch'd the charwoman going out with her load in the morning before she thought I was up and brought her to mistress with her whole cargo. Mary, what dost think she had got, in the name of God? Her buckets were foaming full of our best beer, and her lap was stuffed with a cold tongue, part of a buttock of beef, half a turkey and a swinging lump of butter, and the matter of ten mould candles, that had scarce ever been lit. The cuck brazen'd it out and said it was her right to rummage the pantry; that she was ready to go before the Mayor; that he would never think of hurting a poor servant for giving away the scraps of the kitchen.[30]

One Gloucestershire gentleman, getting back home from a visit to Bath, discovered a fine state of affairs. The servants had been keeping:

... open house in the Housekeeper's room, Landing and Servants Hall; each giving entertainments according to their rank; which cost me eleven hogsheads of Liquor, and Ducks, and Fowls ... the entertainment consisted not of Tea, but Suppers ... Tomorrow, I begin by turning out the old Lady of the house, namely the housekeeper; or so I may properly style her, a house *destroyer*; next the Steward; and so down in station ...[31]

Swift revealed all in his *Rules and Directions for Servants*.[32]

Chamber-pots, he insisted, should not be carried downstairs, but emptied out of the bedroom window. Furthermore, there were other firm principles that a good servant should have in mind:

Never come till you have been called three or four times, for none but dogs will come at the first whistle.

When you have broken all your earthen vessels belowstairs – which is usually done in a week – the copperpot will do as well; it can boil milk, heat porridge, hold small beer – apply it indifferently to all these uses, but never wash or scour it.

Clean your plate, wipe your knives, and rub the dirty tables with the napkins and tablecloths used that day, for it is but one washing.

When a butler cleans the plate, leave the whiting plainly to be seen in all the chinks, for fear your lady should not believe you had cleaned it.

A butler must always put his finger into every bottle to feel whether it be full.

There are several ways of putting out a candle, and you ought to be instructed in them all: you may run the candle-end against the wainscot, which puts the snuff out immediately; you may lay it on the ground and tread the snuff out with your foot; you may hold it upside down until it is choked in its own grease, or cram it into the socket of the candlestick; you may whirl it round in your hand till it goes out.

There were important rules, too, for service in the Eating Room:

If you are a young sightly fellow, whenever you whisper your mistress at the table, run your nose full into her cheek, or breathe full in her face.

\*

High society – above and below stairs – had its comic as well as its nerve-wracking aspects!

The circumstances of history certainly do place men and women in very different situations. Mr Parker and Theresa were not responsible for being placed in a position of high rank and property, or for the fact that their friends were able to eat, drink, and converse in such delightful surroundings; to relieve themselves in pewter in a setting of such artistic taste. Neither were their menials responsible for the fact that, sometimes, they had to hurry and scurry like a company of black-beetles under the floorboards.

Given such a situation, however, there was no doubt that those in authority had to take a firm stand in relation to those beneath.

*A Statute Hall for the hiring of servants*

# 4 THE LIBRARY

## *every Distance and Dimension of the World . . .*

Books! Rank upon rank of rich leather volumes. Shelf upon shelf. The golden age of the private library: when books were privately bound, and lovely to hold and handle . . . and to read! Wealth can be forgiven much if only for the creation of libraries.

The cynicism of Robert Burns:

> Through and through the printed page
> Ye maggots take your windings,
> But oh! – respect his lordship's taste
> And spare the golden bindings!

– was a little severe on at at least some of the masters of great households. Mr Parker needed the library for poring over his political pamphlets, and the increasingly disturbing newspapers – which were beginning to report speeches from the House of Commons which could be read by every manjack in the street who had learned to put his letters together. But his books, too, were a pride. Laurence Sterne and old Uncle Toby, Adam Smith and his disquieting arguments[1], and the large volumes of great voyages and the new lands and peoples which they opened up . . .

From a seat in the library you could explore every distance and dimension of the world.

\*

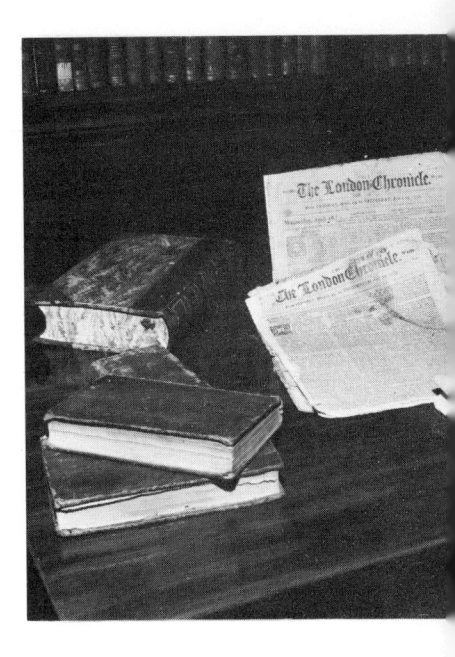

Reading, however, was not the only pleasure that a library afforded. Amateur art, amateur architecture, the planning of house improvements, the designing of gardens . . . all could be contemplated here. An easel, brushes, colours, a folding chair, were among the common equipment of a man of culture. John and Theresa Parker were, in fact, much devoted to the arts, and continuously on the look-out for painters and pictures. Theresa herself did some drawing, but, in the practice of painting all was overshadowed by Sir Joshua, who was now President of the Royal Academy and very often at the house. His painting was almost a family concern. John Parker's name was in his pocket-book more than most others – despite his over-riding concern for exhibition work. Theresa pressed him, for example, to add her little boy, Jack, to her own portrait:

I carried my Little Boy yesterday to Sir Joshua Reynolds, you remember the picture of me three or four years ago, which like all the others that he does not think worthy of a place in the Exhibition lay by and stood no chance of being finished. About two years ago I wished to have the child added to the picture, but he made such faces it was impossible to do anything. However, this year he has consented to put him in, and though he sate but an hour you would be astonished to see how strong a likeness it is. He has caught the character of the child so exactly that I am quite delighted with it and indeed it is impossible to say how much he does excell in that point particularly with respect to children.[2]

Beside Sir Joshua's picture Theresa's drawings seemed very slight, and any effort made by John Parker would have seemed poor daubs! A riding crop came much more readily to his hand than a brush and pigments.

Gardening, however, was greatly in the fashion too – and that was another matter. If he could not wield brushes – he could plant trees.

*

Saltram had its open deer-park, and was capable – as Mr Capability Brown was saying on wealthy estates all over the country – of improvement outside as well as in. Trees could add so much of nobility and grace and shelter – besides being a good economic proposition if they grew to maturity – and John Parker gave much attention to this. The planting of trees formed a considerable item in his account book. In one of her letters, Nanny – who spent much of her time at the house, enjoying the company of Theresa – told her brother of Mr Parker's persistent efforts:

We had a very hard frost, but not so much snow as there has been in other places, and the Devonshire sun is so warm that it really is quite delightful in the middle of the day. The Ice House is filled – which was never known to be possible before Christmas. I am very much afraid for the plantation, for the trees that came by the ship are not yet planted, tho' their roots are all secured, and they say are safer being together, than if they had been fresh planted separately, there are 38,000 of them.

A new arch and lodge was designed for the park entrance, too, and – whatever Mr Robert Adam had to say – he would have *stags* on it, and not *lions!* Whatever they did in London, or in Rome, his grandfather had fenced off a deer-park here – not a tropical menagerie such as some houses were establishing for their gaping visitors, and he would stick to the native creatures of the place.[3] Besides, they were a more noble animal. Nothing was better than to see them stand, with their wide spread of antlers, quiet, dignified, proud, under the trees. But other and more gentle planting was done. On one occasion, Nanny, being compelled to leave the Parkers for a while, to visit London, wrote:

... it is really a pity to leave this place, the House is in the greatest beauty, the trees in full blossom and the House full of roses, violets, carnations, lillys of the valley, mignonette, and everything that is sweet and delightful, we have had a good deal of snow, but it is all gone, and as gently as can be . . .

The designing of gardens was the rage. The old Tudor idea of sheltering a garden by walls and dense yew hedges in this island of winds, frosts and sudden fits of weather, was decidedly on the wane. Open vistas of Nature were the vogue. It was a creation of *artificial* Nature: with contrived lakes and trickling, dimpling brooks with cascades and rock-wort, and shadowed walks, with, in the midst of it all, a craggy outcrop and a delectable ruin (in a mist if you could conceivably get it!) to crown the whole landscape with romance. It was artificial Nature – romanticised.[4] The spirit of the world was not looked for in the pleasing actualities of nature where John Parker saw it – in leaf-mould, or roots, or hard bark with petals and leaves breaking out of it, or in the soft nostrils of horses – but in mystical prominences, ornamented sometimes by the statuary, monuments and extravagant imitations of the classical world by Joseph Nollekens and other fashionable sculptors of the time. Both Mr Parker and Theresa found some of these extremes not so much in bad taste as verging on the lunatic! Theresa wrote to Grantham about one example:

*The Duchess of Kingston who envisaged herself in sculpture as the Virgin Mary*

The Dutchess of Kingston has been giving directions for a magnificent monument for the Duke, the design of which appears to me a step beyond the highest absurdity. Nollikins was modelling it according to her Idea. It was to represent the Duke rising from a Sarcophagus and the figure of a woman handing him out for which the Dutchess was to sit and was to express the Virgin Mary. Above was supposed to be God the Father receiving him pointing to a vacant seat left for him. Upon Sir Joshua and others explaining to Nollikins the impropriety of the latter part in particular he spoke to the Dutchess and with great difficulty prevailed upon her to give that up, but she still insisted on being the Virgin Mary.[5]

Artificial Nature indeed! A virgin presenting her dead husband to Jehovah! All that was further required was that he should have his family settlement ready in hand: so that there could be no lack of clarity about his portion and his place!

The love of gardening spread from master, to farmer, to cottager. *The Gardener's Notebook* claimed:

Gardening is at this time so esteemed by almost everyone, that scarce a person from the peer to the cottager thinks himself tolerably happy without being possessed of a garden . . . [and a French traveller noted that:] The English Farmer has not only a kitchen garden . . . but if there are two fathoms of garden before his house he makes a flower garden of it, where he cultivates the rose and the lily of the valley . . .[6]

But Mr Parker, alas, could not give his mind only to trees and stags and the warm, rain-soaked, flower-yielding earth of his native Devon. Politics, the affairs of the County, London – these made their insistent calls!

\*

John Parker entered Parliament just before the end of the Seven Years War. Two years earlier Wolfe had taken Quebec. Two years later the Treaty of Paris was celebrated. The country was rejoicing on many counts, and – to a new and growing degree – England was a world power. Mr Parker's entry into politics was strictly in the influence of those supporting George III – just one year after he was crowned; but it seemed no time before the King seemed set on that same dominion of the Crown over Parliament which had been the trouble for the past hundred years, and soon John Parker was signing the Devon Petition, supporting Mr Wilkes and defending the privileges of a Member of the House of Commons. He had embarrassment, too, over the Cyder Tax – which could hardly be pleasing to the gentlemen and farmers of the west country – and there was trouble and restlessness about the imposing of the stamp duty upon the American Colonies, and a fear that the King and Lord North would do nothing but lose the colonies for the country.

To be a Member of Parliament was becoming a burdensome business.

In the House itself, it might well seem to some that members conducted themselves in a very casual way:

They enter the House in greatcoats, boots and spurs! It is not unusual to see a Member stretched out on one of the benches while the rest are in debate. One member may be cracking nuts, another eating an orange or whatever fruit may be in season; they are constantly going in and out. Whenever one of them wishes to leave the Chamber he stands first before the Speaker and makes him a bow, just like a schoolboy begging

*Wilkes, the rebel, with his distinctive squint*

*Politics and talk, talk, talk . . . The eighteenth-century polling booth.*

permission of his teacher. [They:] address the House without any stiffness of speech. One of them simply rises from his seat, takes off his hat, turns towards the Speaker . . . holds his hat and stick in one hand and gesticulates with the other. Whenever one of them speaks badly or the matter of his speech lacks interest for the majority, the noise and laughter are such that the Member can hardly hear his own words . . . It is amusing when the Speaker calls out from his chair, like a school-master appealing against disorder: 'To Order! To Order!' Often without attracting much attention.[7]

It might also be true that many County seats were so securely attached to particular families that they were rarely contested; only about a tenth of the seats from the accession of George III to the end of the century being ever disputed at all. Nominations to the County seats were simply agreed by the gentry, and politics was still certainly the business of the great landowning families. It was true that there were rumblings of complaint – reported in the Political Register for example – that the House of Commons as well as the Lords was dominated by the landed gentry.

[The power of the great land-owners has:]

. . . become more formidable than ever. Their number, their privileges, their court-emoluments, their *influence* in *elections*, their weight in the law, the army, the navy, the church, and the public offices, are all to an unexampled extent increased . . . The wisdom of our ancestors established it as a fundamental maxim . . . that no Lord of Parliament or peer of the realm ought to interfere in elections of members of the lower house. But to observe how electioneering is, in our times, carried on, one would imagine the law of this land was, That no member of the House of Commons should be elected but in *consequence* of quality-influence![8]

A lot of these things might well be true; but still – Mr Parker was not responsible for the system! What he did know was that it was an expensive task – in time, trouble and money – to keep electors in good mind, good faith and favourable disposition. Devon was a large county, and though the electors were limited to forty-shilling freeholders and those with comparable claims, in Devon there were some 3,000. All kinds of expenses were known to be employed in 'nursing' electors: providing coaches to take them to the voting, entertaining them for months if the seat seemed likely to be contested, giving their families a golden half-guinea from time to time, keeping their rents moderate, allowing arrears of rent to build up, even throwing open the house to supporters at election time – to the despair of at least one poor Countess:

Our doors are open to every dirty fellow in the country that is worth forty shillings a year; all my best floors are spoiled by the hobnails of farmers stamping about them; every room is a pig-stye, and the Chinese paper in the drawing-room stinks so abominably of punch and tobacco that it would strike you down to come into it.[9]

There was always great excitement about elections – corrupt or not, contested or not. Even country parsons felt a warm glow at being asked to join the meeting of the gentry – probably at the assizes – to hear the nomination of the candidate. An election was a fever that the English people loved. Feelings seethed through the whole population, whether they were active electors or not. 'Bloody heads had been seen' in *contested* elections said one German spectator, and this was how he saw a *settled* election in the streets of London:

The voters, dressed in red cloaks and carrying white sticks, sat on benches erected one above another on an inclined slope. The President sat on a chair. The whole of it was, however, only knocked together with wooden posts and planks. In front of

*Election fever: 'Chairing the Member'*

this scaffold, where the benches ended, were laid mats on which those could stand who were to address the people. In the area before all this had gathered a crowd of people mainly of the lowest class. The orators bowed low to this rabble and always addressed them as 'Gentlemen'. [The candidate] had to step forward and promise these 'gentlemen' with hand on heart that he would faithfully perform his duties as their representative in Parliament . . . As soon as he began to speak, the whole crowd was as still as the raging sea becomes after a storm, and all shouted, 'Hear him!' and as soon as he had ended his address a great 'Hurrah!' rose up from every throat, and everyone – even the dirtiest coalheaver – waved his hat.

He was then formally elected by the deputies on the stage, after which a man stepped forward, and, in a well-delivered speech, wished the people and their new member all prosperity . . .[10]

Obviously – a field-day for everybody!

Small boys, [he said,] hung on the railings and lamp-posts, listening to the speech with as much attention as if it were being addressed to them, and showed their appreciation at the end with a lusty 'Hurrah!' and by waving their hats over their heads just like their elders.

And then:

When all was over, the disposition of the English people showed itself in all its vigour. Within a few minutes the whole scaffold – benches, chairs and all – was smashed to bits, and the mats with which it had been covered torn into a thousand long strips. With these they formed a circle, enclosed within it anyone who came in the way, and drew them along in triumph through the streets.

Election proceedings, even in sleepy Devonshire, did not lack colour. Sir Joshua Reynolds – sometimes thought an austere man – was 'in High Glory', Nanny once said, rushing off to Plympton to such a meeting[11]; and Theresa and the whole household became preoccupied with Mr Parker's business as election time came round. Theresa could never understand why her husband's seat was not contested:

Elections begin to take up a great deal of conversation . . . Mr Parker is obliged to go up to Exeter next week to attend the Assizes an attendance proper to be observed as the Election draws near. He very happily has no contest to fear, at least there is no appearance of any. I have often thought it rather extraordinary there should not considering the three people of most consequence in this County (Sir F. Ackland, Sir Richard Bamfylde and Sir J. Chichester) have all sons just of age and coming into the world.[12]

Here, at his desk in the Library, Mr Parker read his reports, conducted his correspondence, and watched the political scene – not with cynicism – but with a certain taciturnity and down-to-earth good humour.

A Member of Parliament had the privilege of sending official letters free. He wrote letters sparingly, but with a certain painstaking pleasure. He enjoyed the quietness of the occupation for a time. He would fold the letters carefully, seal them with wax, and add his signature in the bottom left corner. The town and date had to be written at the top – and this was important because if the letter was not posted on the day it was dated, the privilege was lost. Mr Parker paid for his ordinary mail at the rate of a penny for one stage ... if over eighty miles it would cost threepence, until in 1784 the rate went up a penny to fourpence – with a resulting outcry! Post Offices then stayed open until nine o'clock in the evening. There was a great temptation to abuse the privilege and send private mail under Official frank. Earlier (in 1734), this had led to an enquiry in which it was claimed that the Post Office lost through abuses over £49,000 a year. In Mr Parker's time the loss was probably many times greater; but all these charges of 'corruption' levelled at their M.P.s by the great-hearted people, gave him a grim amusement. If ever he was near to cynicism it was this that drove him there!

\*

Mr Parker and other Members of Parliament learned much about the disposition of the English people, before, at, and after elections. Even the thought of it was a good reason for a strong drink! One thing Mr Parker knew very well – that it was not only the masters of great estates who were capable of corruption. Those who were not able to dole benefits out – were always ready to receive them: with ever open hands!

The disposition of the English people ...

They even took pleasure in smuggling! And it was not the paupers and labourers alone. Magistrates, lawyers, squires, innkeepers, parsons ... they were all ready to receive a gift from the moonlight gentlemen. They would even – up and down all the coasts of the country – take their sides against the Militia:

Had another Tub of Gin and another of the best Coniac Brandy brought me this evening about 9. We heard a thump at the front door about that time, but did not know who it was, till I went out and found the 2 tubs – but nobody there . . . £1.18s.0d. for a Tub of Coniac Brandy of four gallons by Moonshine Buck and £2.6s.0d. for two Tubbs of Geneva of 4 gallons each – by ditto . . .[13]

There spoke an English country parson!

But then . . . everybody had a weakness for smuggling and smugglers. Tea, tobacco, wine, spirits, snuff . . . anything. Even Adam Smith was so much in favour of free trade and the wealth of nations as to take enjoyment in illicit imports – when he could come by them. Smuggling – no doubt on principle in his case – a Scot, and an economist!

Smoking had become rather a 'low' and 'fast' habit now; a nasty business altogether, and he had no taste for it; but here in the Library, he enjoyed a good claret, and much of it, and a pinch or two of snuff . . . A Member of Parliament needed all the titillations he could get when dealing with the dispositions of the English people!

\*

John Parker found other things much more engaging. There were certain aspects of trade, and the troubles over colonial affairs, which were absorbing, even if explosive with difficulties. People would seem to forget that the colonies were, at the heart of them, *companies*. Virginia had been founded by the London Company (of Virginia) under Charter from James I, and the Gold Coast of Gambia by the Company of Adventurers of London, trading to Africa.[14] And some men in Mr Parker's position were still actively engaged in such enterprises. Indeed, a small syndicate had just been formed, including at least one Member of Parliament, to apply for a concession for a new American Colony to be called *Vandalia*.[15] The members wished to buy land in Virginia for £10,000 and calculated on re-selling at a profit of £500,000. Influential families now combined very considerable landed, mercantile, banking and manufacturing resources, and could secure the representation of their interests in Parliament. It was not so

*Mr Parker sitting astride his library chair. A folding desk-support held his maps, papers, or books, and the arms of the chair then formed a comfortable rest on which he could lean forward, with arms folded, to read and study in a relaxed manner.*

much that their family business spilled over into Government, as that they regarded Government as part of their family business. The American colonies (companies) objected to being taxed by an autocratic monarch in whose government they were not even represented; and there were many who thought that their point of view was very reasonable.

On the verge of losing colonies, however, the country was gaining them in much more interesting ways. If Elizabethan gardens were out of fashion, the Elizabethan love of adventuring was not. The great love of voyages which had continued from those times was strong in the country again. With the sea surging into Plymouth Hoe and up to his doorstep – indeed, sometimes flooding his fields – John Parker found this an irresistible interest. Many books of voyages – of Dampier, Anson, Byron, Wallis, Carteret – had their place on his shelves. On Dampier's maps at the close of the seventeenth century, on the globes of the world, there was a large unlined area indicated in the South Pacific, below South-East Asia, named 'New Holland' or 'Terra Australis Incognita' – an unknown land. Just when the fatal taxing of the American Colonies was beginning (in 1768), Captain Cook was sailing from Plymouth in *The Endeavour* – and not, now, on any military exploits, but on a voyage of discovery to the south seas chartered by the Royal Society. Early in 1770, when Lord North took up the government which was to lose the American Colonies, Cook was circumnavigating the two islands of New Zealand. Later in the same year, he reached

*Aborigines – natives of 'New Holland' (Australia) – drawn by a member of Cook's expedition when he landed in Botany Bay in 1770.*

the coast of Australia and took possession of it in the name of King George.

America . . . Australia. Loss and gain. But the value of Australia and New Zealand was little realised in the obscuring fog of smoke and musket-fire that was to crackle out across the Atlantic.[16] A large and significant patch of territory was added to the globe.

*

There was one other question, rooted in trading and colonial affairs, which was troubling Mr Parker.

Slavery!

Just before New Year's Day, 1769, when Cook was nearing Cape Horn, and his men were beginning to complain about the cold, this advertisement appeared in the *Edinburgh Advertiser*:

*Negro Slaves*
*To be Sold*
A BLACK BOY, about 16 years of age, healthy, strong and well made, has had the Measles and Small-Pox, can shave and dress a little, and has been for these several years accustomed to serve a single gentleman both abroad and at home.
For further particulars, inquire at Mr Gordon, Bookseller, Parliament Close, Edinburgh, who has full powers to conclude a bargain.[17]

The buying and selling of a negro in England was a common transaction. And the slave-trade provided a good supply of labour for the colonies. Just as unfortunates on the docksides were press-ganged into the service of the navy and the army, so the unfortunates of Africa – who were hunted and caught – were press-ganged into bondage for the colonies. Many made the 'middle passage' over the Atlantic in the holds of English ships: sailing from Liverpool, Bristol, London. About 192 ships were engaged on the trade, with space for about 47,000 slaves. The negroes:

. . . were chained to each other hand and foot, and stowed so close that they were not allowed above a foot and a half for each in breadth. Thus crammed together like herrings in a barrel, they contracted putrid and fatal disorders, so that they who came to inspect them in a morning had occasionally to pick dead slaves out of their rows, and to unchain their carcasses from the bodies of their fellow-sufferers to whom they had been fastened.[18]

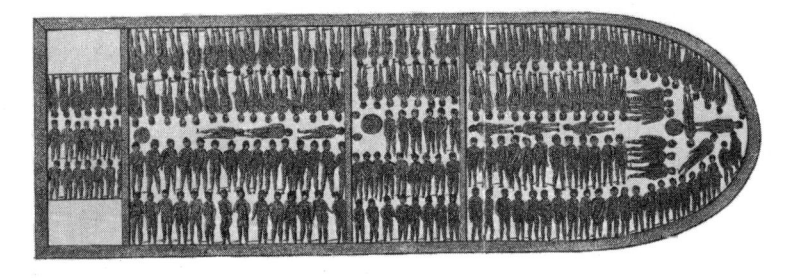

*Diagram of a slave ship to show how slaves were packed into the holds to best advantage – to make the maximum use of the available space. Wilberforce used a model of such a ship for his parliamentary campaign against slavery.*

Horace Walpole, who – like the ill-mannered Dr Johnson – was one of the first to express his utter revulsion of feeling, and to protest, was sickened after one session of Parliament:

We, the British Senate, that temple of liberty, and bulwark of Protestant Christianity, have been pondering methods to make more effectual that horrid traffic of selling negroes . . . It chills one's blood. I would not have to say that I voted on it, for the Continent of America![19]

The Society for the Propagation of the Gospel owned slaves in Barbados, and George Whitefield, a preacher in the evangelical revival, had slaves in Georgia. In later debates in the House, some Moravian missionaries who had been preaching, 'most forcibly, that all men were alike God's creatures', were defended on the grounds that '10,000 negroes had been converted in the Island of Antigua, and their tempers and dispositions had been rendered so much better, that they were entitled to an increased value of £10'.[20] By Mr Parker's day there were about 200,000 negroes in Virginia, and, from 1700, about 600,000 had been transported to Jamaica alone. One estimate was that over 2 millions had been imported into all the British Colonies in America and the West Indies within the past 100 years, and that it would require an annual importation of 58,000 to 'keep up the stock'.

Now, however, so many of good and powerful influence were ranged against it.[21] Dr Johnson, Wesley, Wedgwood, Pope . . . The Quakers were against it, and excluded from their society anyone who was concerned with it. Lord Mansfield – whose library and manuscripts were burned by a mob eight years later – decided, in 1772, in the name of the whole bench, that as soon as a slave set his foot on the soil of the British Isles, he became free. It was moved in the

*Opposite: The Great Room*

*The mirror on the left reflects the Venetian window. Two polescreens stand on either side of the fireplace, and the chimney-piece is that which John and Theresa preferred to Robert Adam's design. The carpet is that made by Thomas Witty, and the roundels in the ceiling were painted by Zucchi. The blue and gilt furniture is probably Chippendale. In the far corner can be seen the candelabra and the table which are shown in the detail on page 74.*

House, four years later, 'that the slave-trade was contrary to the laws of God and the rights of men'.

The motion *failed*.

But there was no doubt whatever that further action in Parliament must arise.

*

The Library . . .

Row upon row of rich, leather-bound volumes. Books of great voyages – on the high seas from Plymouth Hoe to the Pacific; and voyages in the mind and the spirit. Brushes and canvases for leisurely painting. The folders of designs for pleasing gardens, for arrangements of shrubs and beds of flowers to edge the lawns. The drawings for the tasteful improvements of Saltram – made by Robert Adam himself with the warmth of Theresa's taste, her interest, and nobility of heart and mind behind them. Behind them, too, a Member of Parliament for the County – who knew very well politics, power, elections and the disposition of the English people, high and low . . . and who could see, in his mind's eye, even now, a ship taking sail from Liverpool, soon to have some of Britain's living wealth lying chained together, cowed and docile in its corrupting holds.

There were times when John Parker sat in the library window, and did not read, and could scarcely be said even to think. He seemed, at such times, simply to feel himself at the very centre of the world: the world of so much beauty, terror and evil. Its grave realities – and his impotence among them – crushed him. He just watched over the quiet lawns, in the west country where he loved to be, as the late evening, and then the night came on, and, slowly, through a changing sky of almost overwhelming beauty, a complete darkness came down over everything.

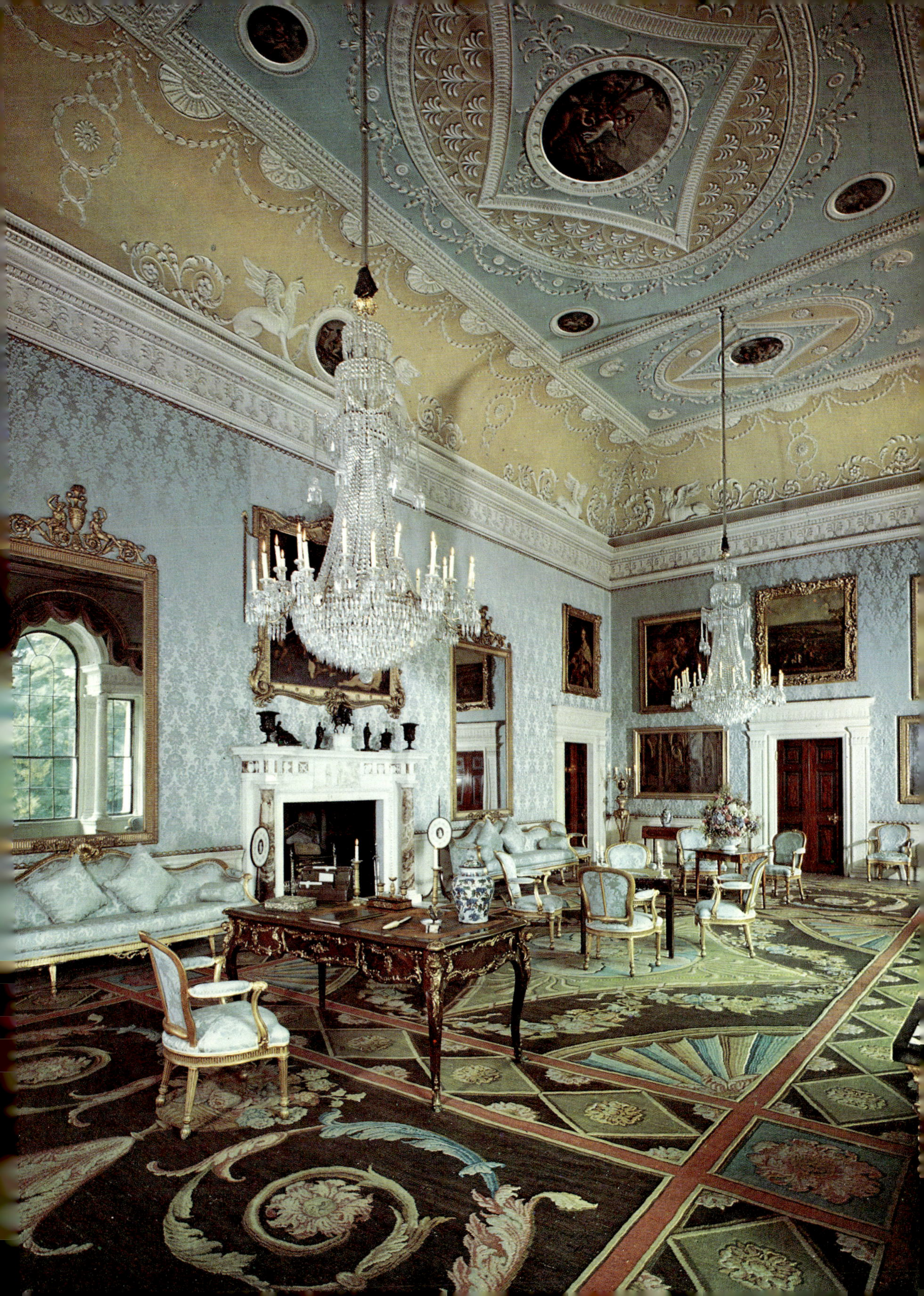

*'Some had been playing cards and some promenading while the play went on . . . Whist was very popular, and* vingt-et-un, *and a good wager always added spice to the play.'*

*The chimney-piece chosen by John and Theresa for the Great Room – with food and wine nearby for the evening's entertaining. This gives a very clear picture of the pole-screen, and on the small table a novel and a glass of wine have been placed by the candlestick.*

# 5 THE GREAT ROOM

## *the Great Age of Candlelight*

The centre-piece of a great house was its Great Room. It was the hall-mark of the wealth, taste and culture commanded by a family.

Even as they were built, these houses became famed as public show-pieces. They were a kind of conspicuous consumption: not only for private use. People travelled great distances to see them – then, as now.

It was certainly John and Theresa Parker's early ambition to create such a house and such a room to their own liking. To do it they went to the man employed and recommended by their friends who was becoming the *only* fashionable choice: Robert Adam. After his return from Rome, Adam's fame grew quickly, but at first his commissions were not to build entire houses, but substantially to alter, re-design and re-decorate their interiors. During the 'sixties and 'seventies, he worked on seven or eight country houses besides Saltram – including Newby Hall in Yorkshire: the home of Theresa's brothers Grantham and Fritz.

Together, John and Theresa pored over the designs which Robert Adam submitted. They were all exquisite – and not assessed easily.

Everything was interlinked with everything else. There were designs not only for the room: but also for all the items within it – like the carpet, the four great wall mirrors and the marble chimney-piece which was intimately to follow the design of the door-frames. Neither of them were sure about the mirrors, or the chimney-piece. They were inclined to something different; it was difficult to decide; and Mr Parker – despite his generous disposition towards the spending of money – was sometimes a little troubled about the problems of his purse!

The expense was going to be very considerable. No purse-strings are unlimited, no matter how well endowed initially, and Mr Parker – by no means a man afraid of decision – sometimes felt, nonetheless, a chill of apprehen-

*Robert Adam*

*A corner of the Great Room. Matthew Boulton's six-branch candelabra stands in the corner. The satin-wood table is that supplied by Henry Kettle, and the chair was probably from Mr Chippendale.*

sion. Was he indulging their ambition, their pleasure, a little too far . . .? But generosity of disposition prevailed! He spared no expense. The Great Room at Saltram was created by making two or more large rooms into one, at a cost of about £10,000. Only two years after their marriage, Theresa, deeply pleased, could write to tell Grantham: 'The Great Room is well finished indeed!'

Robert Adam, however, had not been satisfied with the room itself. It should not be approached abruptly, he felt, but by a classical transition from the Red Velvet Drawing room. To achieve this, he designed classical columns, and accompanying mirrors and tables to flank the entrance.

Ultimately, when all was complete, John and Theresa brought their guests through the relatively warm, relaxed, homely atmosphere of the smaller drawing room, and paused here. But no such entrance could possibly have prepared them for what they were to see when the doors were opened.

*

What were the immediate impressions of all those who walked through these doors? Surely, they were of light, and light colours, and height, and a large spaciousness in a room which was still – a domestic room. An elegant arrangement of the finest art and craftsmanship, within which people could live; within which they could walk, and move, and sit, and converse. The sheltered Elizabethan gardens had gone – replaced by the open vistas of natural landscape; and gone, too, was the sombre tone of the Tudor home, looking out on to its enclosed quadrangle, solid and dark with its oak panelling.

These were Venetian windows: they let a flood of light into a room which had movement in all its lines of walls and ceiling and furnishings. It was, indeed, a re-introduction of the light of the classical world. Europe was struggling with ever more confidence, ever more certainty, out of the dark ages and the tortured purgatory of Medievalism. This kind of room *was* the Enlightenment. Not just a set of philosophical ideas, but also a spirit which infused the designing of things and a way of living within them: of a house and a life which looked out upon the world in reason, enquiry and sensuous engagement, not one shut in upon itself in the dark, dark embraces of introspective dogma.

The people who had *feared* in darkness were seeing a great light.[1]

\*

Adam's work – as Mr Parker's pocket had discovered – was an entire conception. It dealt with every detail: not only the large proportions of walls and ceilings, but also the carpet design, the picture frames, the brass-gilt doorhandles, the smallest fitments. Every element of art and craftsmanship within a room had to blend and match. Adam was not therefore just an individual artist, but a contractor of all those whose skills put his designs into effect. He was the focal point of a large division of labour.

The carpet, designed for the room by Adam himself, was made by Thomas Witty in his Axminster factory for £126. The chimney-piece of Sienna marble (John and Theresa did, in fact, reject Adam's initial design) came from a favourite supplier – Thomas Carter of Piccadilly. The stucco-work of the ceiling was undertaken by a special craftsman; and Adam employed a number of distinguished painters. Antonio Zucchi and Angelica

*An Adam doorhandle*

Kauffmann – who were ultimately married to each other – were two of these. It was Zucchi who painted the roundels in the ceilings.

The world of society, of patronage, of art, was then a relatively small world. It was – as always – a matter of 'wheels within wheels', but then the wheels were big and few. These painters were not only employees of Robert Adam, they were also friends of Sir Joshua Reynolds, and received many commissions – from John Parker and others – as a result of his influence and recommendation. Sir Joshua had befriended Angelica Kauffmann from the time of her arrival in England – she was a very able and cultured woman, well equipped with a knowledge of four languages, and an accomplished musician as well as a painter of considerable skill. Reynolds, she wrote:

... is one of my kindest friends and is never done praising me to everyone. As a proof of his admiration for me he has asked me to sit for my picture to him, and, in return, I am to paint his.[2]

Her portrait of Reynolds was hung in the Staircase Hall. He certainly brought many commissions her way. Nollekens the sculptor, however, who was another wheel within the wheels, had a more caustic view of the dear Angelica. She was, he said:

... a sad coquette. Once she professed to be enamoured of Nathaniel Dance; to the next visitor she would disclose the great secret that she was dying for Sir Joshua Reynolds.[3]

There was one apparently demented man – an engraver, painter and poet of sorts – who poured scorn on this market-place of art. His attitude was odd and eccentric; but one could not deny that it was original – and outspoken!

I consider Reynold's Discourses to the Royal Academy as the Simulations of the Hypocrite who smiles particularly where he means to betray ... Such Artists as Reynolds are at all times Hired by the Satans for the Depression of Art – a Pretence of Art, To destroy Art.
The Rich Men of England form themselves into a Society to Sell & Not to Buy Pictures. The Artist who does not throw his Contempt on such Trading Exhibitions, does not know either his own Interest or his Duty.

'When Nations grow Old, the Arts grow Cold
And Commerce settles on every Tree ...'

The Enquiry in England is not whether a Man has Talents &

*Sir Joshua Reynolds painted by Angelica Kauffmann, and looking less austere than he was usually shown to be. Actually, Reynolds enjoyed other things than delivering discourses to the Royal Academy. He loved shooting and hunting and was worked up to a pitch of high excitement at election times. This picture now hangs at the foot of the stairs in the Staircase Hall.*

Genius, But whether he is Passive and Polite & a virtuous Ass & obedient to Noblemen's Opinions in Art & Science. If he is, he is a Good Man. If Not, he must be Starved.[4]

The man's name was William Blake – but he was a strange, unbalanced man, and then of little consequence.

Robert Adam's division of labour did not stop at skilled stucco-work, carving and fine painting. The carved giltwood furniture was probably designed and made for Adam by Chippendale; but, again, the division of labour went even further than Mr Chippendale himself. If Thomas Chippendale had flourished his chisel over every chair said to be his, he would have been a very busy man. Though obviously a very great craftsman, he was much more than that: a business man, a factory owner, an advertiser, a salesman.[5] *The Gentleman and Cabinet Maker's Director* which he wrote and published was a sales catalogue which advertised his own wares: some of which, he said, 'are the best I have ever seen, or perhaps have ever been made . . .'.

He wasn't backward in coming forward! But nobody spoke of Chippendale furniture then. They would be more likely to talk just of mahogany. Chippendale was a member of the Royal Society of Arts at the same time as Boswell, Dr Johnson, Pitt, Reynolds, Horace Walpole, David Garrick, Oliver Goldsmith and many others – but they never referred to him. He was a tradesman. He had three shops in St Martin's Lane and – according to the record of a fire in his workshop – employed at least twenty-two craftsmen.

Hepplewhite, too, wrote a technical trade book, as did Sheraton, who had the flair of a teacher. Both wrote books. They were large influences, rather than individual craftsmen. Poor Sheraton ended his life as a struggling writer. Adam Black, later to publish the *Encyclopaedia Britannica* was once hard-up in London and worked with him for about a week: 'engaged in most wretched work, writing a few articles and trying to put his shop in order, working among dirt and bugs, for which I was remunerated with half-a-guinea. Miserable as the pay was I was half ashamed to take it from the poor man'. He looked, Black said, like a 'worn-out Methodist minister with thread-bare black coat', working in a house which was ' . . . half shop, half dwelling-house' – trying to make ends meet. Chippendale

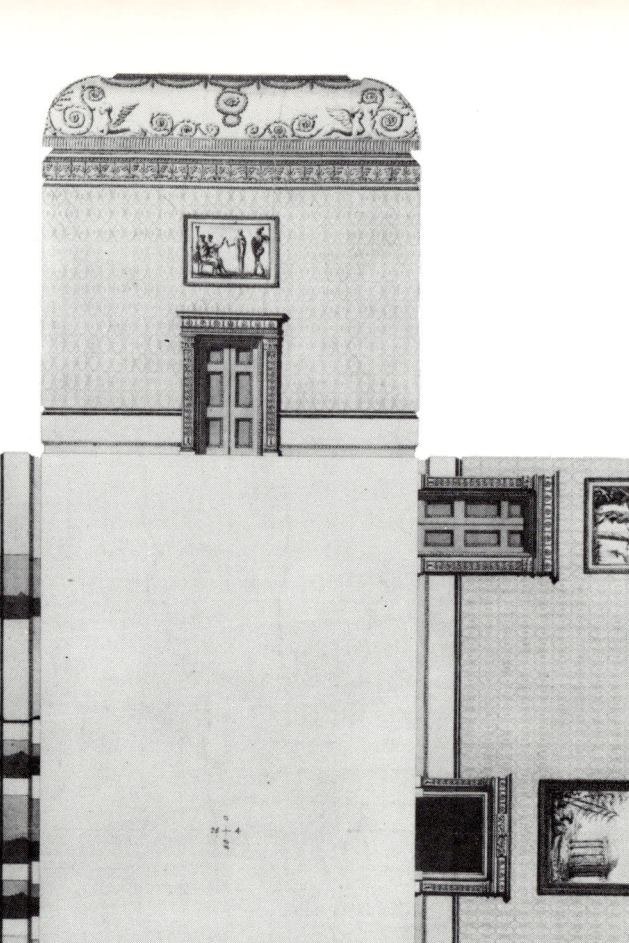

*One of Robert Adam's designs for* The Great Drawing Room *at Saltram. The Venetian window lies on the left. The fireplace, on the right, is one which John and Theresa rejected.*

himself was buried at the Parish Church of St Martin's-in-the-Fields, Charing Cross, for a fee of £2.7s.4d.

Behind Mr Parker's £10,000; behind Robert Adam; lay, then, a considerable division of labour which drew into the Great Room at Saltram, and other rooms of its kind, work and products from all over the country. Matthew Boulton provided six-branch candelabra of the same pattern as he supplied to Queen Charlotte for her drawing room at Buckingham House. A table of satin-wood was supplied by 'Henry Kettle – cabinet maker, upholsterer and undertaker at No. 18 in St Paul's Churchyard, London' – as his label declared. John and Theresa were also well aware of work in the 'Blue John' stone from Derbyshire, and of the ware being produced by Wedgwood in his new Etruria works; but even details of this kind – and there were many – were not the end of the creative work which made and sustained this splendid achievement.

Any sensible housewife would wonder how a room of this size could possibly be protected from cold, damp and streaming condensation; and this was, in fact, one of the continuous problems and preoccupations of the time. In Mr Smollett's novel *Humphry Clinker*, when Miss Tabitha Bramble left Brambleton Hall for any length of time, her chief anxiety was that the house should be kept warm. Her letters to Mrs Gwyllum, her housekeeper, were full of it:

Pray take particular care of the house while the family is absent. Let there be a fire *constantly* kept in my brother's chamber and mine . . .

Make constant fires in my brother's chamber and mine, and burn a faggot every day in the yellow damask room . . . have the feather bed and mattress well aired . . .

Take care to have the blue chamber, up two pairs of stairs, well warmed . . .

Damp was a perpetual enemy!

How, then, was a room of this great size sufficiently warmed – and lighted?

Beyond the walls of blue damask, beyond the marble fireplace and the splendid grate of iron, work-people of another kind were busy with their necessary tasks.

*

Round the sea-coasts of Britain, across-country by rivers and a few canals, ships and barges were carrying their cargoes of coal to ports and inland places. Roads were impossible. A whole fleet of ships was sailing between Tyneside and the Thames. Along rivers from east-coast ports, barges were reaching East Anglian towns. From the mouth of the Severn, boats were sailing to the west and west midlands. A few miles from Manchester, along a new subterranean canal, the boats were going 'by the light of candles to the very mouth of coal pits and were laden underground'.[6] With a shortage of timber, coal was in great demand – for domestic fires and for its new use of smelting iron.

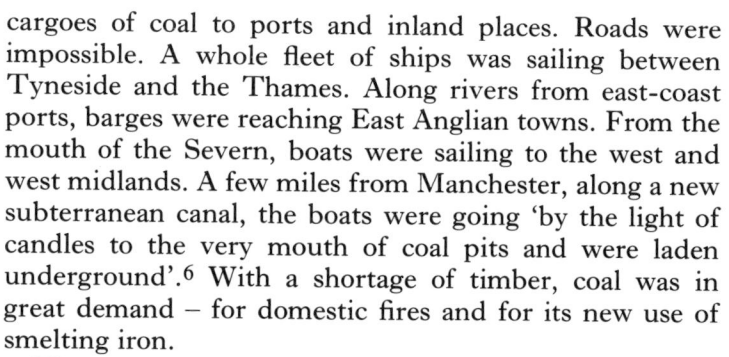

The coal trade was an old trade, but – with pumps to prevent flooding, and ventilation to carry currents of air through all the workings – from the wilds of Scotland, through the large coal-fields of Cumberland, Tyneside and Yorkshire, down to the small shafts of the Free Miners in the green, ferny, glow-worm lighted tumps of the Forest-of-Dean coal-pits were deepened and extended.

Here was another division of labour.

In Scotland, miners and their families were serfs – in bondage for life to a particular mine: transferable with the pit if it changed owners. 'The Black Folk', they were called. A collier went to the pit with his sons at about eleven o'clock at night. His wife and daughters – who began this work at seven years of age – followed about three hours later to carry the coals to the pit-top in large baskets:

> ... it frequently takes two men to lift the burden upon their backs ... The mother sets out first, carrying a lighted candle in her teeth; the girls follow, and they proceed to the pit bottom, and ascend the stairs, halting occasionally to draw breath, till they arrive at the pit-top, where the coals are laid down for sale ... We have seen a woman take on a load of at least a hundredweight and a half, travel with this 150 yards up the slope below ground, ascend a pit by stairs 117 feet, and travel upon the hill 20 yards more ... The weight of coals brought to the top by a woman in a day amounts to above 36 hundred-weights. The wages for this work are eightpence a day![7]

Improvements in the lives of colliers' families could be made, it was pointed out, by substituting horses for women.

One visitor went down the Cumberland pits:

> Occasionally a light appeared in the distance before us, which advanced like a meteor through the gloom, accompanied by a loud rumbling noise, the cause of which was not explained ...

till we were called upon to make way for a horse, which passed by with its long line of baskets, and driven by a young girl, covered with filth, debased and profligate, and uttering some low obscenity as she hurried by . . . All the people we met were ragged and beastly in their appearance, mostly half-naked, blackened all over with dirt, and altogether so miserably disfigured and abused, that they looked like a race fallen from the common rank of men, and doomed, as in a kind of purgatory, to wear away their lives in these dismal shades . . .[8]

One task in the coal-pits was that of the 'Trappers' – boys and girls between 5½ and 10 years old – who looked after the ventilation doors:

They sit in a little hole, scooped out for them in the side of the gate behind each door, and pull it the moment they hear the trucks at hand, and the moment it has passed they let the door fall to, which it does of its own weight . . . they are in the pit the whole time it is worked, about 12 hours a day . . . these little creatures are doomed to spend a dungeon-like life, for the most part passed in solitude, damp, and darkness. They are allowed no light; but sometimes a good-natured collier will bestow a little bit of candle on them as a treat.[9]

Miners and their families were generally known to be an uncouth and unruly lot. John Wesley encountered them when taking the Gospel to Yorkshire and Newcastle:

A wilder people I never saw in England. The men, women, and children filled the street as we rode along, and appeared ready to devour us . . . [they] . . . were such as had been in the first rank for savage ignorance and wickedness of every kind.[10]

Arthur Young, too, who met miners in his travels – as well, it seems, as people in every other walk of life in Great Britain and France – thought they were: 'a most tumultuous, sturdy set of people, greatly impatient of controul, very insolent, and much void of common industry . . .' Some, like the Tynesiders, even had the insolence to strike:

Cut off from the light of heaven for sixteen or seventeen hours a day, they are obliged to undergo a drudgery which the veriest slave in the plantations would think intolerable, for the mighty sum of fourteen pence . . . But the more they are kept down, the more their masters will be enabled to venture ten thousand guineas on a favourite horse, or the accidental turn of a card.[11]

The sane, gentle, sensitive, humane Mrs Montagu who

*Mrs (Elizabeth) Montagu*

founded the Bluestockings in the drawing rooms of London was herself a colliery owner. After her husband's death, she visited the north-east:

> The Tyne valley where I live used to look green and pleasant. The whole country is now a brown crust, with here and there a black hole of a coal pit . . . it has mightily the air of an ant-hill: a vast many black animals forever busy. Near fourscore families are employed on my concerns here. Boys work in the colliery from seven years of age. I used to give my colliery people a feast when I came hither, but as the good souls (men and women) are very apt to get drunk, very joyful, and sing, and dance, and holloo, and whoop, I dare not on this *occasion,* trust their discretion to behave with proper gravity; so I content myself with killing a fat beast once a week, and sending to each family, once, a piece of meat. It will take time to get round to all my black friends. I had fifty-nine boys and girls to sup in the courtyard last night on rice pudding and boiled beef . . . It is very pleasant to see how the poor things cram themselves, and the expense is not great. We buy rice cheap, and skimmed milk and coarse beef serve the occasion.[12]

Mrs Montagu gave clothes to the most needy. Each year, on May-Day, she also gave a feast to the 'climbing boys' of the chimney-sweepers. But, even so, she could not feel comfortable:

> I cannot yet reconcile myself to seeing my fellow-creatures descend into the dark regions of the earth; tho' to my great comfort, I hear them singing in the pits.

A great division of labour tunnelled the earth of Britain, providing coals for heating. But what of the problems of lighting?

\*

The most pleasing description of the eighteenth century was: the great age of candlelight – and it was deeply true. For all this hidden, nocturnal life in the tortuous underground galleries of the country was carried on by the flickering light of candles. Seven mines in Wales and Cornwall used between them, in three years, nearly 162,000 lbs weight of candles – which cost about £4,000;[13] but candles lighted not only pits and work-shops, but great houses and cottages alike. Rushlights were the common thing among the cottagers:

> You get the meadow rushes when they are green. You cut off

both ends of the rush and take off all the green skin. The rushes being prepared the grease is melted. (The grease might be the scummings of the bacon pot, or mutton suet.) The rushes are put into the grease, soaked in it sufficiently, then taken out and laid in a bit of bark. [They:] are carried about in the hand or fixed in stands made for the purpose. They give a better light than a common small dip candle, and they cost next to nothing. You may do any sort of work by this light.[14]

Neither rushlights nor dip candles, however, were good enough for some things. Blanket weavers worked from four o'clock in the morning to eight o'clock at night – by candle-light in winter – to earn 10s. or 12s. a week. They went to the workhouse when they were no longer able to see.[15] Embroiderers might earn 7d. a day by starting work at five or six o'clock in the morning and working until nine o'clock at night; their candles cost about 8d. a week; but after a time they could not even see the clock across the room. One lace-worker 'went a long way to see a man hanged t'other day, and couldn't see him a bit after all!' A grim disappointment; and grimly pathetic.

The homes of the country labourer

... a wretched, damp, gloomy room, of ten or twelve feet square, and that room without a floor, and over this wretched apartment only one chamber to hold all the beds of the miserable family ...[16]

and the homes of the Scottish miners

... nine sleep in two bedsteads; there did not appear to be any beds, and the whole of the other furniture consisted of 2 chairs, 3 stools, a table, a kail-pot, and a few broken basins and cups ...[17]

– were gently lighted by rushlight and candlelight!

A vast, hidden division of labour, going quite beyond the perfumed hands of Robert Adam, the craftsmanship of Mr Chippendale, the quiet colours of Antonio Zucchi – of the 'common wretches that crawl on the earth' as the Duchess of Buckinghamshire called them – lay behind the noble fire that flickered delightfully in the Great Room of Saltram, and behind the breath-taking beauty of the chandeliers, the candelabra in the corners, and the great blaze of candlelight.

\*

What had the Company been doing here this evening, after dinner?

First, this heat from the fire was much too fierce for a lady's complexion. Theresa's guest would have to be shielded by the pole-screen, as she glanced, perhaps, at Miss Burney's latest novel.

Some had been playing cards, and some promenading while the play went on. Cards were quite diverting, and were, in fact, *the* evening entertainment from the rooms of the Royal Family down through all the cultured drawing rooms of society. Whist was very popular, and *vingt-et-un* – and a good wager always added spice to the play. Gambling was a great excitement. London clubs, of course, were the real place for this! The most casual bets could range from one guinea to many thousands:

Lord Bolingbroke gives a guinea to Mr Charles Fox and is to receive a thousand from him whenever the debt of this country amounts to 171 millions. Mr Fox is not to pay the £1,000 till he is one of His Majesty's cabinet . . . Mr Sheridan bets Lord Lauderdale and Lord Thanet, twenty-five guineas each, that Parliament will not consent to any more lotteries after the present one voted to be drawn in February next.[18]

The State Lotteries themselves brought in hundreds of thousands of pounds.[19] Fortunes were gambled on matters as trivial as the sex of a French visitor who for thirty-five years had worn women's clothes but was thought a man. The question was brought to the courts:[20]

Witnesses for the plaintiff gave evidence that the Chevalier d'Eon gave a free disclosure of her sex, had proceeded so far as to display her bosom, and had even permitted one to have manual proof of her being, in very truth, a woman. Lord Chief Justice Mansfield, for the defendant, pleaded that this was one of those gambling, indecent and unnecessary cases, that ought never to be permitted to come into a court of Justice; and he hoped the jury would reprobate such wagers. Defendant's Counsel did not attempt to contradict the plaintiff's evidence, by proving the masculine gender.

Actually, when she died, she was a man!

John Parker himself loved his game of cards – here, at Saltram, and in London. The excitement of gambling – in any form – quickly fired his feelings; he never needed much temptation. He liked to play whist – and sometimes

*'Chevalier d'Eon de Beaumont' – woman or man? This detail shows the 'Chevalier' involved in a fencing match.*

*quinze* – almost every evening at Boodles when they were in London, and his account book told the tale:

> February 17th, 1774 lost to L. Shelburne £144.7s.6d.
> March 5th, 1774 lost at Boodles £126.0s.0d.
> March 6th, 1774 lost at Boodles £945.0s.0d.
> March 22nd, 1774 Won at Boodles £105.0s.0d.
> March 27th, 1774 Won at Boodles £105.0s.0d.

The Duchess of Devonshire, too – with whom (like every man in Society) he felt more than a sneaking affinity – was a wild thing with the cards, as with everything else. It was said that her debts were so enormous that no-one could possibly know their true amount. As for Theresa and Nanny: they would, and did, join in the play; but cards – like too much Company – were, for them, a deadly bore:

> I am waited for below to play at that stupidest of all games vingt et un, it so happens that we cannot all agree upon any other game. Mr Parker can't play at Cribbage, Sir John can't play at Whist, Captain Jervis won't play at 21 if I could help it, you will see by this long account I am in no great hurry to begin.[21]

Some entertaining, chosen entertaining, was pleasing, indeed; but some of these formal evenings, with all the County families preening themselves and making their pretences at worldly polish and gaiety was enough to drive anyone out of their wits.

The age of candlelight was the age of the social round: of theatre and opera, and balls and assembly rooms at the Spas, and tea and coffee and chocolate parties. The walks at Bath: 'were covered with Ladies completely dressed and gay to profusion . . . rich cloaths, jewels, and beauty dazzle the eyes'.[22] They danced, quizzed the women through their glasses, the women practised a code of coquetry with their fans, and all of course, were dressed for the occasion: the ladies with hoops and great quantities of petticoats, and sacques and loose gowns and bosoms much exposed, and – their crowning item – their hair! These were the days not only of wigs, but of fine feathers and frizzlation.

*The Spectator* commented:

> There is not so variable a thing in nature as a lady's head-dress; within my own memory I have known several ladies who were once very near seven foot high, that at present want some inches of five.[23]

*A pretty fellow. The extreme 'Macaroni' style for men, 1782.*

The excesses (or should one say pleasures) of fashion were even the subjects of lectures – given sometimes by clergymen bordering on the lunatic:

On Wednesday, the oration will be: on ruffs, muffs, puffs manifold... pantoufles, buskins, pantaloons, garters, shoulder-knots, perriwigs, head-dresses, modistries, tuckers, farthingales, corkins, minikins, slammakins, ruffles, round robins, toilets, fans, patches – being a general view of the Beau Monde from before Noah's Flood.[24]

The men also shone beside the ladies. A pretty fellow might wear a close-fitting, flowered, brocaded waist-coat; a skirt-coat of satin or velvet trimmed with gold or silver lace; breeches of crimson or black velvet; stockings of black or white silk; a gold-laced hat; ruffled shirt and neckcloth; and carry a gold-headed cane and a tortoise-shell snuff-box with a miniature portrait on the lid. He might even have the joint of a toe removed to improve the set of a shoe; and one of the 'musts' for the fashionable 'Lounger' was: '... a glass suspended from the button-hole by a string ... for very few men of fashion can see clear beyond the tip of the nose'.[25]

Bickersteth nicely captured the attitude of the 'gallant' in his verse:

> A coxcomb, a fop, a dainty milk-sop;
> Who, essenc'd and dizened from bottom to top
> Looks just like a doll for a milliner's shop
> A thing full of prate and pride and conceit;
> All fashion, no weight;
> Who shrugs and takes snuff, and carries a muff;
> A minnikin, finicking, French powder-puff.[26]

Among such extravagances was extravagant gossip. John Parker did not much like extremes of sophistication, but, with the warmth of gambling, of company, of good food and good wine, his earthy humour found much to enjoy in some of the stories which were going the rounds, and – given the laxity of alcohol – some amused him to the point of tears:

The fat Bubb-Doddlington, when created Lord Melcombe, was found before a looking glass in his new robes, practising attitudes and debating with himself upon the most graceful mode of carrying his coronet.
Unfortunately, on being presented to Queen Charlotte, his

breeches in the act of kneeling down, forgot their duty, and broke loose from their moorings in a very indecorous manner.[27]

He also always enjoyed any new stories about the Duchess of Devonshire – of which there were always plenty. Indeed, he sometimes wondered what society women would find to quack about on these drawing room evenings if it wasn't for Georgiana. A man couldn't help liking a girl who so continuously set society by the ears; and when in this mood he couldn't help but be amused by what he fancied was a certain touch of jealousy in Theresa's and Nanny's reports about her. Even good-natured Nanny would think a story like this worth the telling:

There is a story of a quarrel between the Duchess of Devonshire and Lady Cranbourne. They were playing and romping (which is the fashion now for young ladies) and the Duchess told Lady C. that her feathers were very ill put on and she would alter them upon which she with great violence pulled one out when unfortunately her curls followed it which as you may imagine provoked Lady C, very much and she told the Duchess she could attribute her behaviour to nothing but her being drunk![28]

Theresa and Nanny themselves were, on occasion, nearly lost in splits of laughter about some of the conversation. There was Montague, doing his best, in Company, to talk about such things as fashionable tables and Wedgwood ware – which, indeed, he bought for his house at Whiteway – but always coming back, in clod-hopping fashion, to hares and foxes and pheasants and partridges, and each success in hunting better than the last! There was Lord Chichester, too, with what Theresa could only call his 'jockey-coxcomb' antics. But, from table to table, the gossip went on . . . and on:

As I have heard the story, Sir Joshua persuaded Mr Chambers who is going to the East Indies it was absolutely necessary he should marry before he went. Mr Chambers left the matter to Sir Joshua, he recommended Miss Wilton who is very handsome, Mr Chambers saw her last Friday, proposed on Saturday, was married on Sunday, was presented today and goes to the East Indies with her on Monday. I think that is business enough for one week.[29]

I also hear they are much afraid Lord Egremont will marry Lady Barrymore. She has certainly refused him but his character is being very obstinate and inclined to be jealous. Her answer was not a bad one, if she has resolution to stick to it. She said that at home her mother pinched her, when she married her husband horse-whipped her. She was now her own mistress and very much at ease and would not subject herself to the like treatment. . .[30]

Sometimes, the stories were more serious, as, for example, about the daughter of the Pelhams – with whom they were very friendly:

There is a shocking account of Miss Pelham's way of going on. After her great loss last Spring at Lady Harrington's she spent the Summer in repentance and vowed never to touch a card more; but the going to Town put an end to all good resolutions, and she now has devoted herself entirely to it. She plays constantly at the Club, loses great sums as well as her Temper, and composes herself terribly, pays ill, and has employed somebody indifferent to her, who is selling out of the stocks for her every day.[31]

Sometimes, too, there were accounts of how some relationships foundered – not so much tragically, as stupidly and miserably – in the midst of such trivialities:

Lord and Lady Craven's breaking is the story of the day. It has been coming on some time. The French Ambassador's attentions and very general admiration which she has met with, these last two years have made her discover that she detests Lord Craven and as he took no pains to counterbalance them by attentions on his part but on the contrary was constantly drunk, and neglected her, it was not till this winter that he perceived he was in danger of losing her. He has carried her into the country and talks of keeping her there three years. but I suppose they will part in form soon. They say Lord Craven is miserable, they have been both to blame and have thrown away their happiness in a state that admits of a great deal, but is very seldom managed so as to enjoy it . . .[32]

Theresa's values were never lost sight of, whatever the superficialities of society. Beyond a certain point in the evening, however, and a certain point of drinking, Mr Parker began to lose all touch with who was married to who, who had left who, who was addicted to the gaming-tables, who had pulled whose curls off . . . and, what was more, he was not in the slightest degree concerned. He and Montague were by no means soul-mates; indeed, they sometimes had hard and bitter differences; but – after an evening of

*Gaming tables in a London club.*

gossip like this – for two pins, he would have gone off with him to find a couple of horses and go for a quiet, enjoyable ride in the dark. It would have been not only refreshing, but also profound – enlightened – to talk about rabbits, or the new bullet-gun, or the fishing nets, or how the trees were shaping . . .

*

Cards, empty glasses, a fan, a snuff-box carelessly left behind, the dregs of wine, the remains of cold meat . . .

They were all gone now; off in their coaches, or up to their bedrooms – for better, for worse – exchanging the latest story; glowing or lamenting or fuming over the golden guineas that had passed from one pocket to another.

The servant was moving alone among the desolate tables. The candles were being snuffed.

*

Over the quiet roofs and chimneys of Saltram house; over all the brilliant spa towns of Bath, Cheltenham, Tunbridge Wells and Harrowgate, alive with their lights, music, entertainments and dancing; over the ferny pits in Dean Forest and the black holes of Scotland; over the women straining at their baskets, and the girls cursing their horses in the dark galleries underground; over the barges on the dark waters of the Manchester canal; over the ships ready to sail from Liverpool and Bristol for their cargoes of slaves; over John Wesley resting a tormented, saddened head in the north-east; over Mr Thomas Chippendale worrying about his rateable value in St Martin's Lane; over Montague who had decided to make his way back to Whiteway that same night and was riding slowly along, enjoying his loneliness; over Nanny looking out to the shadowy trees from her bedroom window; and over John and Theresa having a last word of warm satisfaction, before bed, about the Great Room, and how well everyone seemed to have thought of it . . . Over all those whose work had gone into the making of it within the rough coasts of Britain . . . darkness fell.

The great age of candlelight went out.

# 6 THE STABLE BLOCK

## *'Saltram' : a name on the Turf*

The clock-tower was a distinguishing feature of the entrance to the stable-block. Whenever the bell struck the hour – ringing from its cupola across the woods and lawns of Saltram – it was a sound pleasing to Mr Parker. Wherever he might be: in the Library, mulling over political reports and county affairs – sometimes busy, sometimes absorbed, sometimes bored beyond measure; or in the Drawing Room or the Eating Room – caught up with guests in some entertaining or other; wherever he was . . . the bell always reminded him that one of his greatest joys lay outside his window: horses, riding, racing – and, with them, the whole of the life out of doors.

Stables were a necessity for the household; the only travel was by horseback or coach; but to maintain a fine stable, not only for domestic and estate uses, but also for racing: this was the great joy, if a costly one.

It was, or course, no accident that fine horses were kept and bred in the households of great landowners. The entire structure of authority in Feudal Society had really reflected the employment of the horse in war. The power of crown and feudal nobility; the bond of vassalage between knight, lord and king, had rested largely upon the satisfactory provision of horses and knights trained and ready for battle. Estates were granted for this purpose. The order of chivalry was an order of armed men on horseback. Like marriage, then, the keeping of horses was not an accidental, private matter, but one aspect at the heart of the institutions of property, power and authority. All this, of course, had changed fundamentally, but the 'sport of kings' and of great families, followed upon a practice that had had much more serious roots.

All that aside, horses always meant much to John Parker. Whenever he was ill, the surest sign of his recovery was that he could scramble on to the back of his horse, to take the air. For Mr Parker, the sound of Saltram bell signified a great deal.

\*

Fifty years after Saltram was built, the *Veterinary Monitor* made this recommendation:

Particular regard should be had to the materials of which a stable is built. It should not be built of stone – as in damp or wet weather it is apt to sweat; and the continual evaporation of moisture through the walls will make it very unhealthy for the residence of horses; in so much that disease and sometimes death must unavoidably be the consequence. Nothing can be more wholesome than brick-built stables – this is warm and dry.

Mr Parker's stables, the most modern of their time, were in fact begun in the middle of the century and mainly completed by 1771. They were built to house hunters – and road and carriage horses were always kept in a stable of their own – near the entrance to the courtyard so that they would not disturb the other horses when required suddenly, or when returning from a long journey late at night. Geldings were usually chosen to carry out all the humble duties – domestic and sporting – for the members of the household. And geldings pulled the coaches. They were usually heavy, strong-shouldered, open-chested horses, and – being castrated males – were quieter and more easy to handle than either stallions or mares who were rejected on account of their passions and continual state of irritation. Carriage horses stood about sixteen hands high – about five foot four measured from the ground to the highest point of their withers – and would often cost about £150, though prices varied considerably. To keep the horses fit for the road and the chase their coats were always kept short or 'fine'. Clipping when required was done with a pair of specially bent scissors and a comb, and a horse was given a 'short back and sides'. It would take a groom about three hours to clip a horse out.

Even the feeding of horses was a difficult art to learn, and demanded much attention and intelligence from the groom. No two horses have the same appetite and the right variety of fodder had to be carefully assessed to keep the horses fit for their duties day in and day out. The basic fodder consisted of oats, hay, split beans, peas, bran, served cold or warm with ale or brandy. Potatoes washed clean helped the horses into a good condition for the road. Turnips in small quantities were often given but carrots were considered indigestible and never used.

The groom's daily routine began at six o'clock in the morning when the windows and doors were opened and the droppings removed by hand. Then the horse was groomed – the first of many groomings throughout the day – taken to a stream to be watered and at a quarter to seven given its first feed. At the same time the grooms had their breakfast. Then at a quarter past seven those horses not required for hunting or carriages were exercised. At nine o'clock the grooms cleaned the clothing of any of the horses which were out and on Sundays washed the stables, the windows, and scrubbed all the woodwork. At ten-thirty horses needed for hunting or carriage work were prepared and this was the time that John Parker visited the stables. He looked over each horse carefully, rubbing its coat with a cambric handkerchief. If the handkerchief was soiled the grooming would not have been satisfactorily carried out.

Then the grooms began to clean and polish the previous day's harness and saddlery which had been hung out all night to dry and every detail was stripped and thoroughly cleaned. This was a recipe for black harness polish:

> Equal amounts of lamp black and linseed oil. Where a shine is wanted linseed oil is omitted and small ale substituted in the proportion of about a pint to an ounze of lamp black. A little brown sugar is added to the composition plus half an ounze of gum arabic or the white of an egg.

The grooms' work continued throughout the day with watering and feeding, further grooming, preparing the stalls, washing the saddlery and harness, cleaning and inspecting the carriages . . . until eight o'clock at night when the horses were watered and fed for the fourth and last time and set fair for the night. It was a long, hard day, from six in the morning until eight at night, and sometimes later – for a weekly wage of seven shillings.

The head groom took a pride in the good health of his horses. He had his own medicine cupboard, and knew, for example, how to treat a horse with a headache – with a special snuff blown up the nostrils three or four times a week. If a horse caught a cold a special drink was prepared: made from liquorice, hore-hound, aniseed and despente, all boiled together in a quart of ale with honey added; but the most common ailments arose from work – saddle and harness wounds; and for this the groom would prepare his own ointment. The horses' shoes were heavy and there was a law which made the blacksmith liable for damages if he shod a horse in the quick – that is if he pricked a horse's foot with a nail.

Mr Parker paid much attention to the good maintenance of his stables, and saw to it that the grooms took great care of their charges.

\*

There were good reasons, too, why the horse should be well-cared for. Pleasure aside – it was not too much to say that civilization rode on its back. Apart from the muscles of men, the horse was the great engine and the great vehicle, of English agrarian society – in agriculture, transport, trade and communications. And the golden age of agriculture was witnessing a new expansion of travel: indeed a new zest for travelling!

Wealthy families made their tours of the continental cities; while others – all over the length and breadth of Britain – were intent on seeing beyond the boundaries of their own localities.

Britain was still a tangled half-civilized landscape.[1] Communities were substantially isolated between stretches of thick forest, untamed bogs and fens, straggling black heather and rocky wastes. Willows marked the way over swamps.[2] In eastern parts, a land-lighthouse guided travellers over the shapeless wastes at night.[3]

Over these primitive distances, men began to struggle more insistently by horseback, waggon and coach – by track, lane and by-way – scarcely by road! Turnpike Companies and Road Acts by the hundred did not seem to make much difference. Arthur Young praised four roads in the country. Of the rest, he said that it was a 'prostitution of language to call them turnpikes':

> I know not in the whole range of language, terms sufficiently expressive to describe this infernal road. It is a principal one, and one would naturally conclude it to be at least decent; but let me most seriously caution all travellers to avoid it as they would the devil; for a thousand to one but they break their necks or limbs by overthrows or breakings down. They will meet here with ruts which I actually measured four feet deep, and floating with mud from a wet summer; what, therefore, must it be after a winter?[4]

Still... nothing could prevent people from travelling.

Some went by horseback alone. The adventurous Scots clergyman took a full month to ride from Clunie to London, marvelling all the way at new methods of farming, the varying prices of coal, the subterranean caves of Derbyshire – and one which especially intrigued him, which seems to have had the name of 'The Devil's Arse', the Duke of Bridgewater's canal, men dangling forty feet high in their chains from gallows, and – ultimately – at all the sophistications of London, including the sheer magic of East India ships on the Thames:

> Come in prospect of the East India Fleet just arrived in the river; six millions of pounds sterling. Get alongside of the Phoenix, East Indiaman. See on board an Elephant, a present to

her Majesty the Queen of Britain. See there also a curious monkey, some Java sparrows, an elk, and several sheep of the Cape of Good Hope ... Great luxury and elegance on board the East India ships. Take leave of our friends and sail up in an open boat to Wapping by the light of the moon.[5]

But along all these tracks small companies of travellers in vehicles of various kinds crept, and creaked, and shuddered at eight miles an hour and more. Large, clumsy, covered waggons with broad wheels to grip the broken roads and span the ruts carried goods and people over 25 to 35 miles in 24 hours – and in such a civilized part as Tunbridge Wells to London. Stagecoaches were lighter and much improved, though without springs, but the journey from London to Edinburgh could take 16 days. A family would pay £100 to travel from Suffolk to Dawlish – in 8 days. Even on the best 'Flying Stage', the journey from Exeter to London took 3 days, and accidents and over-turnings were the expected thing. Elizabeth Montagu, when a girl, used to 'squall with joy' when the coach overturned (her nick-name, as a girl, was 'Fidget'), but others were not so amused. Sometimes horses, travellers, coach and all, were engulfed in filthy pools.

One gentleman who had lived some time in Lisbon was revisiting his sister and paternal home in Norfolk, and had a

*A stage waggon – with wide wheels to cover the rough, uneven ruts in the roads.*

*'. . . . in black, miry pools'. A stage-coach sometimes deposited its passengers in order to traverse a difficult stretch of road.*

fairly smooth journey of three days from London to Norwich. But it was then that his troubles began:

Between Norwich and his sister's dwelling lay 20 miles of country roads. He ordered a coach and six and set forth on his fraternal quest. The six hired horses although of strong Flanders breed, were soon engulfed in a black miry pool, his coach followed, and the merchant was dragged out of the window by two cowherds . . . He was brought back to Norwich, but nothing could ever induce him to resume the search for his sister and to revisit the ancestral home.[6]

That was an end of one family story!

And coach journeys had other hazards for those who wanted to travel cheaply:

There is another way of travelling – not in, but on top of the coach without any seat or handhold being provided. Poor people ride in this way – they are charged only half as much as those who ride 'on the inside'. They sit there anyhow they can, with their legs dangling over the side . . . The coach rolls along the stony street at great speed and every now and then they are tossed into the air; it is a near wonder that they always land back on the coach. This sort of thing happens whenever you go through a village or down a hill . . .[7]

These discomforts of travel were not helped at all by the conditions of wayside inns. Dirt and bugs were so common that the more wary travellers took their own sheets with them, and sent servants on ahead to make sure their rooms were clean, their beds were well made, and that the hostler was ready to clean and feed the horses.

Besides ditches, gaps, ruts, miry pools and flock-beds made up with straw, there were also highwaymen. Though there were some serious shooting incidents, highwaymen however, did not seem too great a danger:

They ride on horseback and often, in their desire to relieve the traveller of his purse, put him in terror with an unloaded pistol. But such men have been known to return part of their plunder to a victim gravely distressed, and in any event they do not murder lightly.[8]

In Devonshire, some of the roads the Parkers had to use were passable, but the by-roads went, without rhyme or reason, over the most difficult hills and slopes. Up hill and down dale was a correct description![9] They were not the width prescribed by law. Huge stones were forced into holes which they did not adequately fill and then covered

*A phaeton ready to drive off from the stable-yard at Saltram*

with small and unbroken stones of no regular size. These were washed away by storms and streams, leaving a ridge of uneven rocks and holes which menaced horses and travellers alike. They were so unsafe, so long and winding, and going frequently over unbridged rivers, that people who dined with friends only two miles away would often stay over-night. Nanny wrote to say how they were once marooned even at Saltram:

I am really quite a prisoner, The Flood last Tuesday night broke down the Arch of the Bridge in the turnpike road just by the lodge so that it is impassable nobody can come to see me but when the tide is out. General Grey called yesterday and Mr Lloyd today but had not time to set down because the tide was turned, and they were afraid the water would deepen.[10]

Travelling on the better roads was no great improvement. John Taylor Coleridge – the nephew of Samuel Taylor Coleridge, the poet – used, as a boy, to travel the 140 miles from Ottery St Mary near Exeter, to school at Eton, on the outside of the coach in all winds and weather, and took seventeen hours. His luggage was picked up from under the elm-tree at Fair-Mile.[11] One of his friends, Daniell, was once $2\frac{1}{2}$ days on the road; his coachdriver having been frozen to death on the box. No wonder that Mr Parker always gave very careful instructions if ever young Jack had to travel back from London without a member of the family. Usually, he had him hire a chaise and pair for any doubtful stretch of the journey:

I have this moment received your second letter respecting Jack's coming down, upon which Mr Parker desires me to say that he sees no real objection to his coming with Mr Leigh, and that he has had permission so to do, which ever way you think safest. He don't like either dilligence or Mail Coaches, he would have Jack take a Chaise and Pair from Honiton to Mr Leys at Exeter. I think there can be no danger his coming that one stage by himself.[12]

97

The traditional patience of the Englishman is easily explained. It has always taken so long to get from one place to another – the region may have been impassable, the weather foul, the roads an abomination, the horses refusing to take the hills, the postillions drunk, the coachmen ill-tempered – that he long ago gave up all thought of actually arriving anywhere.[13] His whole philosophy has had to become one of enduring the journey as well as he may – without expecting any particular destination. Fortunately, this is as sound an attitude as a nation can find for getting through history. Necessity is sometimes the mother of wisdom!

*

Horses were still indispensable in work, transport, manufacture and the growing network of commercial trade. Perhaps their most conspicuous part was in the Royal Mail. The extent of 'community' can always be measured by the distance of the best communications – and then, as earlier, this was a considerable distance:

The Death of Good Queen Bess was not known in some of the remoter parishes of Devon and Cornwall until the Court mourning for her had been laid aside; and in the churches of Orkney, prayers were put up for King James II three months after he had abdicated.[14]

Even God must have experienced a certain dilemma when communications were slow.

Coaches were later introduced by Mr John Palmer, but the promised improvements of the British Postal Service always seem late in coming. At Saltram they did not see much difference for a time. The women-folk – who spent much of their time in letter-writing – were especially concerned:

We are in daily expectation of the Mail Coach which Mr Palmer promised should be down last Monday . . . At present we are worse off than before the reform . . . I received on Saturday a letter which I ought to have received a fortnight ago . . . There has been such an interruption and jumble in our correspondence that it has been the cause of much unavoidable fidgets and confusion . . .[15]

The horse – stronger than the ox, capable of carrying larger loads over longer distances – was still the chief labouring animal, not only in agriculture but in other occupations too. There were 20,000 horses employed in

*The original Bath Mail Coach*

transporting coals in Newcastle.[16] They hauled coal in large panniers of 280 lbs from Worsley to Manchester, and elsewhere towed barges, and hauled trucks through the galleries of mines. Some work in the country was too heavy, too cumbersome, for waggon or coach, and in Devonshire, horses struggled to haul heavy weights of stone and granite by the use of 'truckamucks':

They didn't have wheels, but were a sort of cart with the ends of the shafts carried out behind and dragging on the ground. In fact, the cart was nothing but two young trees, and the roots dragged, and the tops were fastened to the horse. When they wanted to move a heavy weight they used four trees, and lashed the middle ones together.[17]

A good deal of the carrying of goods was done by packhorses. Droves of pack-men and pack-horses moved about the country, picking their way along narrow tracks through which coaches and waggons could not go:

Nothing was carried in waggons then, but on pack-horses, that is to say, no perishable goods. Those were rare times ... There was great skill required in packing; the pack-horse had crooks on its back, and the goods were hung to these crooks ... The packmen used to travel in a lot together, because at times they carried a lot o' money about with them; and it did happen now and then that lonely packmen were robbed and murdered... When they put up at an Inn for the night, there was fun – not but they was a bit rough-like. I mind when one day they found a jackass straying, and didn't know whose it was, nor didn't ask either. They cut handfuls of rushes, and with cords they swaddled the ass up with rushes, and then set alight to him. Well, sir, that ass ran blazing like a fire-ball for four miles before he dropped ... Them was jolly times.[17]

Parts of Devonshire were a labyrinth of very narrow lanes between high hedge-banks topped by a growth of

*The Duke of Bridgewater's aqueduct across the River Mersey*

coppice, and might seem little frequented, but travellers had to beware of brigades of pack-horses which would descend a slope at a very rapid pace if unloaded, and – if loaded – were impassable![18] Even pack-horses could be a peril.

But no less than a transformation of the place of the horse in society was gradually taking place. If roads were not much improved, great changes came with the cutting of canals. Rivers were already deepened and made more navigable by locks; but now completely artificial waterways were linking the important mining, manufacturing and trading areas throughout the country. The Duke of Bridgewater, with his well-nigh illiterate engineer – Mr Brindley – who earned 2s.6d. to 3s.6d. a day and ate well on 6d. – had surprised everybody by finishing the canal between the Worsley collieries and Manchester, and the price of coal at Manchester was at once halved! Before long, Kendal was linked with London by the way of Oxford; Liverpool with Hull by way of Leeds; the Bristol Channel and the Humber by the junction of the Trent and the Severn.[19] Great new highways of water linked communities and their varieties of work in a new richness of exchange, and the effects were seen not only in larger cargoes, but in changing qualities of living:

Cottages in the midlands, instead of being half-covered with miserable thatch, are now covered with a substantial covering of tiles or slates, brought from the distant hills of Wales or Cumberland. Fields, before barren, are now drained, and by the assistance of manure, conveyed on the canal toll-free, are clothed with a beautiful verdure. Places which rarely knew the use of coal are plentifully supplied with that essential article on reasonable terms; and the monopolizers of corn are prevented from exercising their infamous trade; for, communication being opened between Liverpool, Bristol and Hull, and the line of the canal being through countries abundant in grain, it affords a conveyance of corn unknown in past ages.[20]

The grimy hands of machine-industry and commerce had a transforming touch of which the golden fields of agriculture had given little sign. The canal habit soon had England by the heart; everywhere their possibilities were explored. In Devonshire plans were discussed for linking Exeter with Crediton, the Tawe with the Exe, Tavistock with the Tamar.[21] A network of waterways was envisaged from the Bristol to the English Channel. Canals opened Britain up to the benefits not only of internal, but also international trade. Trade from other nations could now move easily through all the internal parts of the country, rather than stop on the periphery of its coasts. A new vast flow of commerce was in the making – not now of special commodities for a few, but of all ordinary commodities for everyone – and it was linked with the new *mechanization* of artificial device. Canals were new kinds of roadways to mines, textile mills, potteries, iron and steel works. The muscles of the horse were giving way to new kinds of engines and vehicles: in cog-wheels, belts, spindles and shafts – a new kind of horse-power.

\*

Here in Devon, however, the old ways of rural England tended, still, to prevail. Mr Parker's horses were his means of transport from Saltram to Exeter, and on his visits to Plymouth and his furthest Estates; they provided the power to transport his slate from Cann Quarry; but, above all that, they were his pleasure – deep and abiding. Like all landed gentlemen of his time, he hunted and rode to hounds. Fox-hunting, more than any other sport, was brought to its peak of perfection at this time. The hunts tended to be confined to the residents of the county, but now large parties of neighbours ran over large districts, and hunts like the Quorn, the Pytchley, the Badminton, gained their great reputations. Englishmen and Englishwomen alike, enjoyed good vigorous hunting, and hardly an acre of countryside was left untrodden by horses and baying hounds:

The English [said Dr Johnson] are the only people who ride hard a-hunting. A Frenchman goes out upon a managed horse, and capers in the field, and no more thinks of leaping a hedge than of mounting a breach. Lord Powerscourt laid a wager, in

*The hunt, crossing the lawns at Saltram, with the 'Castle' just visible among the trees*

France, that he would ride a great many miles in a certain short time. The French academicians set to work, and calculated that, from the resistance of the air, it was impossible. His Lordship, however, performed it.[22]

Sir Joshua Reynolds was as much, and as excitedly involved in this as anyone. On his visits to Saltram, he noted in his diaries days spent in the hunting field:

September 10th – arrived Saltram at one
September 11th – Hunting
September 12th – Ride to Plymbridge – Mount Edgcumbe by three
September 13th – Hunting
September 14th – Partridge Shooting
September 15th – Hunting

The hunt stimulated a fever of excitement in all the country people round about, whether they could take part in it or not:

Suddenly, from the hillside opposite, mantled with oak, came the sound of the hounds in cry, and then the call of the horn. Down from the scaffold came the masons, head over heels, at the risk of their necks, out through the windows shot the carpenters and painters, throwing aside hammers, nails, paint-pot and brushes; down went the roses in the garden; from behind the house leaped the wood-chopper; the coach was left half-washed, and the horse half-currycombed; and over the lawn and through the grounds, regardless of everything, went a wild excited throng of masons, carpenters, woodcutter, coach-man, stable-boy, gardener . . . leaving only, on the terrace, the baby – a male – erect, with arms extended, screaming to follow the rout and go after the hounds . . .[23]

Fox-hunting, however, was not for everyone – but men of all classes could enjoy the unique peacefulness of fishing with nets, or with rod-and-line for perch. All could enjoy coursing a hare, netting birds, or shooting birds flushed from cover by spaniels. A Duke might manage a bag of 80 cock pheasants, 40 hares, and many partridges in a day[24]; but others of lesser means could go rambling for the day in pairs. There was the joy of gambling even in shooting. Sir Joshua Reynolds had a note scribbled in lead pencil in his pocket-book:

Mr Parker bets Sir Joshua 5 guineas that he does not beat Mr Robinson; and 10 guineas that Mr Montague does not beat Mr Parker; to shoot with Mr Treby's bullet gun at 100 yards distance; and a sheet of paper to be put up, and the person who shoots nearest the centre wins.[25]

Everyone, too, could enjoy bull-baiting:

A bull is tied to a stake, and a number of bull-dogs set upon him. If he is not sufficiently roused by the pain of their attacks, expedients are hit upon to awake in him that fury necessary to the amusement of the spectators . . . One saws off his horns and pours into them a poignant sort of liquid that quickly excites the animal to the wished-for degree of fury . . . Even fire is employed to rouse an exhausted animal to fresh exertions, and there are instances where he has expired in protracted agonies amidst the flames . . .[26]

And men of all stations could enjoy cock-fighting, though Theresa Parker despised it:

We by chance saw more of the neighbours than we generally do, by accident was drawn in to hear a great deal of a vile Cock Match – this may sound like a Fine Lady, but seriously considered can anything be worse than to be reduced to such company and such amusements.[27]

The Cock-Pit Royal near St James' Park was a great institution, and at Newmarket a 'Main of Cocks' was often fought for 1,000 guineas a side, and 40 guineas each battle.

The Prince of Wales himself enjoyed watching the popular sport of bare-fisted prizefighting. Great sums were placed on men like Stephen Oliver, who was nick-named 'Death', and the Prince was at one fight when Tom Tyne the 'Tailor' killed his opponent with a blow to the head which drove him against the rails.

Cricket, too, with two stumps a foot high, a popping-hole, a curved bat, and the ball hurled along the ground – a game of the common people – had become one in which all could take part. It was possible, for example, for Lord Sackville to play in a team captained by his gardener; and it was a game, as usual, in which all could gamble:

Tuesday was played a grand match of cricket, at Chigwell, Essex, between eleven Gentlemen of Chigwell and eleven Gentlemen of the Mile End Club, for 500 guineas . . . Even betting at starting.[28]

Rural England was full of sports and games – especially if there was money in it! But the greatest sport of all, for Mr Parker was the sport of kings.

\*

To race at Newmarket was his greatest delight – even if it was also his greatest expense! He even employed the painter – Sartorius – to celebrate his favourite horses.

Buying horses; breeding them; feeding, exercising, training them; maintaining sound buildings; employing good grooms, stable-boys, coach-drivers; travelling to and from Newmarket especially; all this amounted to a very substantial item in Mr Parker's account book: quite apart from the large sums – which he could not resist – on gambling. Mr Parker stretched his resources beyond the point of risk – but it was worth it! Sometimes he lost considerable amounts – but sometimes he won:

On September 21st, Mr Parker received the sweepstakes at Bath amounting to two hundred and ten pounds.
On the 29th Mr Parker received by a note from Mr George for money lost upon the match at Bath, seven hundred and thirty-five pounds.
On March 30th, Mr Parker carried cash with him to Newmarket, two hundred and eighty-eight pounds, fifteen shillings; and—
On April 25th nine hundred and ninety-seven pounds, ten shillings out of which one hundred and thirty-five pounds spent on a colt and fifty-two pounds, ten shillings on a coach horse.[29]

*Drinks for members of the Hunt assembling outside Saltram House.*

'The grooms' work continued through the day with watering and feeding, further grooming, washing the saddlery and harness ... It was a long, hard day.'

*The stable-yard at Saltram.*

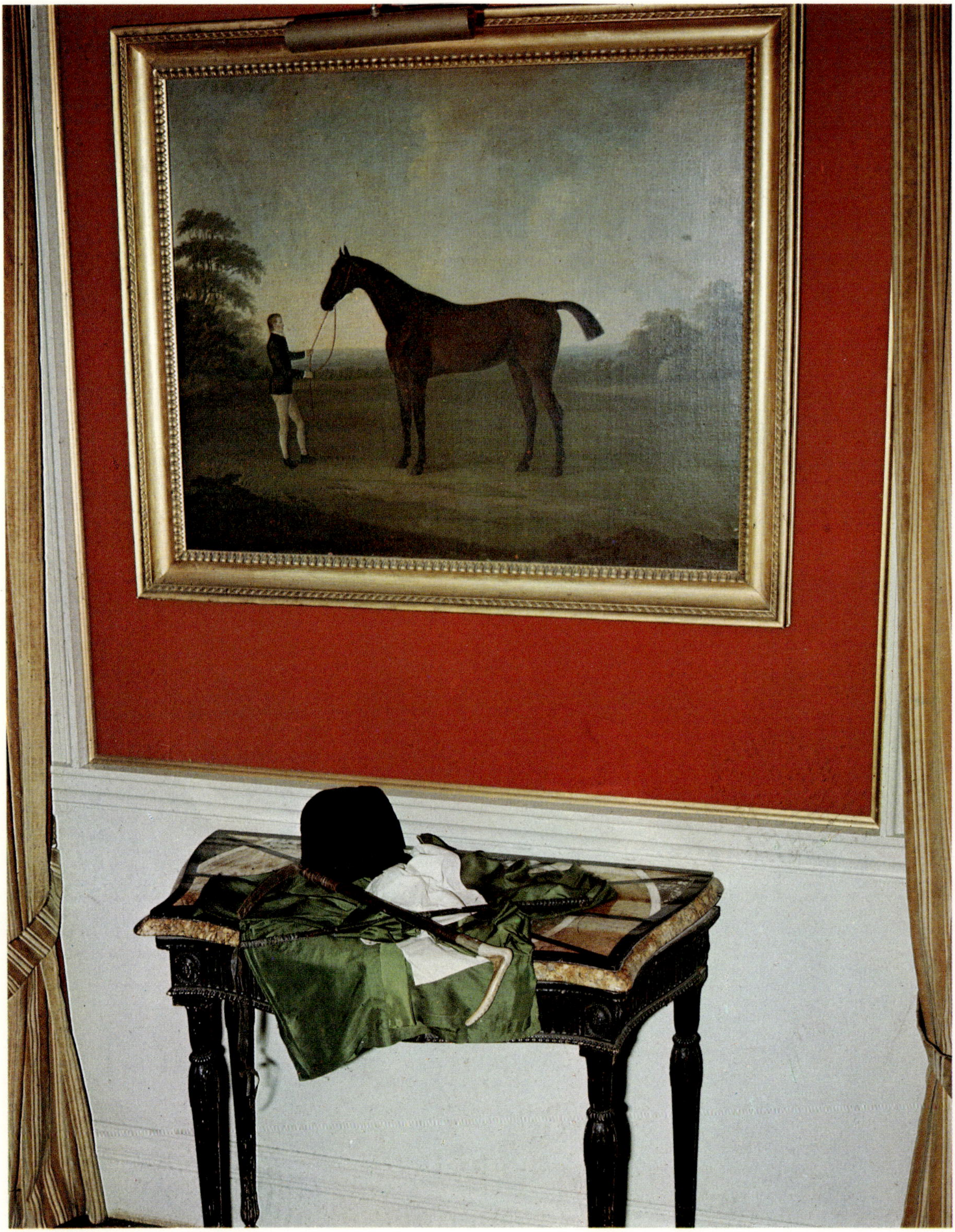

Here, at Newmarket, the jostling, excited crowd contained people of all stations – from Duke to country peasant. Horse-racing was a highly competitive sport. Farmers, gentry and aristocracy all ran their horses against each other, and there was a general fever of zeal, pride, insolence, bristling on the edge of disorder. The expense of keeping a large stable, however, ran into thousands of pounds, and equally large sums could be won or lost in a moment of betting. Some large landowners spent thousands of pounds on racing each year in complete excess of their income. They were urged by their trustees to think better of it, but the fever defeated all caution. Resources were run to danger point.[30] Mr Parker was no exception.

In his early years he was successful, and Theresa was also pleased for him.[31] His stud was of such a high reputation that he was refusing 5,000 guineas for a horse. He won various matches from time to time, but – in due course – Mr Parker had the sweet taste of real success. In the third Derby, run at Epsom, he entered his horse 'Saltram'. The entry fee was 50 guineas – the prize 900. There were thirty-four entries, but, as it turned out, only 6 runners.[32] His jockey was riding in green shirt and breeches and black cap, and, to his great excitement, it was these colours which flashed first past the post.

Saltram was now a name on the Turf!

On that particular home-coming, the whole household celebrated. The bell of Saltram stables – always a good sound – rang even more sweetly in John Parker's ear.

Opposite:

'Saltram' – winner of the third Derby

'Mr Parker's jockey was riding in green shirt and breeches and black cap, and, to his great excitement, it was these colours which flashed first past the post.'

A view of Newmarket: horses being lined up for the start of a race

# 7 CHINESE CHIPPENDALE BEDROOM

*take what you want,*
*says God:*
*take it – and Pay for it*

Theresa loved this room.

It was still as John Parker's mother – Lady Catherine – had made it: with rich oriental wall-hangings, and the most distinctively feminine atmosphere in the whole house.

She was mistress of a large household; helped in her husband's affairs; and shared in all the plans for improving the house and the estate. On some days, she spent a good deal of her time dutifully exchanging visits with neighbours, and – when Mr Parker was away for any length of time – she would take control of the house and deal with some of his affairs. There was much to do:

He has left a variety of letters upon my hands which must all be answered today and tomorrow and the misfortune is, they must all be different as there is one to a Steward, a Gardener, a Groom, and Attorney, and the Commanding Officer of his Militia, about Hats, Swords and Regimentals, however, it also carries his excuse for not waiting upon the Regt. now out at Plymouth, so I don't grumble much at the trouble.[1]

Clearly, a wife was far from being only a feminine ornament.

Even so, more deeply, at the heart of all this, Theresa was a woman – not only of culture and acquired grace, but of natural beauty and warm and generous feeling – who took a deep delight in her own nature, and, indeed, had a many-sided nature of her own to explore. Her deepest joy lay in her feelings of affection for those to whom she was closely attached. She found her own life essentially within these personal relationships. To dwell upon her nature, to deepen it, to sustain her own composure of mind and feeling – here, in this quiet room of her own – was at one and the same time, to sustain her life at the centre of her family.

Theresa had a gift for friendship. The affection which she inspired in others was suffused with all those qualities in which her own nature found its pleasure, happiness, firmness and repose. Her qualities were infectious. It was as though she was inwardly aware of idealities possessing a nature larger than her own – in which her own nature was rooted, but from which it gained dimensions of a greater kind. She was lively, witty, intelligent, good-humoured, accomplished, and could much enjoy the gaiety and sophistication – and even the gossip – of society (at least in measured doses)[2] . . . but there was something beyond all that. There were qualities of seriousness, a certain unforced, unobtrusive, but always present nobility, that shone through her. She was never carried by the throng. She had a mind, a spirit, of her own – a stillness of conviction, a personal grace – which carried a kind of authority of their own. And she had the rare ability of sustaining all her relationships – with her husband, her child, her brothers, Nanny, and all her range of friends, each with its own kind and degree of personal confidence – without loss to any.

People became not only fond of her; they had a curiously warm and tender respect for her, and for her judgements. Though not without her share of prejudice and jealousies – she rarely let them go unqualified: without self-awareness, reflection, and moderation. She was rarely hasty in making judgements. When Lady Georgiana, for example – was about to become the Duchess of Devonshire – she saw all sides of what was involved, and was balanced and generous:

The Duke of Devonshire's match with Lady Georgiana Spencer is all declared and settled. She is vastly well spoken of by everybody that knows her at all and not only by the numerous circle of toadeaters that surround that house. Her manner is remarkably open, good humoured and unaffected and her education has been carefully directed. She is rather too young, as I cannot help thinking it is a misfortune to any woman to marry at 16, but it will be of less consequence to her being upon such a good footing with her Mother and meeting with what I really fancy will make a good husband, though his appearance is against him.[3]

Theresa was a civilized person. She knew that civilization was an art of limitation: a matter of drawing, and observing, limits; and in this, she was deeply and graciously accomplished.

The truth was that in personal character, she held to those same classical qualities which pervaded so many of their alterations to the house. For Theresa, the Enlightenment was not only a matter of ideas, or even of designing houses and things, but a matter of becoming, of being. At the heart of everything, for her, was truth of feeling. After that – simplicity and directness of statement; the temper of reason, and discipline . . . Not the shackled discipline of dogma; not a forced imposition upon unresolved feeling; not a pretence of artifice – but the self-governed discipline of seeking appropriate form. Propriety was not far from a whole morality; taste not far from an ethic.

Yet there was nothing narrow about her. Even within her own nature, the romantic movement grew from the neo-classical, with a ready recognition of spirit, and a ready harmony, in spite – perhaps – of some initial shocks and doubts:

I have just finished Héloise. It is a strange mixture. It struck me as a much more dangerous Book than when you read it to us at Studley, and yet there is a monstrous deal of good in it, jumbled with very romantic and absurd incidents.[4]

Mr Parker – despite his rootedness in the Devonshire earth, and his tenacious loyalty to his Devonshire accent, could have been no west country bumpkin to have chosen, and won, a wife like this.

Beauty, for her, was not an ornament – not a dress one should put on – but the very heart of life as she desired it; an almost tangible ideality which should be known, experienced, cultivated, and which could inform all the actualities of life. The making of art, of character, of the most pleasing qualities of society, were all one with her.

In this sense, and in this sense deeply, Theresa was a woman of beauty and fashion. It should, she felt, be the duty and delight of a woman to enjoy, sustain and uphold beauty in the fashion of her time; but for exactly the same reasons, she was impatient of extremes of fashion. She did not like titillation; exhibitionism; any shouting and clamouring for attention; any extravagance of ornamentation which was rooted in . . . nothing! By and large, however, these amused rather than annoyed her. It was by no means a puritanical objection. Her ventures into London society continually provided comical examples:

You would be amused to the greatest degree for ten minutes to converse with your friend Mrs Earle, an immense quantity of Rouge and being dressed very French has really improved her looks and her manner is so far improved that as before you could only be amused with her absurdities, she is kind enough to carry them to the highest degree. She talks without ceasing, but all by rule, divides her sentences into three parts and gives three reasons for everything she advances and all this in a broken English as if she had never seen England for more than two months. Her Dancing Master comes to her every Sunday morning to teach her Minuets which she sports the Tuesday following at Almacks.[5]

Some prevailing fashions were unbelievable. The new 'Heads', for example:

Heads may be structured two or three feet high, with all kinds of decorations, ribbons, bird's nests, ships, carriages, and waggons in gold and silver in the erection . . . In some are displayed lace, huge bows, feathers and flowers, butterflies in spun glass, and even a sow with a litter of pigs . . . The bodies of these erections are formed of tow, over which the hair is drawn in great curls, rolls, bobs, with false hair added, the whole freely plastered with powder and pomatum.[6]

Some women sat on the floor of the coach so that their towering plumes should not be damaged; and nothing could stop it. The Queen forbade 'plume-headed' ladies to

*'The bodies of these erections are formed of tow, over which the hair is drawn in curls, rolls, bobs, with false hair added . . .' Hairdressing in progress in Theresa's bedroom. The finished hair-style may be seen in the painting on p.32.*

109

appear in court; but she might as well have kept silent. Even her own daughters flaunted plumes. So much went into the making of the heads that some women wore them for many nights, covering them during the day in gauze mob-caps or fly-caps; the ends crossing under the chin and fastening at the back of the head. Pomatum and powder and piles of feathers on a lady in bed were of interest not only to men about town – but also to mice about the pillow! Sometimes a sweet sleeper was frightened into hysterics by a mouse rushing and rummaging through the horse-hair cage.[7] There were other accidents:

About 9. o'clock, the head-dress of a lady in high life, who lives in the neighbourhood of Portman Square, accidentally caught fire, but, by the timely assistance of three engines and plenty of water, it was got under a little before 12.[8]

Theresa thought the fashion of 'Frizzlation' even more incredible! *The London Magazine* carried an appalling, laughable, description:

We have now 600 twists of hair in square inches of paper. These are separately burned with hot irons. In this situation her ladyship looks exactly like a sunflower. The papers being taken off, he daubs her head with half a pound of grease and a pound of meal, and begins with all his dexterity to work her ladyship's pate into such a state of confusion, that you would imagine it was intended for the stuffing of a chair bottom; then, bending it over his finger with one thousand black pins, he nails the hair so fast to her head, that neither the weather nor time have power to alter its position. Thus my lady is drest for three months at least: During which time it is not in her power to comb her head. What is the consequence? Sorry I am to use so filthy an expression! But really – her ladyship stinketh![9]

To what absurd lengths the extremes of fashion had gone were borne out by a bill introduced into Parliament:

That all women, of whatever age, rank, profession, or degree, whether virgins, maids, or widows, that shall, from and after such Act, impose upon, seduce, and betray into matrimony, any of his Majesty's subjects, by the scents, paints, cosmetic washes, artificial teeth, false hair, Spanish wool, iron stays, hoops, high-heeled shoes, bolstered hips, shall incur the penalty of the law in force against witchcraft and like demeanours and that the marriage, upon conviction, shall stand null and void.[10]

The same kinds of extreme – though not, unfortunately, with so light-hearted a consequence – attended the use of cosmetics. Too heavy a white complexion, too continuously laid on, could lead not only to an unnatural appearance, but to an unnatural death from lead poisoning:

A new light is of late thrown upon the death of poor Sophy P. – Dr Hervey, of Tooting, who attended her the day before she expired, is of the opinion that she killed herself by quackery, that is, by cosmetics and preparations of lead or mercury, taken for her complexion, which indeed, was almost unnaturally white He thinks, therefore, that this pernicious stuff got into her veins and poisoned her. Peggy P. – nearly as white as her sister, is suspected strongly of using the same beautifying methods of destroying herself; but, as Mrs Thrale has hinted this suspicion to her, and charged her to take care of herself, we hope she will be frightened and warned to her safety.
Poor foolish girls, how dearly do they pay for the ambition of being fairer than their neighbours! I say they, for poor Peggy looks upon the point of death already.[11]

Fashion, however, is difficult to deny. . . . .

Girls started to paint themselves at the age of fourteen and went on until paint could no longer hide the ravages of time. By thirty many of them were old. Beauty and money were desirable, if not necessary attributes for a woman in society, and beauty was one way in which a wealthy marriage might be secured.

Poor Maria Gunning, who became Lady Coventry, was the daughter of a poor Irish landowner with only her beauty to offer as ransom. She and her sister became the toast of London society; people crowded about their door hoping to see them get into their Chairs; but beauty took its toll of Maria too. Horace Walpole wrote about her ending:

The Lady Coventry concluded her short race with the same attention to her looks. She lay constantly on a couch, with a pocket-glass in her hand; and when that told her how great the change was, she took to her bed the last fortnight, and had no light in her room but the lamp of a tea-kettle, and at last took things in through the curtains of her bed, without suffering them to be undrawn. The mob, who never quitted curiosity about her, went, to the number of ten thousand, only to see her coffin. If she had lived to be ninety like Helen, I believe they would have thought that the wrinkles deserved an epic poem. Poor thing! How far from ninety! She was not eight-and-twenty! Adieu![12]

Theresa disliked the trivialization of woman's nature

which such fashionable notions brought about. She shared the impatience of *The Spectator*:

I have often reflected on this unaccountable humour in womankind, of being smitten with everything that is showy or superficial... Talk of a new married couple and you immediately hear whether they keep a coach and six or eat in plate; mention the name of an absent lady and it is ten to one you but hear something of her gown and petticoat... The toilet is their great scene of business, and the right adjusting of their hair the principal employment of their lives. The sorting of a suit of ribbons is reckoned a very good morning's work, and if they make an excursion into a mercer's or a toyshop, so great a fatigue makes them unfit for anything else all the day after.[13]

Her dislike of unlimited sociability, of unrestrained social intercourse, was rooted in the same feeling. There was something in the dissipation of energies in the crowds of society – and in the perpetual social round – which ruined what could be valuable. The Bluestockings were very near the truth:

The interests of true friendship. elegant conversation, mental improvement, social pleasure, maternal duty, and conjugal comfort, never received such a blow as when Fashion issued out that arbitrary and universal decree, that *every body must be acquainted with every body;* together with that consequent, authoritative, but rather inconvenient clause, that *everybody must also go everywhere every night* ... The decline and fall of conversation has been in good measure effected by this barbarous project of assembling *en masse!*[14]

Daniel Defoe's opinion of the Spa assemblies summed the matter up:

Anciently, these were resorts for cripples and diseased persons principally, but now they are resorts of the sound as well as the sick... places that help the indolent and the gay to commit that worst of murders – that is to say: the killing of time.[15]

\*

The society which Theresa loved most of all was that of her own family relationships. It was enough for her. Her family life at Saltram was a new growth grafted on to her earlier family life – and she drew both together in a pleasing continuity.

Here, in her bedroom, she wrote letters keeping closely in touch with her two brothers, who were in Spain, and

Nanny her sister, who, however, came to stay with her as often, and for as long, as she could. All her experiences of life at Saltram were shared with them, and, through her, a very close union of the two families developed.

It was a continual pleasure to write to her brothers about little Jack:

Here comes this little troublesome Boy who seeing the pen in my hand will make me draw a post chaise. You see some of his drawing or writing whichever you please to call it. It was with difficulty I prevented him scribbling all over the Sheet . . . I shall make him kiss the bottom of this letter perhaps you may distinguish the marks of his lips, it is the only way he can send you a kiss.[16]

And though her observations were always couched in terms of affection and tenderness, she was not without realism in noticing decided and developing traits in his character:

I hope the compleat Art of Coaxing which the little Boy is thoroughly Master of, will not turn out gross flattery when he grows up for it is too engaging at present for me to resolve to check it. He ask'd me whilst I was writing if I was writing to his friend – upon enquiring who his friend was, he said his dear Uncle Grantham. It certainly was merely words, for he can have no Idea of either his Uncle Grantham or Uncle Fritz that he talks so much of, but it was impossible not to kiss him for it.[17]

She was always, too, longing to see her brothers back from Spain, and she told them of Nanny's very peculiar and persistent dreams:

This letter has run to an unreasonable length, so I shall now eat my Sandwich, read a little till twelve o'clock, and if Mr Parker does not come home, go to bed and very likely dream that you are both returned, which, by the by, I do for ever. Nanny says she does the same, but in her dreams she says there is always some great objection to your coming, either you are come by stealth, or upon a melancholy occasion, which so takes off the pleasure of seeing you that she is happy when she awakes to think you are both in Spain, doing your Duty and laying a foundation for a happy meeting in reality. Let that wish'd for time be when it will, you will always find me sooner or later, sleeping or waking, most sincerely and affectionately yours . . .[18]

\*

Here, too – in this room of her own – she could think, and feel, and live a life of her own: exploring the world of her own imagination. It was here that she kept the things she liked to have about her: the books she liked; materials for drawing – which she liked to practise when she could; and the bits and pieces of china and porcelain which especially appealed to her:

I have just been ornamenting a Glass Case you have seen in my Dressing Room with China. The principal shelf with the only China that deserved to be called ornamental I mean the Biscuit, and the others with figures of the same sort of material, which confirms my opinion in favour of the French, the lower shelf being the unglazed Dresden Dogs hunting stags and Bears etc., not bad & the Upper Row Chinese Models – very bad, but not bad of their kind. I think also I may place some of the Wedgewoods best unglazed Black Ware, for that may bear a Comparison with the French.[19]

She had a love of fine porcelain, kept abreast of new developments, and tried not to miss exhibitions in London:

I was at the Exhibition of Dr Honlu this week, there are some new things, but nothing that I wish'd much to have, being satisfied with four of those urns you bespoke for lighting the great Room. I think upon the whole Wedgewood beats them in taste but perhaps it may be owing to his materials admitting to being better executed, particularly with respect to figures.[20]

Here in her own room, too, at leisure, she gave her mind to the collection of paintings which she and Mr Parker were gradually building up. She wrote to Grantham hoping that in his travels to and from Spain he might find some of the things they were looking for; and – in this buying of pictures, too – Theresa's taste and interests were far from being purely fashionable or conservative:

. . . are you likely to pick up any very good Picture to match our Van Dyke as to size and partly as to subject? . . . There remains wanting for the Great Room what I have just desired you to look out for and two very good landscapes. Mr Parker in the Summer offer'd Sir Joshua 800 for the two Claud Lorraines, but he would listen to nothing under 2,000. He will not perhaps catch Mr Parker again in the humour to offer even 800, we bought a Landscape yesterday that I believe is a very good one, at least it is one of the most pleasing I ever saw done by the first Landscape Painter in France his name is Loutherbourg. We called at his home by mere chance and were surprised not only at the beauty of his works but at having stumbled upon one of the greatest reputations in his way. Perhaps you might have seen him in Paris.[21]

The decoration of the room itself reflected the rage there had been for the east and the exotic with the new extension of trade and travel; the taste for the 'Indian' and the 'Chinese'. Theresa, with her own tastes, was more than a little sceptical of this eastern enthusiasm. Mr Chippendale, from whose workshop their delightful bed had come, had called one cabinet a 'Chinese' cabinet on one page of his book, and an 'Indian' cabinet on another. The orient, it seemed, was anything east of Europe – brought by East India ships:

The simple and the sublime have lost all influence. Almost everywhere, all is Chinese . . . Every chair in an apartment, the frames of glasses, and tables must be Chinese: the walls covered with Chinese paper fill'd with figures which resemble nothing of God's creation, and which a prudent nation would prohibit for the sake of pregnant women . . . Nay, so excessive is the love of Chinese architecture become, that at present fox-hunters would be sorry to break a leg in pursuing their sport in leaping any gate that was not made in the eastern taste of little bits of wood standing in all directions . . .[22]

Whatever criticisms one might have, however, the room had such a delicate, gentle atmosphere, such an intricate entirety of design, that it would be wrong to alter it. The bedroom wall-hangings were of Chinese paintings on silk or cotton. The mirror-paintings, the chimney-piece, all were appropriately painted and carved; and there – on the chimney-piece – was a carved motif of bears and bees: an illustration of the Spanish proverb:

>     Take what you want, says God.
>     Take it – and pay for it.

Her dressing room had Chinese wall paper too; and here, Theresa washed and bathed. A lady of good society was as much a prey to primitive sanitation as anyone else. If cleanliness is next to godliness, mankind and womankind were at a great distance from divinity until the invention of the water-closet and the piping of water. The streets of London were fouled by drains in their centre, and the privies of cottages were holed seats over a pit that might be emptied yearly. The valve closet with its stink-trap had been invented, but was still a long way from being generally

*Theresa's dressing room (adjoining the bedroom) showing the limited washing facilities of the time. Water has been carried upstairs and towels have been laid out in preparation for a bath.*

used. Every element of sanitation depended on the fetching and carrying of water, so that baths had been relatively infrequent. A smother of powder had to answer for the absence of soap and water. At this time, however – and perhaps the growth of social intercourse had occasioned it – personal cleanliness and hygiene began to have some attention. Tooth-powder, wash-balls of soap, lip-salve, sweet-smelling powders, orange-flower water and other perfumes, began to do battle with other less pleasing odours:

Washing yourself, and rubbing your body and limbs frequently with a flesh-brush (wrote one nobleman to his son) will conduce as much to health as to cleanliness. A particular attention to the cleanliness of your mouth, teeth, hands, and nails, is but common decency, in order to not offend peoples' eyes and noses.[23]

At least delicacy was observed. A gentleman visiting a lady in her boudoir put the finishing touches to his wig at a powder-stand.[24] From the puff-box he took powder; from the lower tier an ewer of rose-water. He poured a little into the bowl on the top. Then, having repowdered his wig and dipped his fingers into the water, he was ready to be presented.

But water, in terms of carrying it, was too scarce a commodity for this to be an age of sweetness, even if of some light! 'Smell, Madam?' Dr Johnson is reputed to have said, 'I positively stink!' Perhaps he spoke – at least fairly generally – for his time!

*

Wealth could not greatly ease the problems of sanitation – neither could it buy freedom from the ravages of illness and the deficiencies of medicine.

Like Mr Parker, and everyone else at the time, Theresa was often preoccupied and apprehensive about problems of health. Physicians knew of a few drugs like quinine and the pain-deadening laudanum. There was the all-pervasive blood-letting, and methods of bringing about purging, vomiting and sweating. Dr Warren, one of the Parkers' doctors prescribed 'Two Drachms of Soap, made into twenty-four pills, four of which are to be taken twice a day'. It was a matter of getting noxious evils out of the body by any method possible.

Theresa had many fears for young Jack. Rickets was an illness to which babies of the upper classes were prone. The cure was given in Boyle's book of 'Family Receipts':

Open a vein in both ears between the junctures, mix a little Aqua-vitae with the blood, and with it anoint the Breast, Side and Neck: then take 3 ounces of the ointment green, and warm a little of it in a Spoon, and anoint the wrists and ancles as hot as it may be endured: do this for nine nights before bed-time; shift not the shirt all the time. If the Veins do not appear, rub it with a little lint dipp'd in Aqua-vitae, or else cause the child to cry, and that will make the veins more visible and bleed the better.[25]

*The medicine chest in Theresa's bedroom – containing 'Laudanum Poison' and other simple drugs.*

There were then no pain-killing anaesthetics for the drawing of teeth or other operations; indeed, trained practitioners were not always available. Much suffering had to be endured out of a sheer lack of diagnosis, and sometimes this was serious, as in the case of Sophie – wife of Mr Curzon:

I have been attack'd with the most violent pains all on one side of my body, which has entirely hindered my Sleeping of nights and has taken my stomach away. I have been in a Fever with the torturing pain; it was thought Rheumatic for which I have tried many things. Ford has given me James powders which have had a violent effect without doing me good. Ford thought it proper to propose making a *certain enquirie* whether I was with child or not. As I apprehended it to be *absolutely* necessary I consented to the *very* disagreeable operation. I considered that through modesty I was not to give up my life. This morning he has made the examination and declares me not with child . . '. Consider a stoppage of now near 9 months, my body very hard and large, my legs swell'd exceedingly, no breath, violent sharp pains all about me . . .[26]

No reliable diagnosis was ever provided. Nothing was known. Nothing could be done.

Even in matters so serious, however, the situation had its elements of humour. Sometimes, the recommendations of physicians were a kind of wordy, mysterious wisdom – which, nonetheless, was accepted – as from the mouths of witch-doctors:

I was by no means well when I went to bed last night; for I had a nervous heat that banished repose; and the hours due to rest were pass'd by me in sudorific effusions, occasion'd by some analeptic pills, which did me a great deal of service.[27]

Sometimes, too, there was outright comedy, as when the country people were mystified by the new devices of 'electrification' and 'galvanization', but – nonetheless – were exultant about them:

. . . then we was all Lactrified a Think is Imposable to describe Its composed of a Mixture of combuotables that it you Touch it the Fire flys out ot it, besides You have Schuch Shudden Shock with it. We all hold hand in hand about 7 of us when I toucht it, and the Moment I was struck so hard in the Stomch that I could not stand, the Rest felt it as well as me, If there was 500 It would be the same.[28]

Mr Benjamin Douglas Perkins' 'metallic tractors' were

also beginning to come in.[29] These 'drew ailments away from the stricken spot to the extremities' – where they were 'dissipated', and were a 'certain cure for All Disorders, Red Noses, Gouty Toes, Windy Bowels, Broken Legs, Hump Backs...' 'Just discovered,' the advertisement read, 'Grand secret of the Philosopher's Stone, with the true way of turning all metals into Gold.'

Alas... the Philosopher's Stone, once again, proved to be no answer to human ills.

\*

The much more ordinary danger was that of childbirth. Wealth, eminence, beauty, fashion, could not protect women from this. The probability of a delivery without complications was not high. There were no antiseptics, a childbed fever was very common, so that childbirth was almost as great a risk as an illness. Because of family settlements and marriage contracts, some women among the upper classes married very young, some at 16 or 17; but, whether young or not, they had a long period of child-bearing before them, and therefore the risk of an early death. One duchess, for example, though marrying at the age of 30 had 9 children in 14 years and 4 miscarriages, and 7 of her children died in infancy.[30]

Theresa's approach to having children was characteristically serious, and again with that touch of nobility. She was prepared to run the risk. The birth of her boy Jack had been very difficult – but when she learned of her second pregnancy, she was delighted, and began to enjoy all the preparations for the child's arrival:

I think I shall enjoy much more than ever this Summer, it must of course be in a quiet way... We have no visits to make. I propose sitting much in the Green House and drawing a good deal... The place is in the highest beauty.[31]

She was pleased and amused to see how everybody was becoming concerned. 'Connoisseurs' began to foretell whether the baby would be boy or girl, and Lady Pelham was convinced beyond all doubt – and gravely warned Theresa against hoping for a daughter.

She would have to resign herself, too, to all the customs of confinement and the care of the infant – whether sensible or foolish. She would not be able to use her eyes freely for reading or writing for a month after the birth, and the baby would be bound up in the usual prescribed fashion:

A child is no sooner born than it is bound up as firmly as an Egyptian Mummy in folds of linen ... in vain for him to give signs of distress ... the old witch who presides over his infant days winds him up in his destined confinement. When he comes to be dressed like a man he has ligatures applied to his arms and legs and middle to prevent the circulation of his blood. If it be of tender sex, she must be bound yet more straightly about waist and stomach.[32]

She was also pleased that her two families were being drawn even more closely together. Mr Parker, anxious that his affairs should be sound with another child coming into the family, thought fit to appoint trustees on whom he could rely. He had, in fact, come to repose much trust in Theresa's brothers and her sister, and his suggestion to approach Grantham, her elder brother, was a delight to her:

My business is to ask favours, but which Favours I have pleasure in asking, as I am sure you will have as much in granting. The first is a mere form – I suppose you guess I mean to ask you to be Godfather for my little Child ... My next proposal to you is at Mr Parker's desire. An Addition to his Family makes it necessary to make some little alteration in his affairs and the case of the Family is too weighty a consideration to anybody of his feeling, not to pitch upon such persons as Trustees that he had the highest opinion of and could most confide in. You may imagine therefore what pleasure it gave me, tho' God forbid you should ever be called upon, to think that what would be most dear to me in the World would be under the direction of whom I should esteem most capable and deserving. It was natural enough for me to think of it, but highly flattering that Mr Parker should make it his own choice.[33]

Despite Lady Pelham's prediction – Theresa found her mind dwelling with deep pleasure on the possibility of a daughter. Her own values, again, were very evident in the way in which she thought:

I have the great Idea of there being vast pleasure in having a handsome daughter notwithstanding all the anxiety that attends it. I wish very much for one girl at least and think Beauty of such infinite consequence to a Woman, that if it was not the first thing I should ask of La Fée Bien faisante, it should certainly be the second. A little attention to her educa-

*Opposite:*

*Theresa's bedroom with the elegant Chippendale bed and the rich Chinese wall paper. Chinese mirror-paintings can be seen on the wall, and the symbolization of the Spanish Proverb – of the Bear and the Bees – can just be distinguished in the centre of the white chimney-piece.*

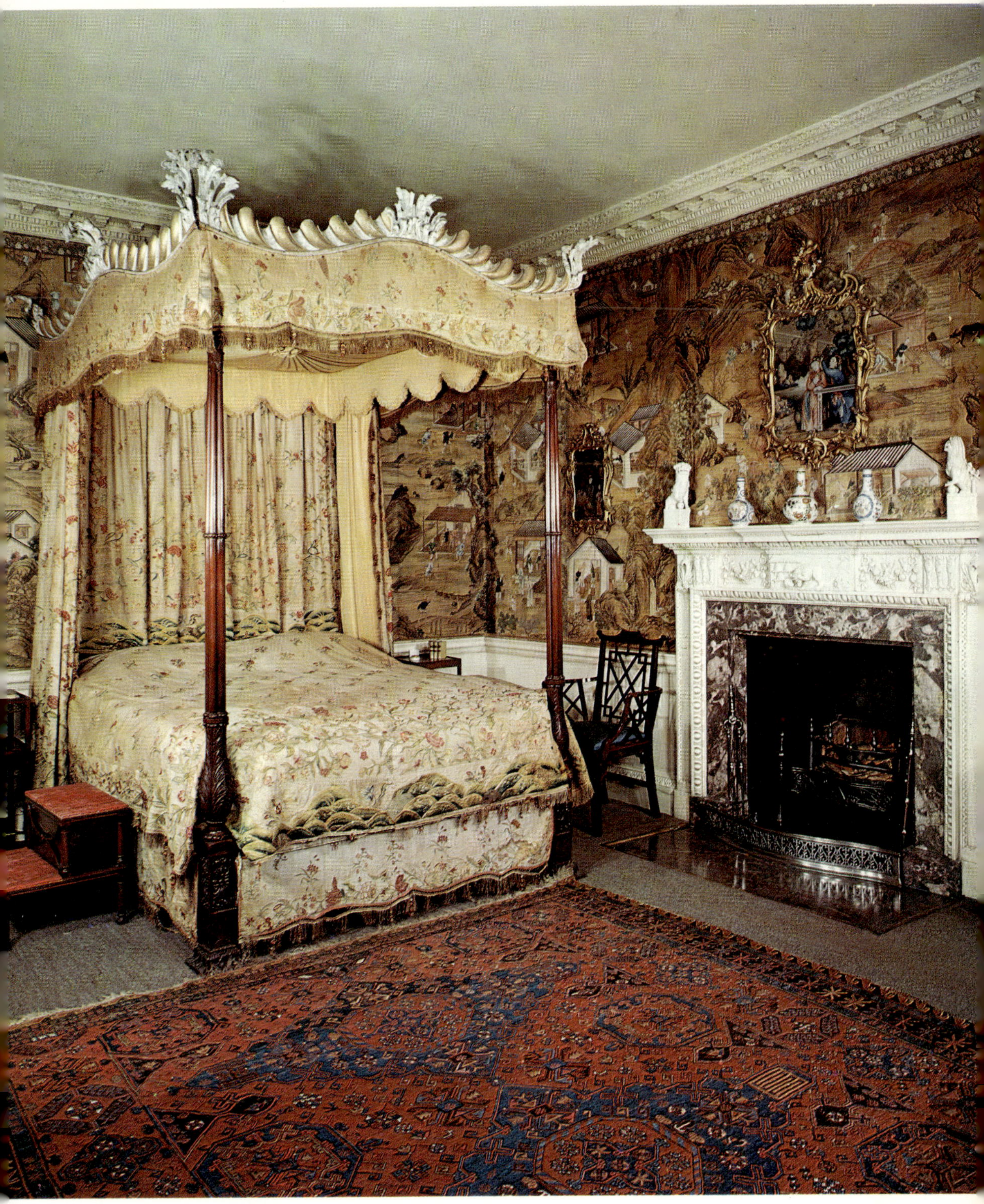

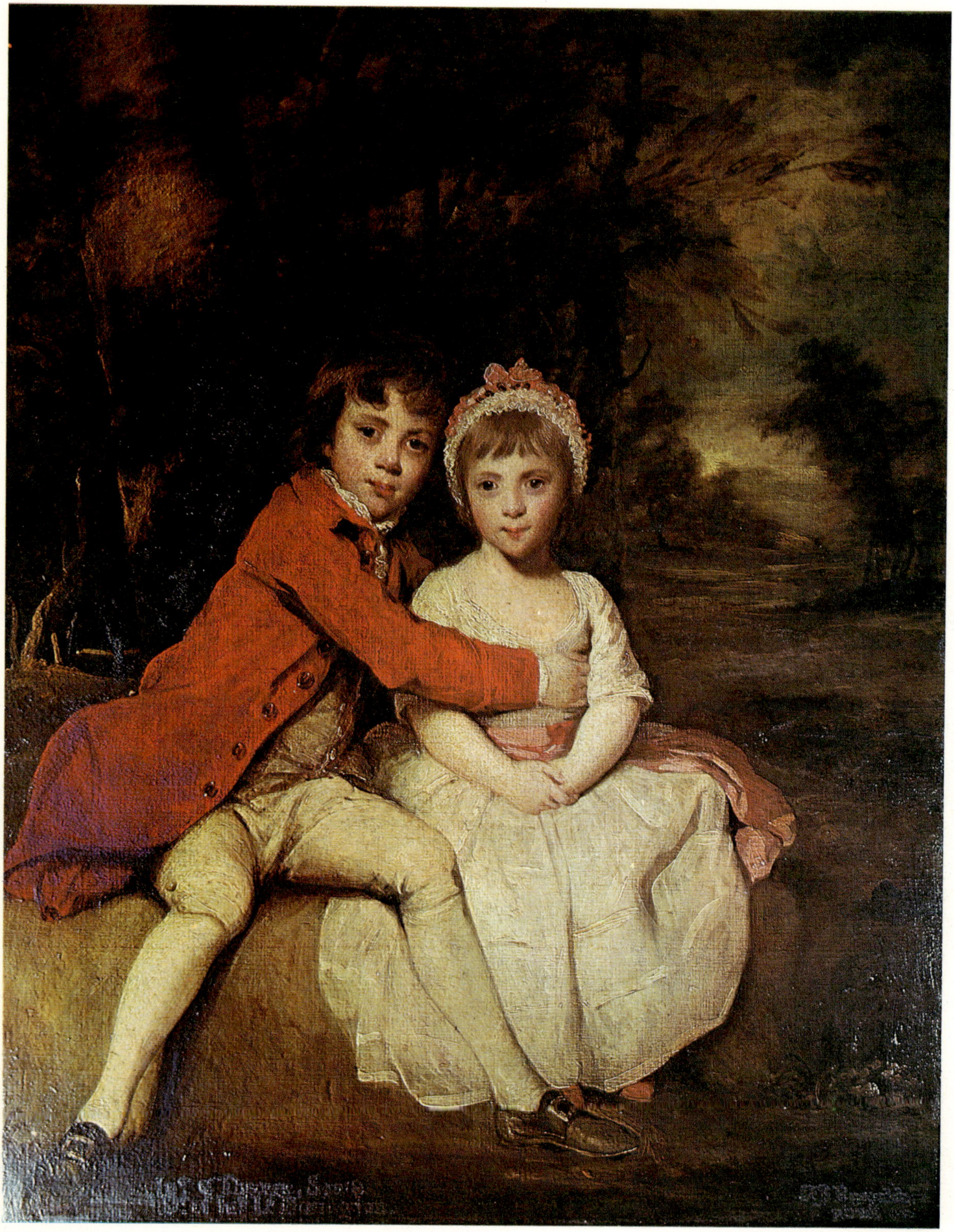

tion will prevent her making a bad use of it, at least I flatter myself I could manage that point. Mothers must give up their boys, but I have no notion of their not forming their girls who are constantly under their eye, in what manner they please. Their marrying well or ill is I believe a constant source of uneasiness to a mother, but I shall teach my Daughter from her Cradle to dread it unless everything conspires to promise Happiness. I think nothing contributes more to the many unhappy Marriages one sees than want of nicety in the young Women at Present, who are much more to blame in that respect than the men. They set their caps at every man of fortune that comes out, are strongly seconded by their mothers and take the first that offers. As my Daughters are unfortunately unborn, I am quite ashamed of having taken up so much of your time about their Education, but should there ever be such beings, you must excuse me if I fill my letters to both of you with my ideas, and begging advice and correction where I am wrong.[34]

Theresa was also touched and amused by Mr Parker's agitation. Remembering the difficulties of last time, John Parker was anxious to get her up to London and in the care of good doctors as soon as possible – even if it did mean leaving the boy behind for a few weeks. He wanted to take no risks:

Mr Parker begins to grow uneasy at my staying so long in the Country, but as I am convinced I am safe if I am in Town by the 1st of October I am not desirous of going sooner than is necessary, tho' in reality I have no objection than that of leaving the little Boy a week earlier, for any other arguments can have no weight with me of course.[35]

Quietly, and with deepening pleasure, Theresa made her preparations. In fact, the child – a daughter – was born before she could leave for London. There was some little trouble, but – within a few weeks – she was well enough to write to her brother, telling him the good news:

Dearest Fritz,

I am happy again to be able to write to you and assure you under my own hand that I am as well as I can possibly expect. My little Girl is a month old today and consequently all the Nurses Authority ceases on this day and I may make free use of my Eyes, for it is against Rules to write or read sooner. I have a great deal of strength to get up, and I must allow a fortnight more to recover the Fever, which was much the most severe part of my illness, but which I have not had the smallest return of, since I was brought to Bed. Altogether I think

*Opposite:*

*Little Jack and Theresa: painted by Sir Joshua Reynolds in 1779.*

myself remarkably well off. It is impossible to describe Mr Parker's tenderness and attention to me throughout he alarmed himself much more than was necessary but had my Fever lasted a few days longer he could not have stood it, as I believe he neither Eat, Slept, or could even compose his Spirits till many days after I was free from every complaint. My little Girl is a very fine Child not very large or small, for her Age perfectly healthy Fair, and Quiet. I think her like Mr Parker but she is rather too young for judgement. The Boy grows a Giant. Mr Parker left us yesterday to attend a foolish County Meeting in his way to Town, how long the Parliament will keep him I don't know. Adieu Dear Fritz, Nanny sends her Love *The Children* are all well and I am ever most affecty yours,

Theresa Parker[36]

But that was Theresa's last letter. Quite suddenly, there was tragedy. She became ill, and doctors were hurriedly called in. Despite their eminence and their high fees – Dr Glass charged £250 for eight visits and Dr Caldwell a £150 for only a few – they could do nothing for her. Mr Parker's fears were justified. Theresa, like many other women, was a prey to the conditions of her time. The fever during the birth was followed by a cold, which – unaccountably – continued. A few weeks later, she died.

\*

Take what you want, says God.
Take it – and pay for it.

It was a strange proverb to be symbolised in a bedroom as gentle as this.

# 8 NURSERY AND SCHOOLROOM

## *the young Parkers*

The world first came to life – for little Theresa, who had been given her mother's name, and her brother Jack – through the sunlight and candlelight, the colours, and faces, and toys, which moved about this rocking cradle. The world woven by their own warm feelings about this doll, and its doll's house . . . the excitement of encountering all that was new . . . a top, a slate, their coloured counting-beads. The world they made in their grave absorption in play: with the warmth of love, and the terrifying gulf with the lack of it. The world of shadows and warmly preserved fancies – fragile, vulnerable, into which the distinctions of reality had to break.

The 'first affections and shadowy recollections' – for them – were born among these things in Saltram's nursery.

*

Reality first disrupted this world with their mother's death. For Theresa, barely a few weeks old, it was the loss of only a warm presence; but for Jack – now three, and vividly aware of his mother's love and protection – the world was suddenly shattered. She had watched her little son grow with tender observation. She had entered sensitively into every part of his childish world and together they had explored every new experience:

You would have been delighted just now to have seen a meeting between my little boy and one of the same age that was sent to see him. Little Jack is always very charming on these occasions, first creeps up and just touches the other, then kisses very gently, then compares their Eyes, Nose, Mouth, to his, and next their Shoes and Buckles, this kinship lasts generally till the other grows more acquainted and I suppose always ends in a quarrel.[1]

To encourage the pleasure and imagination of children throughout their education was an idea now being put forward – by men like John Locke, Rousseau and others.

Thomas Sheridan – the father of Richard Brinsley – put it as strongly as this:

Away with the rod – away with corporal punishments – away with servile fear! Those debasers of the mind, extinguishers of spirit, dampers of genius, the enemies of virtue! Far from the British Isles be they borne to their native soil, the regions of Tyranny and Slavery ... Let pleasure be their guide to allure the ingenuous youths thro' the labyrinths of Science, not pain their driver to goad them on, ignorant of the way, and unknowing whither they tend.[2]

It was very new, but all Theresa's feelings were in sympathy with it. She shared every mishap and every excitement of Jack's young life, and enlarged his world by the pleasure she took in continuously reporting him to those she loved, and bringing him into a closer acquaintance with them:

The present I intended was the little Boy's picture but Small Pox delayed the execution of it. He is now recovering his looks and complexion so fast and has left off his cap that comes very near perfect Beauty. He was delighted with being upon the water the other day and told his Maid he had been to Spain to see Uncle Grantham.[3]

Theresa knew how brief the delight and innocence of childhood was, but she did not know how abruptly it was to end for her son. Now she was dead – and his world would continue to grow – but without her.

*

Mr Parker was completely overwhelmed at Theresa's death. He left Saltram, the children, the servants – everybody and everything – to hide miserably away at Buckland (another of his estates) in Somerset. Theresa's brother, Lord Grantham, wrote to him begging him to pull himself together and return, if only for the sake of the children:

I cannot therefore help ... most earnestly to recommend to you, not to persevere in making the long stay you proposed to do at Buckland where you cannot but confirm and increase your grief. I do not at all wonder at your going there, nor at the not sending for the dear little ones, but for God's sake, do – as soon as you can bring yourself to bear it, *do* see them. They are now with servants and you must not let your dear boy's affection and Dependance look up to anything but yourself and our dear Nanny ... Believe me, no distance can diminish our

*'Nanny' (Anne Robinson). This is the picture now hanging in the Master Bedroom. (see p.26)*

*Little Jack wearing the 'military uniform' specially made for him. This, again, is the picture now hanging in the Master Bedroom. (see p.26)*

feelings. Let us only hear that you are well and keep so and that Reflexion, Religion and Time take something off of the sharpness of your affliction.[4]

Of course, Mr Parker did come back, and did settle into his life again. He had to. And 'Nanny' – who had been so much at Saltram and so close to Theresa – and whose persistent, troubling dreams about a 'melancholy occasion' seemed, as events turned out, to have had such an uncanny, fearful truth in them – came to live at the house: to look after it, and, especially, to look after the children. She became as devoted to them as Theresa had been. Never marrying herself, she became – unobtrusively, but with a full commitment – the heart of the Parker family at Saltram. Before long, her letters to her brothers were as full of delights, concerns, and preoccupations about Jack and the little girl as Theresa's had been.

Together, Mr Parker and Nanny did their best in the upbringing of the children. The life of the family went on.

*

Until he was eight years old, Jack remained at Saltram – surrounded by his toys, getting out and about with his father: learning to ride horseback (which he did not take to quickly), and even going into the camp of the Militia;

playing with his little sister Theresa; watched over by Nanny; and waited on by the many servants of the house. The world all about him was one of cultured elegance. Saltram's park and gardens – spacious and varied, with lawns, fields and woods going right down to the waterside – gave him a wide range of enjoyable activities. The decoration and paintings in the house – the pictures which had been purchased with the advice of Sir Joshua Reynolds and which enriched the walls all around him – reflected his parents' tastes and aspirations. The Library, too, was not there for show! Its range of books was excellent, and newly bound volumes on a variety of subjects were continually being added. Saltram was a world in which it was good to grow up.

Soon, however, Mr Parker employed tutors for his children: a dancing master, Mr French, for Theresa and a local writing master, Mr Pierce, for Jack. Both he and Nanny agreed that – whether pleasurable or not – all the signs indicated that some instruction was needed:

The dear little boy has been writing to his Uncle Fritz and is rather affronted with me that I will not send his letter but as it contains nothing but a few pencil marks I do not think it worth paying postage for. Perhaps you will say the same of this therefore I will not detain you any longer.[5]

Jack began his grounding in classical learning from this quite early age. He had a quick mind, a lively curiosity, and his education was never merely formal. The Library contained beautifully illustrated books of voyages at sea, and Jack was always excited by the stories he heard from his father's friends from nearby Plymouth – like Admiral Ourry and Captain Pole. Like many boys of his age and situation Jack loved to sit and read about these foreign lands and the strange peoples who lived there. But Aunt Nanny was very much alive to the dangers and limitations of educating boys entirely at home:

Lord Hinton would be a very fine boy if he had ever been out of his father's house but at present he can talk of nothing but his servants and horses. He seems to regret that he has never been at school.[6]

Young Jack was not to be so enclosed! Even before boarding school in London, he was sent to the local school in Plympton:

The dear little boy got up before six o'clock on Tuesday morning and walked to Plympton School with great resolution and good humour, and has every day since . . . He seems not to dislike it, and I hope it will be a great service to him. I miss him very much in the morning, and often lose my walk for want of his company.[7]

Before long, Jack was sent to board at the preparatory school of Dr Whyte at Hammersmith. The fees were a hundred guineas a year plus an extra ten for boarding, and Mr Parker was expected to pay Master's fees in addition for more personal attention to Jack's education. That the school was good was largely a matter of chance, for at this time schools were uncontrolled and uninspected and varied widely according to the wealth of the establishment and the nature of the headmaster. Some were reliable and sound. In others practically everything was neglected 'but the receipt of salaries'. When the time came for Jack to leave for school his parting was accompanied by tearful scenes.

For Nanny, the parting might have been with her own son:

Jack is just gone to school and a servant is gone with him . . . The Little Boy behaved at parting with propriety tho' I believe there was a shower in the chaise. He took great pains that I should not see it. If the truth was known I am afraid there was a shower – from another Quarter, which was not so excusable. It is the first time we have really been parted.

We were left quite alone and wanted him very much. He went off very properly with great resolution and a sufficient degree of tenderness. I do assure you he behaved better than some he left behind him. He has wrote us charming letters from the road every night where he has slept. Jack says in the postcript to his letter from Hertford bridge to his Papa. 'I am in very good spirits considering who and what I left behind.'

For all of them, the house seemed quiet – empty – a different place without him.

\*

For a boy, education was a matter for serious consideration, but for a girl, it was of lesser consequence.

Under the guidance of a governess at home, or at one of the boarding schools for girls, the education of ladies was largely an acquiring of 'accomplishments'. When young ladies were 'finished' – which was not an inappropriate way of describing their condition! – they might play a little on the harpsichord, dance a minuet, sing some Italian songs, perhaps speak some French and Italian, know a little geography, ply their needles 'in broad-stitch, cross and changes . . . pink, paint, and frill; work upon catgut, cut paper, and perhaps have a very pretty manner of telling fortunes upon cards'. They also learned other ways with the cards:

At some of our Boarding Schools, the fair pupils are now taught to play Whist, and Cassino. Amongst their *winning* ways, this may not be the least agreeable to Papa and Mamma. It is calculated that a clever child, by its cards . . . may pay for its own education.[8]

There was a tendency for parents to seek to educate their daughters to a level (so they thought) beyond their own station; but the education their girls received was not always the education they had expected:

They came home from school, with a large portion of vanity grafted on their native ignorance. Of knowledge they had just enough to laugh at their parent's rustic manners and vulgar language, and to despise and ridicule every girl not as vainly dressed as themselves . . . They spent the morning in bed, the noon in dressing, the evening at the harpsichord, and the night in reading novels.[9]

Some women in society – in what was an age of beautiful, delightful, colourful, but also great and intelligent women –

*Back from college. 'The life of a young lady now too much resembles that of an actress . . . the morning is all rehearsal, and the evening is all performance.'*

were in a state of open warfare against this. The Bluestockings especially:

This phrenzy of accomplishments . . . has women declining in usefulness as they rise in their pretensions to elegance . . . A stranger would be led to imagine by a view of the reigning mode of female education that human life consisted of one universal holiday, and that the grand contest between the competitors was who should most excel in the various shows and games exhibited in it . . . and that they were so excellent in these *unnecessary* things, that their perfection must needs have been acquired by the *neglect* of whatever was *necessary!* To attract admiration is the great principle sedulously inculcated into a young girl's heart . . . The fundamental maxim of the reigning system of the brilliant education of a lady is comprised in this short sentence: To *allure* and to *shine*.[10]

And to allure and shine for one thing only – the hunting of a husband in the sophisticated marriage-market of society! Hannah More, Lady Mary Wortley Montagu, Elizabeth Montagu and others, were scathing.

Women, they argued, were deliberately trained to have the very stupidities, superficialities, frivolities – the very brainlessness – that were taken to be the characteristics of the sex. The education of women did not so much lend substance to the myth as positively create it:

When a young lady is taught to value herself on nothing but her cloaths and to think she's very fine when well accoutred; who can blame her if she lay out her money on such accomplishments? If from our infancy we are nurs'd upon ignorance and vanity; are taught to be proud and delicate and fantastick, humorous and inconsistent, tis not strange that the ill effects of this conduct appear in all the future actions of our lives.[11]

. . . You are studiously laying up for your children a store of premature caprice, and irritability, and impatience, and discontent . . . The chief source of human discontent is to be looked for not in our real wants; not in the demands of nature; but in the insatiable cravings of artificial desire.[12]

It was frightful to think that the fatuous views of Mrs Malaprop – Mr Richard Brinsley Sheridan's character – were not only a butt for farcical comedy, but widely held as being true:

Observe me, Sir Anthony. I would by no means wish a daughter of mine to be a progeny of learning; I don't think so much learning becomes a young woman; for instance – I would never let her meddle with Greek, or Hebrew, or Algebra, or Simony, or Fluxions, or Paradoxes, or such inflammatory branches of learning – neither would it be necessary for her to handle any of your mathematical, astronomical, diabolical instruments: – But, Sir Anthony, I would send her, at nine years old, to a boarding-school, in order to learn a little ingenuity and artifice. Then, sir, she should have a supercilious knowledge in accounts; – and as she grew up, I would have her instructed in geometry, that she might know something of the contagious countries; – but above all, Sir Anthony, she should be mistress of orthodoxy, that she might not misspell, and mispronounce words so shamefully as girls usually do; and likewise that she might reprehend the true meaning of what she is saying. This, Sir Anthony, is what I would have a woman know; – and I don't think there is a superstitious article in it.[13]

The model of womanhood, of wifeliness, of motherhood which was being held up in the present education of women was simply belittling and absurd:

If the life of a young lady, formerly, too much resembled the life of a confectioner, it now too much resembles that of an actress; the morning is all rehearsal, and the evening is all performance . . .

A young lady may excel in speaking French and Italian, may repeat a few passages from a volume of extracts; play like a professor, and sing like a syren; have her dressing room decorated with her own drawings, tables, stands, flower-pots, screens, and cabinets; nay, she may dance like the Queen herself, and yet be very badly educated . . . When a man of sense comes to marry, it is a companion whom he wants and not an artist. It is a being who can reason, and reflect, and feel, and judge, and act, and discourse, and discriminate; one who can assist him in his affairs, purify his joys, and educate his children.[14]

Nanny was decidedly of the same opinion. If Theresa was kept at home it was entirely because she and Mr Parker wanted to give her the best they could provide – not at all because her education was taken lightly. Her mother had been a cultured and reflective woman, a woman in whose nature character and beauty were as one, and Nanny was encouraging the little girl to become the same: to have an appreciation of the same arts and the same values. She took all the care possible to see that little Theresa had a good governess:

I do assure you she is a very good little girl. She received your French letter and understood it perfectly as she read it in

English to her Papa . . . She is reading L'Ami des Enfants, which we brought her down as a present from Sir Joshua, and yesterday she gave me one of the stories translated into very good English, very exactly done, and very well spelt . . . I flatter myself we have got a treasure in her governess. Her not speaking English is the greatest advantage as she has no temptation to mix with the other servants and be spoiled. She dines with the little Girl, and is never out of the room but when she walks out with her.

Theresa was gently and carefully nurtured at home.

\*

Theresa frequently corresponded with Jack – and often in French – when he was away at school:

Jack and his Sister are corresponding in French and write it much better than I thought they could, especially Jack, as he has not had the instruction in it that she has.

But – French, classics, music, dancing, education aside – they were happiest of all when it was time for the holidays! Theresa was all agitation and excitement when Jack was coming home; and Nanny and Mr Parker were just as anxious to see him:

This morning received your kind letter which gave me great pleasure as it fixed the day we are to have the happiness of seeing the dear little boy here, which I hope nothing will prevent this day seven-night, he will be so overjoyed that I am afraid he will be almost too riotous. I have wrote to him . . . and hope he will behave well upon the road, and not eat too much tart . . .

Theresa found it hard to restrain her tears if he was at all late – which he was almost bound to be with the state of the roads and the vagaries of the weather:

[The Little Boy] is perfectly well, tho' by his not arriving till six o'clock he allarmed us much, the Dear Little Girl behaved better than you can immagine, she could not help shewing her disappointment, by the tears running down her cheeks tho' she did all she could to stop her crying, but the moment she heard the Gigg she expressed her impatience, in the most natural and joyfull terms.

There he was – at home at last! School was over for a while. The house – and the whole countryside – came to life again; and there were long, glorious days to look forward to: boating, riding, walking, and all kinds of indoor games.

*Young Jack at the age of twelve*

Even during the holidays, Jack was not allowed to leave his school work completely. Mr Parker – who was spending a lot of money on Jack's education, and wanted to see that it was well spent – saw to it that Jack applied himself thoroughly to his home-work. Aunt Nanny supervised this as she did everything:

Jack is at present employed in doing his task and I hope well. I must find him something for him to learn or translate some French when he has done his task to keep him from being quite idle. He is a very good boy and does everything I tell him with respect to reading, lessons, etc., and we pass the time very well with walking, riding, and driving, when we have nothing else to do.

But there were all sorts of good things to do when work was finished; and sometimes unexpected presents:

The little boy is as happy as possible with his Magick Lantern... He liked his holiday very much as he Hunted Foxes and Hares in the morning and Fitchey at night in the Hall, which my Brother would have liked very much if he had been here....[15]

Jack, too, was developing. By the time he was twelve years old school-work and Magick Lanterns alike were not quite enough for him. He was beginning to apply his mind to different, manly stuff:

Jack continues perfectly well, in great Spirits, and when they don't get the better of him, is vastly good, he has just been writing to Leveson a political letter for he at present thinks of nothing else and is very violent.

Nanny cared deeply for Jack and his welfare, and was much concerned that his holidays should put back the happiness and sheer weight that boarding in London seemed to deprive him of:

He has had great liberty and pleasure these Holidays and has enjoyed them much. He came down rather thin and pulled by the discipline he had undergone just before, but he is now remarkably well and quite fat enough. He is much improved and I hope not much spoilt, indeed I must say for him, he is easier managed by indulgence than severity, and that no favour is thrown away on him

Holidays, however, seemed always far too quickly to come to an end, and the prospect of leaving Saltram again brought a desolate feeling – for him, and for all of them:

His time draws very near . . . the middle of next week he sets out and has but little prospect at present of finding his way down at Xmas . . . he complains much of the emptyness of the town.

And soon, all the days of infancy – whether at school or on holidays – were over. It was time for a change.

Mr Parker wrote one of his very rare letters to Uncle Grantham who had recently been Foreign Secretary in the Government of Parker's great friend, Lord Shelburne:

I am very much flattered that you think Jack is improved and hope he will continue to merit your friendship and protection. If you approve of it I mean to move him to Westminster School, at Lady Day next, but I shall never take any steps concerning him, without first begging your assistance and advice which will always govern me.[16]

\*

The grammar schools took a mixture of boys from families of different station, but the son of a large landowner like Mr Parker, had a private tutor for at least part of his education, and was then, most probably, sent to a boarding school, though the standards in some of these had fallen so low that many families kept their sons to a private tutor alone. Charles Bosanquet, for example, described his experiences as a pupil at Newcome's Academy at Hackney:

The smaller boys were neither more or less than slaves. Children of tender age were often sent on a cold November evening to pilfer turnips from a neighbouring field and many were the logs of firewood or kettles of boiling water I had to carry up the dark and winding staircase. Compared with one of us Caliban was a sybarite and our Prosperos ever ready with hand or stick . . . The Sabbath, though free from lessons, was a dismal day. The formal walk to church in a line of two abreast, headed by the master and closed by his usher; the droning organ, the long-drawn spiritless sermon . . . The habit of swearing was so inveterate that I never got rid of it. It was a most profligate, abominable school. I was kept there seven years, learned very little, and was most unhappy.[17]

Westminster, however – the school for which Jack was intended – was one of the better schools of the time.[18]

Whether a boy was educated at one of these chools, like Eton, Harrow or Rugby, or by private tutors – the curriculum would be much the same. It consisted very largely of the classics: especially Latin – Greek was not so strong;

but there was sometimes English literature – some plays, some history; and sometimes French, accounts, drawing, fencing and dancing. Among schools and private tutors alike, some concern was also shown for propriety of conduct:

In the Morning, after you have got up and dressed yourself, and finished your duty to God (that is your prayers), then wash yourself, and comb your hair before you go downstairs . . . When you receive orders to go into the Room where your Parents are, bow, and enquire after their health, in these or like words: how do you do, sir? or, Papa, I hope you are well? I Hope you have had a good night's repose? In the same manner you must salute your Mamma.

Stand still till such time they bid you sit down, or inform you what is their pleasure with you . . . sit still, upright and silent . . . Play not with anything about you – Buttons, Handkerchief and the like . . . Put not your fingers in your mouth, bite not your nails, make no noise with your feet, put not your hands in your pockets, turn your Toes out, lay not one leg over the other.

. . . It is very vulgar in any one to make a noise in coughing and sneezing . . . and have a special care not to make any kind of Faces; that is, such as grinning, winking, or putting out your tongue, and the like; for that will make you despised.[19]

*A boarding school of the time. The Fourth Form room at Harrow.*

There was some criticism of bullying and flogging – but the tyranny of parents and masters could not have been always severe. Two visiting observers thought English education astonishingly liberal:

Education, the aim of which should be to direct and temper the natural disposition, has little or no influence upon the English. It begins with teaching to read and write at home. The principal object of this groundwork of education is, not to put any constraint upon the tempers of children, nor any bias upon the operations of nature, in unfolding the faculties either of the body or mind[20] . . . English boys remain true to nature until a certain age. What a contrast when I think of our six-year-old, pimpled, pampered Berlin boys, with great hair-nets and all the paraphernalia of an adult even to being dressed in lace-trimmed coats, and compare them with the English boys in the flower of youth – lithe, red-cheeked, with open-breasted shirts, hair cut and curling naturally! This free and natural dress is worn until they are 18 or 20.[21]

One of these visitors was shrewder than he knew, when concluding that the education of the wealthy classes was yet one more avenue for making family connections:

The public schools and the universities bring together persons of all ranks... A spirit of emulation reigns there, connexions are formed, which often lay the foundation of the greatest fortunes.[22]

*

Propriety was also stressed in the education charitably provided for the labouring poor. Dissenters and Anglicans, and the societies they supported – for the Propagation of Christian Knowledge, the Gospel in Foreign Parts, the Reformation of Manners – organized a large-scale provision of charity schools.

They taught reading and writing in a very elementary fashion. They taught children to be industrious and pious; and acquainted them with bowing, curtseying, and the Church Catechism. Above all, instruction in morality was most necessary for the lower sort.[23]

> Be good, and God will love and bless you...
> Keep your clothes clean,
> Wash your hands and face,
> Comb your head,
> Tye your shoes...
> Learn to spin Wool and Linen.
> Learn to sew Shifts and Shirts and Caps.
> Learn to knit hose.
> Learn to bake and brew and wash.
> Learn to clean Rooms and Pots and Pans.
> Do no wrong.
> It is a sin to steal a pin.
> Swear not at all nor make a brawl.
> Use no bad words.
> Live in peace with all as much as you can.

The insistent moral, however, was in the opening prayer:

Make me dutiful and obedient to my benefactors, and charitable to my enemies. Make me temperate and chaste, meek and patient, true in all my dealings, content and industrious in my station...

Dr Watts wrote simple poems and hymns which were used in these schools, and was quite satisfied that they taught the poor their proper place in society:

The masters and mistresses of these schools among us, teach the children of the poor what their station in life is, how mean

*Isaac Watts: quite satisfied that the poor were educated for their proper place in society.*

135

their circumstances, how necessary 'tis for them to be diligent, laborious, honest and faithful, humble and submissive, what duties they owe the rest of mankind and particularly to their superiors.[24]

But even this degree of education might lead to political discontents. Some associated the education of working people with newspapers and French politics.

The Scots clergyman, for example, on his adventurous, parsimonious ride from Perthshire, seemed to see Mammon everywhere (though chiefly in England!); not only among the Vauxhall ladies of pleasure, but even in a quiet country yokel – if he could read:

Saw with some surprise, indeed, a shepherd reclining on a green hill busied in reading a *Newspaper!* 'Curse on French Politics,' said I, 'for they will ruin our Country.' What business has he with this newspaper? I like Liberty as much as any man ... but this fellow would be better employed taking care of his sheep![25]

'Enlarging the views of the peasantry of a country to the power of making uncomfortable comparisons between themselves and their employers' said the author of the report on the agriculture of Devon, indulging in gratuitous comments on a topic which, he felt, could not be passed over in such a publication, 'can end in nothing but creating dissatisfaction and ideal misery among them, injurious to the existing orders of community and government.'[26]

He looked forward 'with a sort of dread' to the 'illumination', or the 'mental enlargement' of the peasant's mind, and respectfully submitted to the Honourable Board (of Agriculture): 'the propriety of opposing any measures that may rationally be supposed to lead to such a fatal issue'.

A girl in one charity school told of one of their lady subscribers who came back from a winter passed in London:

She held it little less than criminal to teach poor girls to read and write. They who are born to poverty, said she, are born to ignorance, and will work harder the less they know. She told her friends that London was in confusion by the insolence of servants ... but she was resolved for her part to spoil no more girls ... In less than a year the whole parish was convinced that the nation would be ruined if the children of the poor were taught to read and write ... Our school was dissolv'd.[27]

It was generally agreed that the 'lower sort might be so

*A school mistress: the interior of a charity school*

far civilized as not to be disgusting . . .' and that their children need not be 'wholly ignorant . . .' but still '. . . a very moderate share of scholarship was sufficient . . .' otherwise the labourers 'might be spoiled for field work'.

The principle was clear:

The ignorance of the Poor affords their masters the best security of their unremitting Utility, Faithfulness and Obedience. To instruct them in Reading and Writing generally puffs them with Arrogance, Vanity, Self-Conceit, and . . . unfits them for the menial stations which Providence has allotted for them.[28]

\*

As time went on, Jack began to feel and to enjoy a new sense of independence. He felt a new zest in the important business of exploring and becoming acquainted with society. When at Saltram, he made the round of visits to the neighbours – among them, the Edgecumbes who lived a little way across country. Nanny still took the most detailed interest in all his comings and goings:

Mr Edgecumbe called yesterday morning and Jack returned with him to dinner and to stay all night. He is not yet come home. He went to the Ball last Tuesday, and danced, he dines on Monday next at Captain Berlin where they are to have a Hop and sleeps at the Commissioners so you see he makes the best use of his time.

In London, Jack frequently visited the theatre and the opera, or dined with Sir Joshua. Charming, if still a little awkward and gauche, he was developing a mind of his own and was not afraid of letting people know what it was. His godfather, Mr Ley, wrote to Mr Parker in quite glowing terms:

We talked on all subjects nothing was too serious or too light for us – I was much pleased. And am satisfied there is a good foundation which may be and deserves to be cultivated with great care and attention. Pray don't think I flatter, for I would not say so if I did not think it, my object is only that it may not be neglected, for the time is now approaching when he is to take the complexion which is to last for life.

For a young man of wealth and high station, the restrictiveness of boarding school and the shelter of home, was followed by the rich culture of the universities. It was decided to send Jack to his father's old college – Christ Church, Oxford. The puzzle was – to find the culture! The dreaming spires, the noble edifices, of Oxford and Cambridge were also called a 'Disease of buildings'[29], and this seemed a better description of what was going on inside them. The great universities of England were confined to celibate Anglicans. Their colleges were companies of Church of England monks – who much preferred port and walnuts, with puffy hands folded over plump bellies in snoozing common rooms – to teaching the young. Gibbon, the historian, was admitted to the fellows' table of Magdalen College, Oxford[30]:

From the toil of reading, or thinking, or writing, they had absolved their conscience. Their conversation stagnated in a round of college business, Tory politics, personal stories, and private scandal; their dull and deep potations excused the brisk intemperance of youth.[31]

The brisk intemperate youths attended the universities from their middle teens. There was no fixed duration of courses. If he came from a wealthy family, and had a good allowance, a student could take with him his own private tutor, his servants, his horses, and lead a life of lavish entertainment in his rooms.

Undergraduates were – even in those days – undergraduates. This was the way in which prospective clergymen behaved:

Hearst, Bell and myself, being in Beer, went under the Dean's window and abused him very much. He came down and sent us to our Proper Rooms, and there we Huzza'd him again and again . . . We waited on him next morning, and he read to us a Statute or two, and says he shall not mention again provided the Senior people do not . . .[32]

When one of them took his B.A. degree, there were celebrations that do not sound unfamiliar:

I sat up till after twelve o'clock, and then went to bed, and at three in the morning, had my outward doors broken open, my glass door broke, and pulled out of bed, and brought into the Common Room, where I was obliged to drink and smoak, but not without a good many words . . . Some of our Fellows went at four o'clock in the morning, for Stow, and all drunk; some in a Phaeton, some in a Buggy, and some on Horse back. I went as far as Weston on the Green with them upon my Grey, and was home by nine o'clock this morning . . .[32]

The courses of study, the disputations on specified questions, and the examinations on various subjects held in private, were a great joke. Lord Eldon claimed that an examination for a degree at Oxford 'was a farce in my time':

I was examined in Hebrew and History, 'What is the Hebrew for the place of a skull?' said the examiner. 'Golgotha,' I replied. 'Who founded University College?' I answered, 'King Alfred'. 'Very well, sir,' said the examiner, 'then you are competent for your degree'.[33]

That was in 1770, and things were little different in the other great university:

A Norfolk clergyman was examined for his doctorate at Cambridge. The examiners put to him the question: 'Does the sun turn round the earth, or the earth round the sun?' Not knowing what to say, and wanting to make some reply, he assumed an emphatic air and boldly exclaimed: 'Why, sometimes the one, and sometimes the other.' This reply so amused the examiners that he was made a doctor on the strength of this piece of fatuous stupidity.[34]

Courses and examinations alike, claimed Dr Knox, deserved 'the utmost poignancy of ridicule'. This was the rich offering of Oxford and Cambridge – the culture of the élite – which the children of the charity schools would never enjoy.

\*

For a young gentleman, however, the university was not the culmination of his education. There was the much more splendid and exciting finishing process of 'the Grand Tour'. With his books, his clothes, his letters of introduction, his passport, his bankers draft, Jack could set off knowing that he was well equipped for what might be a hard journey over rough country, but an already well-travelled journey on the continent. There were dangers on the road – but occasionally good sport to be had, and many acquaintances, adventures and entertainments to which to look forward. To make sure that he did not idle away his time or become uncouth in his habits Jack was no doubt given the kind of advice contained in Lord Chesterfield's famous letters to his son, including their very precise directions on cleanliness and good manners:

I would much rather know that a man's fingers were actually in'

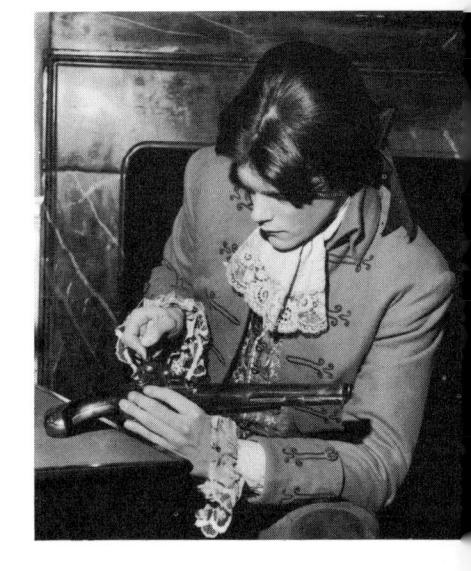

his breech, than see them in his nose. Wash your ears well every morning, and blow your nose in your handkerchief whenever you have occasion; but, by the way, without looking at it afterwards.

Jack, however, was much more concerned about money! He was provided with bankers drafts which would enable him to draw money in towns and cities wherever he might want to go. Mr Parker's resources being less than they had been, there were limits to the amount that could be allowed – nevertheless, the arrangements were very thorough and through his private banker, Mr Parker had done his best to foresee all the details of Jack's foreign visits.

Money was becoming the most serious point of contention between Jack and his father. Mr Parker was generous to a fault, especially towards his children, and would not have liked to appear any other, but he had the disquieting feeling that Jack – in his new expeditions into society, caught up in a new circle of friends – was not only demanding more, but becoming more and more plausible in doing so. His requests never ceased:

... how happy I am to find by Aunt Nanny's letter that you continue well and that your leaving off the draughts have not hurt you, which I own I much feared. I have only one pair of breeches and some things mended since I came here which came to a great deal of money, and I am going to ask a favour which I fear I have no pretensions to, and which I hope that you will have the goodness to acquiesce. It is that you will permit four shirts, four pairs of stockings and four neck cloths ... as I find all these materials are dearer than I expected and moreover being absolutely necessary, one year old ones being very bad, and as I have not money enough nor shall I have till the beginning of May and when I assure you it would enable (me) to go on the rest of the year pretty tolerably which I am sure I can not else do, and save me from Bankruptcy.

Your devoted and dutiful Son,

If I don't hear by return of post I shall conclude that you are so good as to acquiesce in my request.[35]

Nanny was also becoming a little worried. Now that Jack was moving in fashionable circles, she was apprehensive about the possible influences upon him of rather dissolute and wayward young men. It was not for her to choose Jack's friends – but some of them were odd and questionable choices to say the least. She could not bear to have them hanging about at Saltram, indolently drifting their time away:

Sir Lionel is still here, I wish he may be gone before Jack comes. I am sure he will do him no good. Sir Lionel is very idle and lazy, very inactive and no application to anything, not even Whist which seems to be his only amusement or study. I wrote Jack word Sir Lionel was a very idle young man, and much to be pitied for not having apply'd when a Boy at School.[36]

Aunt Nanny was also troubled by the feeling that she might have *cause* to be worried: for Jack was showing signs of foppishness and of inclinations to follow extreme fashions which his father would certainly not approve of. In the most tactful way, for example, she had written to him about his perfume, and his reply to this displayed a kind of skilled plausibility (Theresa, long ago in his infancy, had called it 'the compleat Art of Coaxing') which did not leave her happy:

I cannot return your sufficient thanks, my dear Aunt Nanny, for your kind little notes and the hints contained therein dictated, I am sure by love and affection towards me. You will not I trust, think they are flung away, when I assure you that I never will either now or in the future make myself a fool and dupe to any such follies as perfume . . . or any such frippery. For however immaterial they may be in themselves I am thoroughly sensible how much they will prejudice people against me and I am sure no one can more fully coincide in everything you allege upon the subject than myself. The perfume you allude to was when I left Saltram very little in quantity and was at the end of the journey nearly gone. I am certain I never carried it on the clothes in which I carried it to London. It has now been gone more than a month and I trust you will do me the justice to believe that my folly does not extend to the spending of money on so foolish an article; and you will recollect that I did not buy that.

For better, for worse – Jack was not to be tied to his family for long. Now fluent in French and Italian, he had joined a society at Oxford known as the 'Literati' and, together with some of its members[37], he was ready to embark on the Grand Tour as his father had done some twenty-five years earlier. The countries chiefly visited were France and Italy: Paris, Geneva, Genoa, Florence, Rome, Venice; and some time was spent also in Germany and the Low Countries.

*The Grand Tour: Venice, a detail from a painting by Canaletto*

France was the 'mistress of Europe', the 'Queen among the Nations'. Here the Enlightenment was an invigorating reality: in ideas and philosophy; in literature and the arts; in palaces and courts which were treasuries of culture; in fashion and dress; in commerce and wealth.

The French language was the cultural currency of the world. Italy was visited for its architecture, and its paintings and sculptures – some of which a young traveller would bring back with him for his collection. The Tour might take four or five years.

An elder son would have as lavish an allowance as was possible, and took with him a tutor, two or three servants, and his horses. The Duke of Kingston, for example, extended his tour over ten years and spent something over £40,000. Younger sons enjoyed only a shortened tour costing only a few hundreds of pounds, but they would be moving towards a career in some profession, whereas the elder son was acquainting himself with the best that culture had to offer for the way of life of a man who was to become the head of a great family and estate.

English visitors on the continent were marvelled at for their extravagance, their energy, and – sometimes – for their eccentricity. Sometimes the cultural values of the exercise were caustically, cynically, questioned:

This is one of the advantages of travell, to come home with a vamp'd Corregio, and some shabby marbles, and then neglect the real antiquities and old pictures at your family seat![38]

The Duke of Kingston was an excellent example. When his gambling losses were so high that he was urged by his guardians to marry, settle down, and put his estate to order, they were dismayed at his response:

... in plain terms ... if ever he marries it shall be to have a woman to breed out of and not for a companion, and that neither the consideration of continuing his family or clearing his estate shall ever determine him to do it before 30, if he ever does it at all.[39]

Even at Saltram, Mr Parker and Nanny saw examples among their neighbours in the County:

Sir John Chichester visited us this morning ... He does not hit me at all. There is nothing in him. His travels have given him an opportunity of talking of many places, people and things, which he manages without the least judgment and pays very little regard to truth, He is a great Coxcomb in his dress which, is not amiss at his age, and just come from abroad, and really drepes very well in London, but he is a sort of Jockey Coxcomb in the Country which is a sad style . . .[40]

In London, however, the profligates gathered in their plenty, and critics were more scathing:

They come home, the unimproved illiberal and ungentlemanlike creatures, where one daily sees them, that is in the park and the streets, for one never meets them in good company; where they have neither the manners to present themselves, nor the merit to be received. But with the manners of footmen and grooms, they assume their dress too, for you must have observed them in the streets here, in dirty blue frocks, with oaken sticks in their hands, and their hair greasy and unpowdered, tucked up under their hats of enormous size. Thus finished and adorned by their travels they become the disturbers of playhouses; they break the windows and commonly the landlords, of the taverns where they drink: and are at once the support, the terror, and the victims of the bawdy-houses they frequent. These poor mistaken people think they shine and so they do, but it is as putrification shines, in the dark.[41]

Parents gave their sons opportunities to become mature men of the world, men of experience, only to see them dribbled away into frilled shirt-fronts, fancy waistcoats, lace sleeves, sweet nosegays, and hats that looked like nothing short of an artificial poll-parrot!

\*

Education – then, as ever – was a mystery. The poor were trained to keep their station – but seethed with rebellion. Young ladies were trained to become 'accomplished' – only to drive their husbands deeper to drink by their trivialities, and gamble them into the ground. The Grand Tour sought to produce men of experience who would manage their estates responsibly – only to produce rakes who ran them savagely into debt before they even started. The one thing common to all forms of education seemed to be – that the effect they produced was the exact opposite of that aimed at!

Education seemed to be a net of anxieties thrown by one generation over the next – and which the next had to throw off, in order to survive.

Somewhere in all this, there must have been a moral . . .?

\*

Mystery or not – education is always something which the young are compelled to undergo. For better, for worse – none can escape it. Young Mr Jack Parker was like all others.

The world which had first come to life, for Theresa and himself, among the things of the nursery at Saltram ... was now at an end. The distinctions of reality had not so much broken into it, as shattered it! The doors of the schoolroom were closed. The doors of the Grand Tour, the Great World, the Real World – such as it was – were opened before him.

Into that world, he had to go.

*The Grand Tour: The Forum at Rome*

# 9 THE RED VELVET DRAWING ROOM

## *times of Contentment, perhaps the happiest times of all*

Sometimes, and more frequently now, there were quiet evenings.

They were the best of all.

No company, no visits, nothing whatever to attend to.

After dinner, they came into the small drawing room, and settled down to whatever it was they wanted to do – entertaining themselves, or each other – just as they felt inclined.

These family evenings had a quality of their own: a peacefulness – long, slow, undisturbed.

\*

Mr Parker loved one thing especially – to hear some music; and he was especially pleased that Theresa, who was growing up quickly, was already quite accomplished in her singing and playing. He had been much concerned to find a tutor for her, and the best instrument he could lay his hands on. He had Nanny, too, writing to her brothers to explore every possibility:

Mr Parker desires me to trouble you with a commission. He has determined that the little Girl should learn Musick this summer. There is an old man in Plymouth, who is a pretty good Master, but there is no such thing as a harpsichord, bought, hired, or borrowed. He would therefore be very much obliged to you if he could prevail upon you to get a tolerable good one second hand that will not cost much and have it sent down as soon as possible.[1]

It was said that the Puritans – in the service of morality – had tried to stamp out minstrelsy, and all harmonious music, as everything else remotely resembling pleasure.[2] Mr Parker was not sure about this ... but what was certain was that England had been a great musical nation at a time when half the musicians of France couldn't read a line of music at sight, and, despite these dark attacks, it was still widely enjoyed. The fiddler was still a colourful figure in country communities, leading the dancing and seasonal festivities. Each church continued to raise its little orchestra; its small knot of men who guarded their instruments and traditions with loving care; their viols, their sackbuts and perhaps their lutes, put to bed between a warm rug and a blanket – but not between sheets, which might have a little moisture in them ... Music was still a fashionable and a popular art.[3] Nothing could kill it!

To know and appreciate music, and to be able to entertain Company with a little singing, or playing on the harpsichord, was certainly an accomplishment to be desired in a lady. Mr Parker was intent upon giving Theresa as good a grounding in music as was possible.

This, however, was not her only accomplishment.

Her French was coming along rapidly under the guidance of her excellent governess, and she was reading more. In a good and careful home, a girl was educated to be accomplished in all those arts of life which were the province of a woman at the heart of a household and family. She should know at least enough of cookery and household duties in general, to be able responsibly to manage affairs. She should be skilled in needlework and embroidery, painting and drawing, and well-versed in etiquette and manners, and all the arts of entertaining. She should be capable of good conversation, and all those arts which gave her qualities of grace and beauty as well as utility. She should know French and Italian, and have a certain cosmopolitan acquaintance with culture. She should come to know London Society. And she should also, in her own person, embody qualities of grace and composure – so that she should learn deportment and become skilled in the movements of dancing.

Mr Parker and Nanny were determined that Theresa should have every care in her upbringing and education towards womanhood. And Mr Parker, especially, liked to take her out and about: to enjoy out-of-doors, and to see something of the world beyond Saltram. She even went with him, sometimes, when he visited the camp of the Devon Militia. She was – as Nanny put it – 'replacing Jack'.

But of all these accomplishments – music was hard to better! Was anything more beautiful than English music – than a young girl's voice, and an English song?

Mr Parker looked at his daughter approvingly. She

was giving them an idea of a new song – 'Drink to me only with thine eyes' – a setting of Ben Johnson's verses. He was not sure that he liked the song: it was one of those new ballads; but he liked to hear Theresa singing it. It pleased him that she was able, now, to try various kinds of composition; but, all that aside, he just liked to hear her singing.

\*

John Parker had come to enjoy these quiet, restful evenings. He had been ill lately. His gout was becoming troublesome. He could not easily get out-of-doors, and had to use a stool indoors, and recently some ailment of the chest had taken him, which involved much bleeding and congestion. It worried and distressed him. He had been warned by his physicians to drink sparingly, and to Nanny's surprise he was obeying them – which meant that he really did feel low:

On Sunday evening last, Mr Parker was seized with a violent fit of coughing, which ended his spitting blood as much as either time in London. He immediately sent for Dr Mudge and Mr Yonge, the surgeon who bled him and gave him a sleeping draught by which means he had a good night and has been recovering every day since, and I flatter myself he is not worse for this last attack, but is going on as well as before it happened. His cough and spitting is much lessened, and has had no fresh spitting of blood since last Sunday, and I flatter myself he is not the worse for this relapse, and if it has no return I hope will have done him no harm.[4]

He could not be as active now, and, what was more – and it sometimes troubled him – he did not want to be. Now that he was not so busy with Parliament, or even with County affairs, he found it a great enjoyment to spend a good deal of his time reading – in a leisurely and casual way, following his inclination.

There were now a large number of interesting newspapers and journals. Mr Wilkes used the *North Briton* to attack Lord Bute's *Briton* – which was run by Smollett. There was the *Morning Post* and the *Public Advertiser,* and reading was very engaging now that political debates were printed. The *Gentleman's Magazine* and the *London Magazine* had been forbidden, for a time, to print debates – except in fictitious form – but Wilkes the rebel had forced their hand again: and now the affairs of Parliament were open to the general public. God knows where it would end if Government should become a matter for the people!

Also, there was no shortage of a kind of reading matter in which your imagination could become wholly engaged! The novels of Mr Fielding, Richardson, Smollett, and racy, randy old Laurence Sterne – had a lively and provoking way of commenting on things. You could live in these books, and find characters there who were a sight more colourful and entertaining than those you encountered in the flesh! And now the women were stealing their thunder. Miss Fanny Burney, for example – a gossip if ever there was one! Everyone seemed to think it necessary, also, to write diaries – of their horseback tours across the swamps and forests of the midlands, of their impressions of the nosegay women in St Jame's Park, of anything![5] Every wife in creation spent her days writing volumes of letters. It was a literary age – and a hare-brained and eccentric one, too! It was not only Macaroni madness – Mr Fox and his red-heeled shoes – but much more strange doings.

There was this new passion for ballooning, for example. Why the devil should people want to go up in the air, while there were horses to ride on? The craze had spread as fast as the smallpox. Even Aunt Nanny could not restrain her excitement about it:

We have been letting off balloons every night . . . most of them were burnt, some tore, and but one fairly succeeded . . . The Exeter Paper advertises an Air Balloon to be exhibited on Monday next . . . if it does not go into the sea I think we shall have it upon the lawn here, if the wind should change.[6]

And, of course, Horace Walpole had to have his witty say about ballooning – as about everything else that happened in the wide world:

My servant called me away to see a balloon. I saw it from the common field before the window of my round tower. It appeared about a third of the size of the moon when it sunk slowly behind the trees . . . I amused myself with ideas of the change that would be made in the world by the substitution of balloons to ships. I supposed our seaports to become deserted villages; and Salisbury Plain, Newmarket Heath, and all downs, arising into dock-yards for aerial vessels . . . In those days Old Sarum will again be a town and have houses in it. There will be fights in the air with wind-guns and bows and arrows . . . But enough of my fooleries![7]

Fooleries indeed! Nanny found the idea of travelling through the air an exciting one, and people really did seem to think there was a serious possibility in it. But it was absurd to think of taking heavy cargoes up into the sky!

Stranger entertainments still were being thought up. There were even men in vessels going under water:

> There is a curious bett soon to be decided between Mr Blake and I don't know who, but Mr Blake is to find a Vessell I believe between 30 and 40 ton which is to be sunk 100 foot under water with a Man in it who is to remain there twelve hours and to come up alive ... I heard Dr. Priestley talking about it the other day (which is pretty good authority) and he had no doubt of the possibility of a man breathing in that space without any communication with the outside world for twelve hours even in a more confined space. There will be some difficulty and ingenuity in sinking the Vessel that Depth and also in raising it again. The raising is to be effected by the Man's sawing or knocking off what helped to sink it, but in what manner I don't know.[8]

Such things made you wonder what men would try to do next – especially with this new inquisitiveness of science. It brought good things, certainly – like inoculations, but it seemed also to lead to such fooleries as men getting lost in the sky or drowned in the oceans! There was – about this world – only one thing of which you could be absolutely sure: and that was – that it would be forever changing!

In this mood – absorbed, drifting, amused, carping, critical, good-humouredly assertive in his own mind – Mr Parker loved to dip into book after book – into his perennial love of voyages; into some of the new archaelogical and geographical studies, like those of Sir William Hamilton[9] on earthquakes and volcanoes ... Lately, he had found himself much impressed by the opinions of some of the women: the Bluestockings. They were laughed at by a good many people, but, thinking about the education of his daughter, he found their ideas compelling.

They attacked the trivialities of ordinary drawing-room entertainments – of cards, drunkenness, gossip, and gambling; and the idea that women were capable only of brainless conversation – fluttering behind their fans like so many butterflies. They wanted drawing-room evenings during which men and women could converse seriously – as equals – and about subjects of importance. It was

Mr Stillingfleet, grandson of the famous Bishop of Worcester who was responsible for their 'title'. He had turned up at one of Mrs Montagu's salons wearing 'blue worsted stockings' instead of the customary 'black silk'. Poor Mr Stillingfleet: he could have had no idea that his legs would be forever renowned as a national label.[10]

The Bluestockings were an impressive group, to say the least. Lady Wortley Montagu was not only a cultured woman: it was she, really, who had done all the fighting for the spread of vaccination; and had succeeded! Elizabeth Montagu – who was no sober-sides – did not keep her culture within the walls of her drawing room, but openly sympathised with mine-workers and chimney-sweep boys. Holy Hannah (More) did at least try to *do* something about training the poor[11]. Miss Burney could certainly write! Especially, however, he liked their views on education.

Everything he had experienced in his life with Theresa, had led him to know that the companionship of marriage was only a full companionship when a husband and wife were able to regard each other – in taste, judgement, information – as equals. He therefore greatly admired the stand they took against inequality and subjection. He liked Lady Wortley Montagu's outspokenness; her passionate condemnation:

To say truth, there is no part of the world where our sex is treated with so much contempt as in England. I think it the highest injustice that the same studies which raise the character of a man should be thought to hurt that of a woman. We are educated in the grossest ignorance, and no art ommitted to stifle our natural reason.[12]

Even so, he could only suppose that they themselves were very able in all the arts of rebellion. They did not do so badly in making themselves heard despite their subjection! For this – and surely none could deny it – was an age of notable women.

Even so, he couldn't stand some things. All this cutting out of paper-shapes; all this 'fancy work'; all this tent-stitch, featherwork, netting and knotting – it was sheer tedium!

Mr Parker was too much a lover of the cards and gambling and more active excitements to eschew the sophisticated drawing-room life altogether, and – though

*Georgiana: Duchess of Devonshire – but here in far more formal pose and attire than those usually described by gossip.*

no less a person than Mrs Delaney devoted herself to this stuff, and though it was no doubt pretty, and though the King and Queen themselves encouraged it – to look at it too much was enough to make him long for an outrageous squeal of scandal from the Duchess of Devonshire, and a good belly-laugh in her company.

He chuckled to himself as he thought about it. There were limits to sobriety – and it warmed him simply to think of Georgiana. Whatever her reputation – she was a woman few others could approach not only in beauty, gaiety and outrageousness, but also in good nature, good humour and generosity of disposition. Even Nanny was coming to agree:

I have had the civilest and I may say the kindest letter from the Dutchess of Devonshire that can be. She has been to see the Boy at Hammersmith and sent the Little Girl a pair of Bracelets which was really an attention that was not at all necessary tho' not at all surprising from her. I do assure you the more she is known, the better she is to be liked.

One other fashion was now bringing the travellers teeming down to Dawlish: the fashion of sea-bathing; but this did at least seem to carry some benefits for health. Even Fanny Burney had tried it – though, no doubt, so that she could write about it:

Today for the first time I bathed. I was terribly frightened, and really thought I should never have recovered from the plunge. I had not breath enough to speak for a minute or two, the shock was beyond all expression great; but, after I got back

*Opposite:*

*The Morning Room: showing some familiar pictures in their accustomed places. Montague can be seen near the corner.*

*This was the room for breakfast, and the family would spend much time here. When alone, they would probably dine here – the Red Velvet Drawing Room adjoins this room. The large Eating Room would be used only when there was Company.*

*'Fritz' – the Honourable Frederick Robinson – Theresa's younger brother.*

to the machine I presently felt myself in a glow that was delightful – it is the finest feeling in the world, and will induce me to bathe as often as will be safe.[13]

Mrs Frederick Robinson – Fritz's wife – had been low in spirits for some time . . . and had written from Yorkshire, asking if she might come down to Saltram to sea-bathe, as it was considered beneficial for her health. Mr Parker had Nanny write off at once:

. . . the chief reason of my writing today, is to lose no time in acquainting you that, we are not likely to have any Company except some dinner visits, from the few neighbours around this place. Mr Parker desires me to tell you that you shall have an appartment to yourself where you may dine whenever you please, if there should be too much company for you, or you should not be in Health of Spirits to dine below, in short that you will entirely be at liberty to do as you like, as much as if you was at home. Mrs Robinson will be able to Bathe as often as she pleases, with ease and I hope benefit, I am sincerely sorry that she should have occasion for it. I flatter myself when she has had a little quiet and rest here that she will recover her strength and spirits. I am sure no endeavours of mine shall be wanting towards accomplishing it.[14]

Nanny sometimes thought that sea-bathing might even do Mr Parker himself some good and had wondered if she ought to suggest it to him, but she was doubtful whether she could persuade him to try. She had become completely identified with the family since her sister's death, and now knew Mr Parker's whims and moods almost as well as if she were married to him:

He keeps strictly to one glass of Negus only, though allowed to drink plain wine. He is rather low, and has a very bad opinion of himself, which I own I have not, and I believe that is one reason of his great impatience to see Jack . . . We have not heard from Jack this week, and Mr Parker grows so very impatient to see him . . .

\*

Mr Parker's occasional melancholy, however, was not only an outcome of brooding over his own illness, though, sometimes, he did have a deep apprehensiveness about it. The continued lack of any progress in the treatment of it was such as gradually to depress his hopes of recovery, and he had not seen any great reasons why his faith in physicians

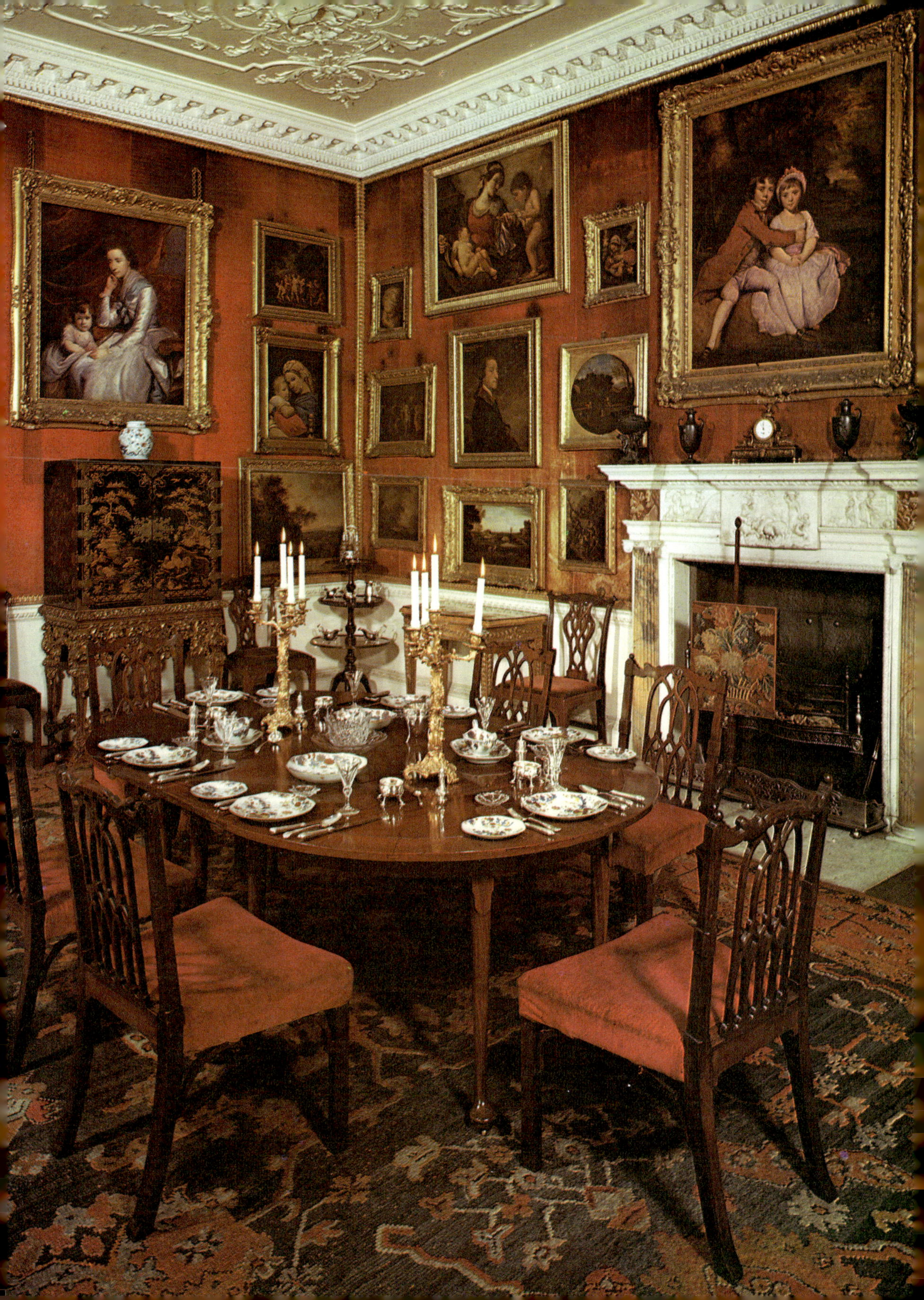

*Spillikins in the Red Velvet Drawing Room*

'... his hands, rather stiff and awkward now, were becoming almost useless at this game. He tried – again and again – but was much too clumsy to manipulate the slim ivory picks.'

should increase! Still – he was not a man who was unable to look inevitabilities in the face – when they were proved to be so; and meanwhile he could enjoy the many pleasures and the warm affection which lay about him.

The truth was that he had arrived at an age when troubles mounted; when the limitations of life impressed themselves more forcibly than its promise; when the course of personal events seemed no longer of the nature of changes only, but of culminations. Circumstances sometimes seemed to be closing upon him. Their insistence sometimes enveloped him in a sober tone and atmosphere.

He had never, whether with Theresa or with Nanny, made much of relationships with the neighbouring county families. Even so – as a native of Devon – he had known them longer and more intimately than they had, and it was saddening to find that he was not alone in his illness, but that friends of very long standing were in the same, or sometimes a worse, plight:

Mr Parker is very much hurt at his two oldest Friends being both very ill, Sir John Chichester is still alive but in the greatest danger, and Sir Tho' Acland tho' not much in immediate danger, is so weak that it is doubtful whether he can get to Bath, which is the only thing likely to do him good. Mr Parker has not been quite well himself and has had some return of his Complaint, but without fever . . .[15]

Much more seriously distressing for himself, Nanny, and the whole family – had been the death of poor Grantham. Nanny had received continual reports of an illness – from Grantham himself, who had clearly made light of his ailment, and from Fritz. But none of them had realised its gravity. Fritz's letter with news of his brother's death, had been a great shock. Nanny had not known how to reply:

My dearest Dear Fritz,
What can I say to you, indeed I can give you no comfort, I have none to give for I can feel none . . . your welfare may give me some, you are all I have left. Let me recommend to you (tho' I am sure there is no occasion) to place your whole confidence in your dear & good wife, whose good sense, and ready attachment to you will do every thing in her Power to enable you to go through the arduous situation you are in . . . but lett me at the same time entreat you, for her sake, not to put too hard a task upon her, but to support yourself as much as you possibly can.

If example could be of service let me add, that nothing but the *two* Dear ever dearest Children, could have enabled me to have gone thro' what I endured, above ten years ago. Oh my Dearest Fritz, this is an opening of old wounds, hardly healed. I must have done. This is no letter of comfort, let us see you here as soon as you can, this is Mr Parker's wish as well as mine. God Bless you my Ever Dearest Fritz I know you will take care of yourself, you have one comfort which is that you have neglected nothing and fulfilled every – more than every – duty. Once more God Allmighty Bless and preserve I am your most Affect$^e$ Sister.[16]

Grantham's going had been a distress to them all, a great disturbance to the family. Fritz had now to step into his brother's shoes in the conduct of many affairs, and, in particular, was now vested with the duties of trusteeship for Mr Parker's children. Fritz was anxious about his own position and status. He and his wife came to stay at Saltram for a time, and efforts were made to secure a place for him in the Treasury, or some other appointment. Mr Parker advised him to apply to Mr Pitt, and later in the year such a meeting was arranged. Nanny stayed in the closest correspondence with him:

On November 11th, 1786:

I shall be impatient to hear from you after you have seen Mr Pitt.

At the end of November:

... I was particularly obliged to you for giving me so full and early an account of your conference with Mr Pitt, from which I must own I think you have a good chance of succeeding, & I hope you will have no difficulty with respect to the Irish pension.

Two days after Christmas:

I wish you could hear something from Mr Pitt before the parliament meets.

And at the end of January in the new year:

I received your kind letter of the 26th yesterday and take the first opportunity in my power of thanking you for your early and full inteligence respecting the Irish Pension. I am extremely glad it is in so fair a way of succeeding as I know it will be a great reliefe to you, & certainly advantageous to all the different partys, indeed the more I think of it the more I am convinced of the propriety of the measure, you may be sure of my being ready to sign or do anything that you tell me is necessary on this or any other occasion to serve you, with respect to 6000 £ I should suppose the Funds the best security, but you are the best Judge. I am glad to find Lord Hardwick is so liberaly disposed at present, and hope he will continue so. I wish you could hear something good from Mr Pitt, if you had not given up your profession or had been in the Church he would have had no difficulty in providing for you, as there seems to be nothing to be had but in the Law & the Church at present. I hope however he will find out something *soon* . . .[17]

It was an unsettling situation; and one not yet satisfactorily resolved.

Also – illness and death aside – Mr Parker had reached an age when even close personal relationships could lose such saving graces as they had once possessed, and harden; when earlier sentiments which had given them at least some savour, some pleasure, seemed worn away – leaving only a stark expediency of calculated interest where at least some personal attachment had been professed and assumed. His relationship with Montague, his younger brother, was an example, and much distressed him. Montague, with his rooted country ways, had been accustomed to spending much time at Saltram, and things had not been bad between them; but problems of property, complicated by marriage settlements, easily gave rise to conflicts and resentments – not only between brothers, but also between brothers and their wives. A long time ago, when Theresa was alive, he had agreed to an exchange of lands with Montague – for which Mrs Montague's consent was required – and ever since, relations between them had worsened. At the time, Theresa herself had written about her visit to the House of Lords to help in settling the matter:

I went the other morning before a Committee of the House of Lords to give my consent to a Bill now depending for an exchange of lands between Mr Parker & Mr Montagu, part of which being Whiteway, which you know was settled. I was obliged to give my consent before it could pass. Mr Montagu's Estates that he had given in exchange for it lay round Saltram, & were under the same predicament, his consent therefore & Mrs Montagu's were also necessary. Mr Parkers illness prevented his going down. It was not a very long ceremony & the Committee was composed of Ld. Pelham & others that I knew or did not Mind. It is hardly necessary to add that this exchange is rather in my favour tho' it is giving up Whiteway. Mr Parker would never have consented if it had not & it is the fairest bargain that was ever made between the two brothers.[18]

Through all the years following, feelings had rankled, and it had become such a grievous and intense matter as to enter into the most ordinary social intercourse. Nanny had become indignant about the lengths to which it was taken:

We are just returned from Ketley from a most unpleasant dinner owing to Mr Montague's dining there. Whether by design or accident we cannot tell. It was either the most impertinent or the worst judged thing that Mr Bastard could do, knowing as you do Mr Parker's feelings and situation he is in with respect to Mrs Montague. You will not be surprised to hear it is the last visit we shall ever make there. He is as you may naturally suppose very much Hurt. I must own I was much shocked at finding him there.[19]

Since that occasion they had tried to avoid meeting.

Age saw earlier incidents working, almost inexorably, towards definite and unpalatable conclusions. There seemed as much a fatefulness in the working out of events as in the natural growth towards illness and death.

Mr Parker was by no means of a melancholy disposition, and gloom never for long prevailed with him, but sometimes the 'sea of troubles' seemed to surge very close, and it was then – more than at other times – that he felt a longing to see Jack back at Saltram, and when he dwelt more deliberately, with a deeper and warmer appreciation, upon these simple evening activities in the drawing room: with Nanny always loyally near at hand to humour him, and sometimes politely to argue with him, and little Theresa giving him the deepest joy of all – just by her presence.

*

Sometimes, they played games here.

A family in the country was not without an enjoyable round of entertainment – should they want it. Strolling companies of players quite frequently performed Shakespeare, Congreve, the Beggar's Opera – in the Court House or some Public Rooms, and there were all the seasonal festivities on the farms and among the County families round about the Christmas Feast, and Singers, and the festivities at Harvest Time. The country was far from being a dull place in which to live. Even so, they liked these quiet games amongst themselves – cards, chess, dominoes, spillikins. Sometimes, visitors played cards with Nanny and Mr Parker – but she would leave the betting to him:

We have had a thorough match at Whist, and trimmed the Duke and Duchess most handsomely. They play three or four rubbers, never win more than one of an evening and not often that. Mr Parker and I always play together and they bet with him. There is no other company here at all.[20]

Onc game they liked to play when they were alone, was spillikins, but Mr Parker found that his hands — rather stiff and awkward now — were becoming almost useless at this game. He tried — again and again — but was much too clumsy to manipulate the slim ivory picks. It exasperated him; made him irritable. If only Jack were here. He would have played with Theresa, and Mr Parker himself could have relaxed and let his mind dwell on other, more important things. Whenever his mind turned to Jack, however, his feelings were a confusion of love, irritation and distress. He was growing a little afraid of his illness, beginning to wonder about the seriousness of it; and — in this mood — dearly wanted to see Jack at home. Yet, at the same time, the boy was becoming more of a problem. Sometimes, he seemed to have lost all sense of what was right and proper. There was the matter of franking letters:

According to your desire, I shall no more date my letters on the Cover, my only reason for ever doing it was to prevent that day being lost, which Aunt Nanny complains, and as the liberty of doing is by no means an appendage of that of franking it is very common for people out of Parliament so to do.[21]

Mr Parker was very sensitive that in his present financial state he could not indulge Jack to the extent he would have liked, but need the boy remind him so continuously how short money was?

I am glad you are going to sell all your useless Horses, and you receive my permission to sell my ... pony for as much as you can get, upon conditions that you will accept the profits arising therefrom. I am most exceedingly sorry to hear my Mare is so sickly, it was at this time of year, when I was here, that your stable boys or somebody spoilt the grey mare. My old Boots, as you know, full of holes and patches, are too small that I cannot wear them, may I ask your permission for another pair which if I come to Devon will be absolutely necessary. In winter amidst dirt and frost ... to have no boots would be very disagreeable. My black breeches are hardly decent ... You do not I conclude, think of any more ponies. I think it ought to be publicly given out that you are provided.[22]

His difficulties seemed almost a matter for shame when they were written about in this manner, and he could scarcely believe that Jack could be so insensitive as not to realise the effect on his feelings. It was disquieting: almost as though he did not know his son at all.

Theresa, of course, could play spillikins much better than her Papa. Her nimble fingers were used to more delicate pursuits, sewing and stitching, and she was good at cutting out paper flowers like Mrs Delaney – whom she admired so much. The King and Queen had received Mrs Delaney and had declared themselves delighted with her work. Even Sir Joshua said that she was unrivalled. Theresa had come to idealise her: not only for the art she practised, but also because of her character; and, decidedly, there was an element of romance in Mrs Delaney's history. Few novels provided a more colourful story.

When she was Mary Granville – a girl of seventeen – she was staying with her friends, Lord and Lady Lansdowne. She was amused 'to great mirth' by a 'fat, snuffy, dirty, gouty, and sulky' old Cornishman of sixty, of enormous 'unwieldy bulk and crimson countenance'. Then, to her horror, she discovered that this was the man it had been arranged that she should marry. She did marry him out of a sense of duty, and lived with him in a remote old castle with broken-down ceilings, during the seven years until he died – during the greater part of which he was brought home drunk at six o'clock in the morning. Only after twenty years of widowhood did she ultimately marry Dr Delaney, a man of her choice, and even this was almost prevented by her brother, who thought Delaney's family of too low a station. As Mrs Delaney – a friend of Elizabeth Montagu, and of Swift – she was to become very well known throughout Society[23].

Theresa much admired Mrs Delaney's strength of character – but felt that she herself could never possibly have made the same kind of sacrifice. In fact, she had no fears that any such thing would be asked of her. She had a complete trust that her father would arrange a suitable match and that the man chosen would be someone of character whom she could admire. Here at Saltram she was happy and secure among the people she loved most in the world, and it was only occasionally, as yet, that she thought of marriage – and even then without any real knowledge of what lay in store for her. Even so, no young lady could escape this central fact of her destiny, on which her entire happiness depended – her marriage.

Mr Parker was well aware of this, and thought about it from time to time, although he was not disposed to hurry matters. In this, more perhaps than in most things, it was best to bide your time. He could not stand the feverish pitch of the marriage-market; the stupidity of fitting girls out with superficial 'accomplishments' as a set of baubles to attract husbands. It was as though, from her very cradle, a girl was thought of only in terms of a prospective 'match':

There, you . . . behold lilliputian coquettes projecting dresses, studying colours, assorting ribbands, and choosing feathers; their little hearts beating with hope about partners and fears about rivals; their fresh cheeks pale after the midnight supper; their aching heads and unbraced nerves disqualifying the little languid beings for the next day's task . . .[24]

Tied to such a competitive frenzy, the upbringing and education of a young girl lost all its true parts and qualities. It was simply put on – like a sparkling head-dress – to catch attention and to please. It was learning to do tricks – like performing monkeys for payment and applause. It was not a training of the mind, of the person, but the swallowing of a book of quotations:

The swarms of Abridgements, Beauties, and Compendiums, which form too considerable a part of a young lady's library, may be considered in many instances as an infallible receipt for making a superficial mind . . .
Talents which have *display* for their object despise the narrow stage of home: they demand mankind for their spectators, and the world for their theatre.[24]

*Mrs Delaney*

Marriages were arranged, and had to be arranged, and, as with Mrs Delaney, a young girl could be a pawn for political advancement through marriage. Sometimes her future happiness was negotiated away while she was still a child; and in her teens she was then married, according to plan, with no thought to her personal desire. With these kinds of restrictiveness, this kind of riding roughshod over considerations of personal choice and happiness, 'runaway marriages' were only to be expected. There were clandestine and irregular marriages in churches and chapels where no formal ceremonies, banns or licences were required. Marriage was in a state of chaos: of arrangements and mis-arrangements, of constraints and disorders. The mixture of morality and immorality in law and religion was almost beyond belief – but a colourful mixture for all that.

'Public Penance' was still carried out in some churches. The penitent put on a white sheet, and had to make open confession in the church:

> I do here, in the presence of Almighty God, and this congregation, humbly confess and acknowledge, that I have most grievously offended his Divine Majesty, in defiling my body, by committing the heinous sin of fornication, with William, for which, my said foul offence, I am heartily sorry, and do sincerely repent thereof, and beg of God, mercy and forgiveness of the same . . .[25]

*Little Theresa at the age of twelve*

Parish Authorities could still force couples to marry, in order to control the movements of the poor, and their expenses on them. A country parson recorded such a marriage as a matter of course:

> I married Tom Burge of Ansford to Charity Andrews of Cary by License this morning. The Parish of Cary made him marry her, and he came handbolted to the Church for fear of running away, and the Parish of Cary was at all the expense of bringing of them to. I received of the overseer of the Poor of Cary for it – 10s. 6d.[26]

At the same time, wife-selling was not an uncommon occurrence among the lower sort until after the end of the century:

> On the 11th of last month, a person sold, at the market cross in Chapel en le Frith, a wife, a child, and as much furniture as would set up a beggar, for eleven shillings.
> A Butcher sold his wife by auction the last market day at Hereford. The lot brought £1 4s. 0d. and a bowl of punch.

There were examples all over the country – Hull, Knaresborough, Sheffield, Smithfield.[27]

The marriage-market was a fearful business – sometimes a despicable business – at all levels. But Mr Parker knew that it need not be so, and was not so, if care was taken over the personal choosing. He was determined that Theresa's education should not be inflamed by such a poison. Come what may later; at home, she would be introduced to true and important qualities. The arrangement of a marriage and a marriage settlement need not exclude the most careful consideration of personal qualities and personal choice. A marriage would certainly be arranged for Theresa – but nothing would be proceeded with which held the slightest suspicion of a prospect of unhappiness for her. Theresa was fully confident of this, and Nanny, knowing very well the importance which her mother had attached to marriage, continually reminded her of her mother's attitudes and words:

I shall teach my daughter from her cradle to dread marriage unless everything conspires to promise happiness. I think that nothing contributes more to the many unhappy marriages one sees than the want of nicety in young women at present who are much more to blame in that respect than the men. They set their caps at every man of fortune that comes out and take the first that offers.

Some things were being done about the nature and condition of marriage generally, and the new 'public marriages' were much talked about. Since Lord Hardwicke's Marriage Act (of 1753) it was required that all marriages should be 'public': that they should take place in a parish church after the banns had been published on three consecutive Sundays. The 'public marriage' was still quite an event, particularly in the country, and people flocked to see it, as to a public occasion. Fanny Burney – when she witnessed one – was not sure whether to be delighted or afraid:

*The public wedding – a new experience and new social event after Lord Hardwicke's Act of 1753.*

We have just had a wedding – a public wedding, and very fine it was I assure you. The bride is Miss Case, daughter of an Alderman of Lunn, with a great fortune; the bridegroom is Mr Bagg. Our house is in the churchyard and exactly opposite the great church door – so that we had a good view of the procession. The walk that leads up to the church was crowded – almost incredibly a great mob indeed – I'm sure I trembled for the bride – oh what a gauntlet for any woman of delicacy to run! How short a time does it take to put an eternal end to a woman's liberty! I don't think they were a quarter of an hour in the church altogether ... when the bell began to ring so merrily, so loud, and the doors opened – we saw them walk down the Aisle, the bride and bridegroom first – hand in hand – the bridegroom looked so gay, so happy! She looked grave, but not sad – and, in short, all was happy and charming. Well of all the things in the world, I don't suppose anything can be so dreadful as a public wedding – my stars! I should never be able to support it.[28]

The contemplation of marriage – all sides of it – was

intriguing to young Theresa: but she was pleased that it was still some way off. The society of the neighbouring families at Saltram; Jack's visits on holidays; the fire in the hearth; the music; the spillikin ivories on the table . . . these were a world of happiness, enough for now.

\*

Whilst the other two were busy with their games, music and reading, Nanny liked to work on with a little sewing or embroidery. She enjoyed making things for herself, and was pleased when her work turned out well:

I have made up my Habit and it is the surprise and admiration, and Envy of everybody that sees it, I set the highest value upon it, but not for the above reasons as I hope you will easily immagine.[29]

She had stepped very successfully into her sister's shoes. The way of family settlements was such as to leave the daughters of a marriage, as well as the younger sons, with only limited provision. If she was not fortunate in marrying, the only occupations for a woman were those of governess or housekeeper. The spinster in the household had become almost an institution!

There existed in the families of most residents in the country, a certain antiquated female, either maiden or widow, commonly an aunt or cousin. Her dress consisted of a stiff-starched cap and hood, a little hoop, a rich silk damask gown with large flowers. She leant on an ivory crutch-cane, and was followed by a fat dog of the pug kind, who commonly reposed on a cushion, and enjoyed the privilege of snarling at the servants, occasionally biting their heels with impunity. By the side of this good old lady jingled a bunch of keys which opened cupboards and corner closets of all sorts . . .[30]

Nanny was very far from this caricature; but without such an occupation, a spinster was dependent upon the other members of her family – and moved from house to house to stay with them. Sometimes this was an embarrassment of dependence since her resources were limited.

In earlier years when her sister Theresa had been alive, Nanny – though very close to her and staying often at Saltram – had been as independent as her limited allowance would provide; but often she had felt the strain on her pocket, particularly when she wanted to go to Yorkshire to visit her brothers and the family home. Theresa had, in fact, written tactfully to Grantham on her behalf, and he had responded at once:

. . . the long journey is a little upon her mind, and not very convenient to her pocket. But she manages her affairs with great Prudence and Propriety and takes care not to go beyond the mark . . . Nanny received by the same post your very kind intention toward her. I hope it is by no means inconvenient to you, for I am sure she would be miserable if she thought so. When I hinted to you that her journeying to Yorkshire would be expensive I knew she would be obliged to retrench some of her other amusements and as her expenses are all upon a small scale, and she manages very well and properly I know your very kind attention to her will more than set her at perfect ease.[31]

But this could not be pleasant for a sensitive person; and a maiden-aunt was often a very considerable boon to a family. The dangers of child-birth were such that it was sometimes a wife who bore the children and a spinster sister who brought them up – as with the Parkers. Nanny, however, was no pug-dog carrier rattling a bunch of keys. She, too, was a woman of fashion. She continued to entertain with Mr Parker – though she disliked doing it without him; and she went to Court on occasion:

I was at the Play on Wednesday in the Stage Box directly over against the King and Queen, having done the same thing a fortnight ago I thought it quite right to go to Court yesterday, and was most graciously received. The King asked after you both, and when you came to Town, and whether my brother had not his usual call to Town this year before Christmas . . .[32]

Nanny enjoyed the normal management of the household: deeply pleased to commit herself to what had been her sister's dearest interests. Mr Parker had come to look to her for guidance, and trusted her opinion about many things. She took an interest in all the improvements of the house – the new Eating Room and Library, the planting of trees on the estate; and was devoted to the children. Like her sister, and Mr Parker himself, she liked Company – but only in small measure. More than anything, she liked to sit here, busying herself with some work of her own, and feeling pleasure in the presence of those to whom she was so closely attached – with what was now, in effect – her own family.

Nanny also supervised the shopping for the household, and this was especially pleasing, because – apart from the ordinary food stuffs which could be had on the home farm – meat, vegetables, bread, fruit – other goods had to be fetched from a distance: from Plymouth or from London. Sometimes, someone who was known to be in London would be commissioned to bring things back. This was a practice throughout the length and breadth of the country. From the moors and dales of Yorkshire to the red cliffs of the west country – wives and daughters waited in anticipation for the packages which were to arrive on the coach. There was great excitement when the parcels arrived; a special delight in unpacking them – so long waited for – to see whether they were all that had been expected. The very limitations of shopping added a spice of excitement to it; and then, too, the shops of London were open at all hours, giving careful personal attention no matter what time of the day or evening it was:

I did not receive your letter till after eight o'clock in the evening . . . and was obliged to set out the next morning . . . so I

*Shopping in London in 1789. The lady is stepping from a Sedan chair.*

took a coach, and did your commissions as well as I could by candle-light, which is not the best time to chuse many things... I fear you will not like your China much. I saw only one set of twelves and that was the old pattern, foreign, with a great deal of blue, and gilt edges. He had only one set of Nankin for which he asks £47. I saw some very ugly Common – £27 – 18 dishes, 2 Terreens, 5 doz plates, 2 doz Soop Dit, a very poor quantity... Mr Cooper has no choice; he did not shew me any new or pretty patterns. Since their misfortune, Wedgewood's shop is never open after dark, otherways I should have bought the China there... I hope I have not omitted any other of your commissions, but the rest of the things will all come with me...[33]

*

Tea was taken after dinner in the drawing room, and Nanny enjoyed this more than any other period of the day. It was a particularly restful time, with everybody relaxed, quietly and pleasantly together. Though not the caricature of the spinster with the bunch of keys, she did, however, since tea was so expensive and servants only human, take care against pilfering, and carefully guarded one key – the key to the tea-caddy.

Tea had become the fashionable and universal drink.

The habit had spread like a fire among all classes. It could form quite a large proportion of a servant's wages:

February 19th – to Jane Dowie – for nine months wages – fifteen pounds, fifteen shillings. Her allowance of tea – one pound, six shillings.

At the beginning of the century about 20 thousand lbs were imported; by the end of it, about 20 millions – and, smuggling or no smuggling, the price remained high! In 1710 tea could be had for about 16s. a pound (though cheaper black tea was from 12s., and green tea from 10s. a lb, and the best Bohea tea was 30s. a lb) the tax per lb being 5s. In 1780 the average price was still about 16s. Mr Parker's account books recorded the costly items:

By cash to Mr Simmonds for tea, nineteen pounds, twelve shillings.
To Bradley for tea, fifteen pounds, seven shillings.

Remembering that an average labourer's wage was about 7s. to 8s. a week, it is plain what an extravagance tea-drinking was to them. In fact, they used an 'adulterated' tea.

*

Tea, in the evening, in the Red Velvet Drawing room, with nothing much happening.

These long evenings, for Mr Parker, Nanny, and little Theresa, seemed as though they would last for ever; so slowly they passed.

They were times of contentment; perhaps the happiest times of all.

# 10 LEAVE-TAKING

### *the lead coffin trundling over the West Country road . . .*

Nanny wrote to Fritz at once – within half-an-hour of the event. It was a day she would never forget: a Sunday, the 27th of April, not yet the end of the spring month, and the gardens of Saltram were beginning to bloom fully – in all their usual beauty:

Poor Dear Lord Boringdon died a little before five, after a struggle for breath which lasted less than an hour. His last moments were perfectly calm and easy and I have the comfort to think that no care or attention was wanting towards him, and which I hope in some measure contributed to alleviate his sufferings thro' his long and tedious illness which he bore to the very last with the greatest Fortitude, only wishing to be relieved . . . Poor Jack is just as he should be, and most truly miserable except when he is employed in writing letters, which I have told him to do.[1]

The house was in mourning.

\*

Riding alone through the misty mornings, the drenching rain, the quiet nights, round his loved home of Saltram; sitting alone in his bedroom – watching the grace of a single candle flame; John Parker had sometimes been overwhelmingly aware of the transience as well as the miracle of life, the tragedy as well as the wonder of the world. These feelings and forebodings were well-founded and true.

Time is a measured and unyielding master.

Twenty years ago – almost to the exact day in April – he had inherited Saltram when his father died. In the early summer, barely a year later, he had brought Theresa to the house, which – together – they had transformed as the home of their family, and which they had loved. Now, an all-too-brief twenty years later: it was time for his own last leave-taking.

\*

During the last few years of his life, still making efforts to maintain his active interests – in racing, planting trees,

167

*John Parker – 1st Lord Boringdon – a new portrait by his friend Sir Joshua Reynolds.*

Opposite:

*The 'Escutcheon and Atchievement' – nowadays termed the Hatchment.*

*'... a tablet fixed to the front of the house for a year after death showing the Boringdon armorial bearings.'*

politics, and in watching over the interests of his friends – John Parker had known the conflicting experiences which come with middle and old age.

He had tasted the satisfaction of success, and was deeply pleased by a great distinction for himself and the family.

Four years before his death he was elevated to the peerage. The Viscount's robes, coronet and armorial bearings, symbolised a pleasing culmination to his long engagement in political life, and a fitting conclusion to the aspirations and ambitions – natural in their time – which he and Theresa had had in making their family home one of the most beautiful houses in the land.

There was great elation among his friends. The notebook of Sir Joshua Reynolds, his lifelong companion, received yet another conspicuous entry:

Before the Royal Academy Exhibition closed, Mr Parker, Sir Joshua's lifelong associate – the man whose name occurs oftenest in his list of engagements ... was raised to the peerage, and henceforth stands Lord Boringdon in the pocket-book.[2]

Lord Boringdon!

Nanny, Theresa, and John Parker himself, gloried in the magnificence of the 'Letters Patent' from the Crown: beautifully coloured in blue, red, brown and gilt, with ornate but graceful gilt lettering inscribing the name of King George III; and also the smaller, attendant document which granted the armorial bearings. The cases in which they came seemed as large and impressive as the documents themselves, and, since one of the very heavy seals seemed loose in its semi-circular compartment, they wrapped it carefully in a page of the *Morning Post*. They were then put safely away in a cupboard.

But mixed with this gratification were grave financial worries. He had not thought himself unduly careless in his spending on the house and estate; on cards, horses and racing. Yet money problems loomed large. Perhaps he had been too lackadaisical in his business affairs; too good-natured in placing confidence in his steward. Some debts, for sure, seemed to have been owing to him over a period of six years, and some of his debtors – for slate supplied from his Cann Quarries, for example – were labelled 'Runaway' or 'Insolvant'.[3] The payment of rents, too, seemed to have been haphazard and unreliable.

IN CÆLO QUIES
1788

*The Letters Patent received from the Crown when Mr Parker became Lord Boringdon. This was accompanied by a smaller, but similar, document granting Armorial Bearings. The seal shown above is the size of a saucer, and about half an inch thick. It was the seal of the smaller document which was found wrapped up in a page of the* Morning Post.

His chief anxiety was that Theresa and his son Jack should be well provided for. Jack – though sometimes puzzling and troubling him – seemed now to be settling down to some solid work and study. He was making continually greater demands as he moved towards manhood, with his university education and Tour before him – just at the time when his own debts seemed very large.

It was plain that he would have to retrench in some direction. His loved horses, his Newmarket racing, were the most obvious; and Nanny encouraged him:

I am afraid Lord Boringdon has had a bad meeting, by the Papers. However, I flatter myself he won't have many more . . . He is really and seriously going to part with all his horses as soon as he can, he finds it so very inconvenient to come so far every year to see them that the trouble is not worth the pleasure and I am sure if they are no pleasure they are not worth keeping for the profit.[4]

With this mixture of success and trouble, he had also endured a gradual worsening of his illness over some seven years. His gout was bad enough, but the bleeding of his chest increasingly troubled and incapacitated him. But he endured the inevitabilities of age well and did not make much of his condition. His character retained all its pungency. There was no yielding in him.

He disdained unnecessary letter-writing to the last:

Lord Boringdon is much the same upon the whole. He had a very hard day on Saturday . . . I do assure you his writing to Mrs Robinson was great exertion. I believe she is the only lady in the world he would have wrote to.[5]

As long as he possibly could, he scrambled on to horseback:

Lord Boringdon is at present without complaint, his cough is gone . . . and the spitting better . . . He goes on horseback when the weather will permit or goes out in the chaise, and is in better spirits than he has been for some time.[6]

His native, ironic humour did not fail – even shortly before his death:

He does not gain ground, though at the same time I don't think he is worse . . . He says his State of Health is just like the present state of politics: at a perfect standstill![7]

Loving his world, his children, Nanny, his friends and the home about him – stoical and uncomplaining –

keeping his thoughts to himself, Mr Parker endured what he had known would come. The very day before his death, Nanny wrote:

He grows weaker every day; he was so fatigued and distressed with getting up and going to bed on Monday, that he has not been up since . . . He is as calm and clear as ever, he desired me only last night to write to you about two Tables which he says he gave Lord Pelham and which are at Hayward. He desires that you will take them for your new house if Lord Pelham does not.

Whatever his successes or failures in other activities, there was one thing in which Mr Parker had known the deepest kind of happiness. The personal relationships he had enjoyed – with Theresa, Nanny, the children, Fritz, Grantham and friends like Sir Joshua – had all been marked by a staunch loyalty and a warmth of genuine affection. Even his troubled relationship with his brother Montague was, happily, resolved to some extent towards the end. Montague visited him early in March, and Nanny wrote:

Lord Boringdon continues to have tolerable appetite and good nights; but he grows weaker, and coughs more . . . Mr. Montague's coming was a great Event, he was rather hurried* with it at first but upon the whole glad to see him. He is still here and seems quite happy and at home. He is in very good Spirits and good humour, tells very long stories, and is very fond of the Children.

Nanny reported his death with this same feeling:

I must own that the Friendship and Habits of twelve years (I may almost say nineteen) can not be easily or soon got over; forgot they can never be by me . . . I have so liberally and so confidentially shared in all the happiness, comforts, and advantages of his House and Fortune, that I cannot but think myself under many and great obligations, and must ever retain a grateful and tender remembrance of the real Love, Esteem, and Regard I know he had for me . . . and I am much better pleased with the last kind marks of his attention and affection, than with any increase of income or sum of Money he could have left me . . .

A lead coffin carried him to his burial at St Mary's Church in Plympton.

The familiar, fitting words were spoken:

*Ill at ease, flustered.

Man that is born of woman hath but a short time to live, and is full of misery. He cometh up and is cut down, like a flower; he fleeth as it were a shadow, and never continueth in one stay . . .

*The last leave-taking from Saltram. Funerals commonly took place in the evening, with flambeaux carried by the mourners.*

*

If time is an unyielding master, however, so too are the necessities of living. If life is transient, it is also urgent, insistent, rapidly changing. Nothing can stop it. The world did not die with Lord Boringdon; neither did the life of Saltram come to a stop. Nanny – alone now at the heart of the family – kept her hands loyally on its affairs during a very difficult period of adjustment. The house was immediately filled with a new range of activities – some trivial, some of the greatest importance.

For the year before he went to university, Jack was sent to live in Yorkshire with Uncle Fritz – who, with Mr Ley, was now Jack's guardian – and he took with him as his tutor, Dr Andrews (later Dean of Canterbury), and a manservant – Tom. Nanny saw the necessity of this with the new straitness of their circumstances, but, nonetheless, it cast an additional sadness over the house:

I am perfectly convinced of the propriety of Jack's being from home and in some degree weaned from me and indeed me from him. But I cannot help feeling at present the great length of time it may be before I shall have the comfort of seeing him again. However in the meantime I must and do trust that I shall have constant accounts of his being well and happy. I am sure the little girl and I shall pass our time very quietly and well, our hours are all settled and we are a good deal together. She dines with me and is in very good spirits though as you may imagine very low that her brother went.[8]

But the sadness was soon sharply disturbed by a different feeling. Within three months of Lord Boringdon's death it became clear that Tom – the manservant – had been courting Molly – the nursery maid. Nanny wrote to Fritz in some agitation:

... to speak out plainly to you, she is seven months with child ... she behaved very properly and was in very great distress not knowing where to go or what to do, she said he had promised to marry her . . . I told her she might stay for his answer upon condition that she might give out in the house that she was going away on account of her health . . . If he won't marry her she must be ruined for ever, she says it will break her father's heart; and if he does marry her it is ruin to them both, what can he do with a wife and family at one and twenty, and she is two years older . . . I think, however, that *you* should speak to him . . .[9]

Whatever it was that Fritz said – it was very effective. Nanny was soon writing again, and in a much relieved manner:

Tom came on Saturday evening, he could not get the licence till yesterday afternoon . . . He don't seem to repent at all, he showed me the licence last night and seemed in great spirits . . . They were married this morning at eight and both set out for Bath at nine. I am much obliged to you for having settled this so well . . .[10]

In no time at all, too, there were the usual, completely unforeseen accidents:

Old Anthony is now quite recovered from a terrible fall he had about a week ago, from the Bridport Poney, being *younge* and *foolish* he chose to try if he could carry him and the fishing net which the poney not liking he kicked them both off and hurt Anthony very much in the back and knocked out the only three teeth he had left.[11]

The household was also thrown into confusion for weeks by a perplexing robbery. Large sums were stolen from the steward's office. The local Justices came and questioned the servants in turn. Handbills were printed in Plymouth offering a reward of 'Fifty Guineas over and above the Sum of Forty Pounds allowed by Act of Parliament' for anyone helping to discover the 'Offender or Offenders'.[12] The robbery even became public knowledge in London: but the culprit was never found.

Far from being a place of quiet mourning, Saltram seemed – to Nanny – suddenly to be seething with new and unforeseen activities, and yet, in the midst of all these, she had to give her mind to the immediately pressing, and more serious, financial problems. Soon she was trying to manage with a much reduced number of servants, and supervising the cutting as well as the planting of trees:

All the money is received and safely lodged in the Bank at Plymouth for the sale at Merafield, the . . . Housekeeper and all the servants discharged so that we are now one family and I hope shall live with great economy . . . I shall begin tomorrow upon the Scotch Firs and hope to have them all down by this day sevenight.[13]

Fritz was acting as executor to the estate, but it was Nanny who was the mainstay of the Saltram household at this time.

*

In many ways, John Parker's life was one of much achievement. He considerably improved his father's property. He made a successful marriage, and together, he and Theresa completed – with all the artistic excellence available in their time – the re-creation of Saltram which his parents had begun. The home of the Parkers was famous for its beauty even within their own lifetime. His parliamentary career was led among men of the greatest distinction, and the life he and his family could enjoy in London was one of wide interest and excellent connection. There is no evidence that he procured pensions or sinecures; that he successfully used parliamentary privilege to build up his own fortune (which was accepted practise then), but this was probably because he lacked either the ability or the desire. These rich pickings came chiefly with high office. At the same time he was raised to the peerage – and this was the fairly common road for a propertied family into the House of Lords – which could, perhaps, more properly have been called the House of Landlords. John Parker, however, was never of orthodox or easy persuasion in Parliament. He really *was* of independent mind. The year before his elevation to the peerage, his last recorded parliamentary action was that of voting for Parliamentary Reform. As good an action as any on which to go out!

It is true that he experienced tragedy in marriage – his marriage to Theresa, as well as his earlier marriage, was tragically short. Even so it was one of great happiness. His children survived, and lived enjoyable and successful lives, and two things were especially true. First: Mr Parker enjoyed his life – his shooting, riding, racing, his devotion to home and family; and this, really, was success enough. Second: he was rich in the happiness of friendship. From the beginning to the end of their story – so many of John's and Theresa's relationships were those of deeply felt affection.

Yet, on his death, it seems that Mr Parker was to be considered a failure. He left an estate very heavily encumbered with debts.[14] Twenty years earlier he had inherited large estates and a sum of £32,000. Now he was between £56 and £58,000 in debt. Something approaching £90,000 is a lot of money to lose in twenty years.

One drain was probably inefficient estate management. It is impossible to estimate the capital value of his estates (though Mr Parker had himself mortgaged them for £20,000 before his death) or the total income they yielded – but there was certainly a laxity and unreliability in the payment of rents. Even so the income from them could not have been much more than to pay for the upkeep of house and servants.

A large expense was the house itself. The wages of perhaps thirty servants would have been quite substantial – but not really a large sum. His improvements to the house were the greater cost: £10,000 – it seems – spent on the Great Room alone, and substantial alterations to the Eating Room, Library, Kitchen. So much outside building had been undertaken, too: the Orangery, the 'Castle', the Stables. And as Member of Parliament, Mr Parker had also to rent a London house which carried additional running costs.

But there is no doubt that it was his gambling and his horse-racing which were his chief extravagances. The expense of his long-maintained racing connection with

Newmarket was very high. The largest sums recorded in his account book were those he carried to Newmarket:

1774 April 25th. To Mr Parker to carry to Newmarket £997.
1777 March 29th. To Newmarket – besides £1,235  –  £500.
1778 April 19th. Mr Parker carried to Newmarket  £1,478.

At cards, too, his stakes were high. Though he lost and won variably at Boodles in London, his account book sometimes showed net losses of £900 in a month. Sometimes he lost in one or two evenings enough to pay the entire servants' wages for a year. Racing and cards together – at this rate – would not take long to dispose of £90,000.

Such sums, however, may exaggerate the seriousness of the situation, and Mr Parker may have had other involvements about which nothing is known. The family estate certainly managed to continue without serious disruption, and affairs were gradually brought to order; but on his death, some debts had to be dealt with immediately, and there were several large sales.

On June 3rd – thirty-one mares, colts, fillies, coach horses, pack horses, and phaeton ponies were sold for £586, and a coach and three phaetons raised another £60. Before October, cattle, sheep, and pigs had been sold to realise about £1,400. A sale of stock took place at Merafield – one of Mr Parker's properties – which, together with a waggon and a few carts, raised just under £600; and the tenant of Merafield – Nicholas Barraball – was discharged. This and other adjustments to the estate were considerable, but it speaks well for the health of the estate that – in only fourteen years – such large debts were settled – some £56,000 having been received. A recovery of £4,000 per year was not a bad rate of progress.

Also, of course, there were the immediate bills for the funeral to be settled. The English were renowned for the concern they showed over the manner of their burial and at least one foreigner thought they took 'more pleasure in dying than living'.

Some noble burials were vastly extravagant: the funeral train, the dress and other magnificence could cost half an inheritance. This was a fairly modest funeral compared with many. The expenses amounted to about £200. Of this, £114.12s.6d. was paid to Mr Birdwood for 'Mourning Goods' – probably the black drapes which were hung round the darkened rooms of the house; and Thomas Ealis received over £30 for making the 'Escutcheons and Atchievement' which was a tablet fixed to the front of the house for a year after death showing the Boringdon Armorial bearings.

The death of Lord Boringdon, far from bringing quietness to Saltram, had brought much hard work, and some anxiety.

After twenty years as master of Saltram – the splendour of the great house, the peer's coronet, the auctioneer's hammer, and the lead coffin trundling in a cart over the west country road . . . were significantly connected at the ending of John Parker's story.

*

Sometimes, however, the things people make are of greater value than their income; than their profit and loss account. The work they do may prove less transient than they. The end of John's and Theresa's lives was not the end of what, by their taste, devotion, energy and love, they had created. Their house, Saltram, 'bosom'd in its own woods and backed by Devon Hills'[15] – an embodiment of the finest art and craftsmanship of their age – remained; and, only one year after John Parker's death, it received a gracious recognition. It was given over to the Royal Household for their visit to the west country. These rooms which had so recently known the presence of John Parker, Nanny, Jack and little Theresa, were now, for a time, occupied by King George III, Queen Charlotte and a large number of their servants:

Arches of flowers were erected for the Royal Family to pass under at almost every town, with various loyal devices, expressive of their satisfaction in this circuit. How happy must have been the king! The greatest conqueror could never pass through his dominions with fuller acclamations of joy from his subjects than George III experienced . . . We passed through such beautiful villages, and so animated a concourse of people, that the whole journey proved truly delectable – till we came to the end of our aim, Saltram.

The house is one of the most magnificent in the kingdom. It accommodated us all, even to every footman, without by any means filling the whole. The state apartments on the ground floor are superb; hung with crimson damask, and ornamented with pictures . . . Its view is noble; it extends to Plymouth, Mount Edgecumbe, and the neighbouring fine country. The

*Fanny Burney – later Madame d'Arblay – for some years Mistress of the Robes to Queen Charlotte. She came from Kings Lynn. Her mother was said to be one of three women who could read there.*

sea at times fills up a part of the domain almost close to the house, and then its prospect is complete.[16]

This record was written by Fanny Burney – who was Mistress of the Robes to Queen Charlotte – and who stayed at Saltram with them, in what she called a 'sweet parlour with the most beautiful view of any on the ground floor, and next door to the library'. No royal family ever more unwittingly placed a reporter in the midst of their retinue!

King George III – 'Farmer' George; the man noted for his much-rumoured, strange, unaccountable illness; the man notorious for losing America; the monarch who threatened the privileges of Parliament – here loved and enjoyed the quietness, simplicity and charm of Saltram. Like John and Theresa themselves – whom he knew – for him a little of the grandeur of things was enough! He preferred a limit to his social life. He admired the splendour of the Great Room – but did not care to use it. He preferred the quiet, more intimate atmosphere of the smaller Eating Room. There was pomp and circumstance during the visit – but he preferred quiet rides round the estate and strolls by the ampitheatre – where, perhaps, the playing of those same horns entertained him which had first greeted Theresa twenty years ago.

*The Amphitheatre at Saltram, where George III liked to stroll and where Theresa had been entertained on her first homecoming. The two men in livery standing just behind the statue are playing the horns which probably greeted both Theresa and the King. These horns still hang on the wall of the Garden Room at Saltram.*

Fanny Burney herself – busy writer that she was – found much to enjoy and record. There were the exciting activities on the docks at Plymouth:

The dockyard is a noble and tremendous sight... It was a sort of sighing satisfaction to see such numerous stores of war's alarms! – ropes, sails, masts, anchors, – and all in the finest symmetry, divided and subdivided, as if placed only for show. The neatness and exactness of all the arrangement of those stores for tempests, filled me with admiration; so did the whole scene – though not with pleasure!

She herself preferred it when 'The Royals' were out visiting, and she could enjoy ferreting through Mr Parker's bookshelves; browsing in the library he had loved, and going out into the quiet woods – sitting there alone and reading:

This morning the Royals were all at a grand naval review. I spent the time very serenely in my favourite wood... The wood here is truly enchanting; the paths on the slant down to the water... and it abounds in seats of all sorts. Today was devoted to general quiet; and I spent all I could of it in my sweet wood, reading the 'Art of Contentment', a delightful old treatise, by the author of 'The Whole Duty of Man', which I have found in the Saltram Library.

The Art of Contentment!

*

Some would say that the art of contentment had died with John and Theresa.

At the very time that Fanny Burney was peacefully turning the pages of her book in Saltram wood – the August sunlight dappling down on to its leaves – almost to the month, the Bastille was falling in Paris to an angry mob; a tumult which was to have its repercussions throughout Europe, signifying not only change, but a vast transformation.

More and more conspicuously a new world was taking shape about the quiet woods and waters of Saltram. A larger world – of trade, manufacture and the political development of great nations – was invading the isolation of these fields and moors. The countryside itself was changing: its human society, as well as its pattern of fields and crops. Trade and manufacture were growing – not only in the midlands and the north – but here: in the quiet places of Cornwall and Devon. Canals and iron bridges, everywhere in the land, were carving new arteries and setting a new blood of commerce flowing. Trade Union organization was raising its rebellious and prophetic head within thirty miles of Saltram. An early kind of gaslight was invented and introduced into carriages and work-places in Plymouth.[17] The world of fields and moors, of rough roads and hedge-banks, of silent, starry, windy skies, was being changed for a man-made world of lamp-lit streets. The tree was giving way to the strong rigid girder; the limited, living, temperamental horse to the controlled, powered machine. Village, market-town and city were giving way to a manufacturing urbanization. Man in nature, was giving way to Man and his deliberately contrived society. A large, clumsy leviathan was slouching through Europe to be born; waking, and flexing its slow, powerful limbs.[18]

Gradually, the beneficial, disrupting monster of industrial civilization was beginning to extend its great grasp over all. The golden age of cultivating nature traditionally but inefficiently, and with only limited human welfare – was yielding to the steel-gray machine age of exploiting natural resources scientifically and efficiently, and with a greater degree of human welfare. The great dilemmas of our modern world were born.

Though they did not know it, John and Theresa, Nanny, Grantham and Fritz, lived on the threshold of what was to

*A new world was taking shape . . .
An early iron works on the banks of
the Severn.*

prove the most rapid, radical and extensive transformation in human history. Behind them – and even still about them – lay a world of limited traditional communities. Before them lay the interdependent, conflictful entirety of the modern commercial and industrial world: the rational globe itself.

In the three life-times between then and now, we have come a long – if a disturbed – way.

Now, a tenth of every generation does not die of smallpox. Our wives and children do not regularly die in childbirth. We are not bled for every ailment. Our teeth are not pulled out without anaesthetics. Our sanitation is not an unhealthy stench in house and street. Our children are not educated by unquestioned privilege or condescending charity. We are not transported for joining working-men's associations. Government now *is* for the whole people – who have rights and a voice in a principled constitution. Yet – the science which serves us also vexes us by a correct and inescapable questioning of our traditional beliefs; and the society which has brought these benefits has also become bewildering in its complexity, and brings its restlessness and discontents.

Our knowledge is so much greater; we are so much more fortunate; but our dilemmas deepen. Still, the dilemmas are the same. The concerns of John, Theresa, Nanny, and of many of the writers of their time, in upholding personal qualities in character and conduct, and firm values in art and education, have a strikingly familiar air.

Accustomed to the close relationships of home, family, neighbourhood, and those of similar station, within a natural community – they were disturbed by the prospect of a larger commercial and urban organization in which these important personal ties and qualities were lost. Accustomed to personal qualities of work and art and service in traditional craftsmanship, they were disturbed by a new kind of impersonal, mechanical making of things – a manufacture directed to exchange on the commercial market for profit. Commerce *was* settling on every tree. Accustomed to a simple self-sufficiency of morality, based upon settled duties and desired qualities of work and character, they were disturbed by a wordly, superficial cleverness, a haughty exhibitionism, an exaggeration of fashion, an affected foppishness, a shallowness of dissipation and wit, which had no principles whatsoever. Sometimes feeling a firm religion and morality desirable, they found religion itself frequently apeing the new wordliness it should have been judging. Looking for sound and pleasing qualities in education, they found education itself pandering to the very fever for which it should have been providing a basis for judgement of its own.

Where there should have been quietness – there was an inflammation. Where there should have been integrity of judgement – there was clever, egotistical wit. Nothing simple and direct would do. Truth and true qualities were threatened by mere show.

One of the Bluestockings put her pen to it:

... if I were called upon to assign the predominant cause of the greater part of the misfortunes and corruptions of the great and gay in our days, I should not look for it in any obviously great or striking circumstance; not in the practice of notorious vices, nor originally in the dereliction of Christian Principle; but I should without hesitation ascribe it to a growing, regular, systematic series of amusements; to an incessant, boundless, and not very disreputable DISSIPATION. Other corruptions, though more formidable in appearance, are yet less fatal – dissipation is the more hopeless, as by engrossing almost the entire life, and enervating the whole moral and intellectual system, it leaves neither time for reflection, nor space for self-examination, nor temper for the cherishing of right affections, nor leisure for the operation of sound principles, nor interval for regret, nor vigour to resist temptation, nor energy to struggle for amendment ...

Look abroad and see who are the people that complain of weariness, littleness and dejection. You will not find them among the class of such as are overdone with work, but with pleasure. The natural and healthful fatigues of business may be recruited by simple and cheap gratifications; but a spirit worn down with the toils of amusement, requires pleasures of poignancy; varied, multiplied, stimulating![19]

A growing, ostentatious profusion obscured a more satisfying simplicity.

But in seeking to appraise the qualities of social life in the time of the Parkers, and to appraise our own life in relation to theirs, the task of judgement is very hard. We sometimes long for the simplicity of the past – but cannot remain blind to its harshness. We sometimes admire the qualities of taste and art in the eighteenth century, as a glowing interval of humanism between the fear-ridden swamp of medievalism and the black tyranny of the age of Victoria – and yet we know that the gaunt moralists of Victorian England put right many of the evils which eighteenth-century libertines no more than sniffed at; and the eighteenth century seems *then* the decadent world out of which modern progress sprang. A settled traditional society – yes – but one in which there were great gulfs between the social classes, and in which the wealthy dominated society by privilege: spending at least a great deal of their heaped-up fortunes in sheer trivialities of culture – whilst slavery sprawled in their ports and colonies, and paupers rotted in their parish poor-houses.

The perspective of judgement can swing with each view; fluctuate with each measure.

But an acquaintance with a particular family like the Parkers, and a house decorated with refinement and with much concern to make it a real home, makes one wonder whether all such definite judgements are not caricatures.

People say that the eighteenth-century upper classes – their marriages arranged for money, property and position – thought little of personal love, and were given up to sexual licence, dissipation, even bawdiness. But John and Theresa – in their arranged marriage – without any doubt whatever enjoyed a relationship of personal love. They shared and took a delight in each others' interests and work. They enjoyed a deepening companionship. From the day she arrived at Saltram to the day of her death, Theresa spoke warmly of Mr Parker's constant affection and attention:

It is impossible to describe Mr Parker's tenderness and

attention to me throughout, he alarmed himself much more than was necessary but had my Fever lasted a few days longer he could not have stood it, as I believe he neither Eat, Slept, or could even compose his Spirits till many days after I was free from every complaint.

People say that in the eighteenth century upper-class parents neglected their parental duties and delegated them to nurse, governess, tutor and school, leaving themselves free for high fashion, cards, gambling and assembly-room dissipation. But John and Theresa were devoted parents – from the deep pleasure they took in looking forward to the birth of their children to their continuing concern for their education afterwards – and for their full development and happiness as persons within the social life they would have to lead. Nanny had shared and continued Theresa's intention. Even before boarding school in London, she had seen that young Jack was sent to the local school in Plympton, and there was certainly no lack of affection in her comment:

The dear little Boy got up before six o'clock on Tuesday morning and walked to Plympton School with great resolution and good humour, and has every day since . . . He seems not to dislike it, and I hope it will be a great service to him. I miss him very much in the morning, and often lose my walk for want of his company.

People say the upper classes were addicted to a glittering profusion of the superficial and the artificial in society. But John and Theresa preferred a quiet life centred very closely upon their family. They liked company, certainly; but they liked to choose and limit it. Theresa scarcely ever mentioned visiting, or receiving company, without some expression of reserve:

We must spend the next week in returning all our Dining visits which we do not enjoy the thought of much . . .
Lord and Lady Chatham who are down upon a wedding visit to Mr J. Pitt have threatened us with their company, I don't love him – but the pleasure of being in company with so remarkable a man would make up for the trouble of receiving them.

Without the slightest trace of dullness, John, Theresa and their friends had not only decided convictions about the qualities of character which they wished to uphold – but also actually and actively preferred them to superficialities.

People say that the interest of the wealthy classes in art was pure affectation – a mere acquisition of what was fashionable. But John and Theresa exercised individual judgement – accepting some of Robert Adam's designs, but not others; seeking and patronising new painters; judging new work – like that of Josiah Wedgwood – in relation to other ware (Chinese and French, for example) which was very much in fashion.

Sir Joshua Reynolds was in no doubt whatever either about Theresa's personal qualities or about her qualities of artistic judgement:

Her amiable disposition, her softness and gentleness of manners, endeared her to everyone that had the happiness of knowing her. Her whole pleasure and ambition were centred in a consciousness of properly discharging all the duties of a wife, a mother and a sister and she neither sought nor expected fame outside her own home. As she made no ostentation of virtue, she excited no envy, but if there had existed so depraved a being as to wish to wound so fair a character, the most artful malignity must have searched in vain for a weak part. Her virtues were uniform quiet and habitual, they were not occasionally put on, she wore them continually, they seemed to grow to her and be a part of herself and it seemed to be impossible for her to lay them aside or be other than what she was. In so exalted a character as hers it is scarce worth mentioning her skill and exact judgement in the polite arts; she seemed to possess by a kind of intuition that propriety of taste and right thinking, which others but imperfectly acquire by long labour and application.[20]

Might it not be possible that there is rumour in history, just as there is rumour about our own age? Is it, perhaps, always the people who like to glitter in the assembly-rooms of society who attract the publicity – about whom the gossip-mongers gather and the fashionable play-wrights write their plays?

One eighteenth-century woman thought so:

There is, in society, a certain set of persons who are pleased exclusively to call themselves *the fine world*. This small detachment consider their situation with respect to the rest of mankind, just as the ancient Grecians did theirs. The Grecians thought that all who were not Grecians were Barbarians, and this *certain set* conceives of society as resolving itself into two distinct classes, the *fine world* and the *people*; to which last they turn over all who do not belong to their little *coterie*, however high their rank, or fortune, or merit. Celebrity, in their estimation is not bestowed by birth or talents, but by being connected with *them*. They have almost a language of their own; they form a distinct *cast*, and detach themselves from others, even in general society, by affectation . . . and only whisper and smile in their own little groups of the initiated . . .[21]

But perhaps in every age the majority of people live according to values which are very different from those who strut in the centre of the stage. Perhaps John and Theresa were more representative of people in the eighteenth century than we can know. Perhaps, indeed, they are more representative of the values of most of us in our own century, now, than we can know.

*

The story of John and Theresa, and their family and friends, raises large questions as it closes. It is only possible, and only correct, to end on a personal note. Nothing that pretended more could be true.

Walking through these rooms, these corridors, these halls of Saltram – empty now – I have found myself moved by two strong feelings.

On the one hand, I so much admire the exquisite qualities of much that was done here: the furniture, the pictures, the colour and elegance of the decoration in the various rooms, the ceilings, the carved woodwork. I find myself won over by the concentrated wealth that could make such art and craftsmanship possible, and feel regret for their passing. I feel the great attractiveness, too, of the relative simplicity of the personal relationships and community life which could be experienced then; the leisurely pace of life that could be enjoyed; the enjoyment of having the time and opportunity to think, feel, and indulge your taste within a certain composure of living. It is quite plain that it would have been very pleasant to be an aristocrat.

On the other hand, such beauty and leisure were only for the very limited and privileged few, and one cannot help but be aware of the massive poverty and degradation of mankind that lay behind the splendour of this façade.

Looking at the magnificent fire-places of marble and stone in Great Room and Hall, it is difficult not to see – beyond them – the miners in Scotland, Tyneside, Wales and the Forest of Dean, working in their inhuman galleries;

living in their hovels. Marvelling at the beauty of the chandeliers in the Great Room, it is difficult to put out of mind those who had to live by rushlight in workshop and cottage; who were blinded at their lace-making and their blanket-weaving. It is impossible not to be conscious of the crowded poor-houses of the time, and the vagrants sheltering by the hedge-banks – not far away from Saltram house – near the moors; and it is difficult to remain undisturbed by an art, an excellence of living, which seemed to rest upon such human indignities. I certainly feel a strong sympathy with those poets, writers, politicians, religious and educational reformers, who wanted to shatter this social world to bits – and then remould it nearer to the heart's desire; who struggled through the sophistications of culture to an art, a philosophy, a society, which was based upon the elemental dignity of the human spirit.

Looking at the pleasing portrait of a contented, well-patronised Sir Joshua Reynolds, it is difficult not to be aware of the ghost of William Blake, hovering nearby and shaking a fist of militant indignation.[22] It is difficult not to see, moving through this splendour, the tall ghost of Wordsworth – pale, dignified, quiet with a noble reflectiveness – probing beyond this luxury to reveal a nature of the world and the spirit in which all could feel the significance of their place; seeking a simplicity of poetic language within which all men could recognise, know, and share their experience of the natural and the sublime. I cannot help feeling that there is a moralist in all of us that we cannot stifle, and that cannot altogether be dissociated from our judgements about art.

What is certain is that the movement towards a just society has removed families like that of John and Theresa Parker from their pedestals. So that now – in our humane, welfare state – we come to their house not as a living home, but as a museum.

And yet there was so much of beauty here; of taste, of elegance, of reason, of genuine classical aspiration.

The story ends with a conflict of questions. One can only feel sure of this – but of this one *can* be sure – that social change involves significant losses as well as important gains: and that in our struggle for excellence in human society we can never afford to blind our eyes to the qualities and achievements of people of the past.

# EPILOGUE

## *a New World . . . the momentous events of War and Peace*

But what happened to Nanny, Theresa and Jack after Lord Boringdon's death?

For a time, despite all her work, care and devotion to the family, Nanny's position – as a dependent spinster – was unsettled, and in doubt. As tactfully as dignity and respect allowed, she made her desire to stay with the family very plain:

If I was to consult my own feelings I certainly had much rather remain quietly here, and not enter into any engagement that may take me from hence, or put me out of my present way of Life, but as I have no other objection and am sure you will be better satisfied and pleased, I am very willing that Either of the Places you mention should be applyed for.[1]

It was a painful and anxious period; and at a time when she had to take upon herself so many new duties in the management of the household. To her happiness, however, and to that of Theresa and Jack, such efforts to place her were not long pursued. She remained at Saltram, and the children remained in close touch and correspondence with her for a long time to come. Theresa stayed with her, and together, they watched over many other changes in the house which Jack himself planned and put into effect – such as the considerable extension of the Library, which involved changes in the room where Fanny Burney had stayed.

Very gradually, as time went on, the social life of the house returned, and the Company who visited provided their usual highlights and oddities. There was the great Mrs Siddons, for example, though Nanny was not much impressed:

Mrs Siddons dined here. With her two daughters and her husband. I had rather a curiosity to see her which is fully satisfied, and I cannot say I much want to be in company with her again. She is very pompous and not entertaining at all . . . She is still acting away at Plymouth, but we have not been tempted to go . . . from what we saw of her here, I don't think there is anything charming in her.[2]

Later, in London, when Theresa had become a Lady in society in her own right, she had not forgotten this Saltram visit:

Only think, [she wrote to Nanny] of my going to see Mrs Siddons at Belvedera last night – a thing I always vowed I would *not do*. So much for a woman's resolve . . .[3]

When she was twenty-three years old – in 1798 – Theresa married George Villiers, son of the 1st Earl of Clarendon. She was quickly at ease with London society, but always retained the values she had been brought up to observe at Saltram, and from time to time, she wrote to Nanny about Jack, who was becoming something of a gay blade and man-about-town in both London and Paris:

My brother is grown quite stout again, and the gayest person in London, going to banquets, Masquerades, and I know not what. I do most heartily wish with you that he would follow *my sage example*, but I despair of it now, more than ever.[4]

Jack was becoming, in general, a lavish person – but his grand manner and grand designs were not only directed to balls and masquerades. He became politically active, and a strong supporter of Pitt's government. Later, like his father, he supported Parliamentary Reform. He was responsible for many improvements of a public nature in and about Saltram and Plympton – the 'Flying Bridge' ferry, for example, which he subsequently replaced by a cast-iron bridge. He constructed dry docks in Cattewater Harbour, and the embankment of the River Plym, and later in recognition of all this, he was awarded the Gold Medal of the Royal Society of Arts. He was also made the 1st Earl of Morley. The making of embankments and the reclamation of 'Chelson Meadows' were not, however, reported with much enthusiasm by Charles Vancouver – the Surveyor for the new Board of Agriculture, who compiled the *General View of the Agriculture of the County of Devon with Observations on the Means of its Improvement* at about the turn of the century. He was most insistent on the difference between:

. . . salt-marsh, ripe and fit for exclusion from the sea, from that which may be prematurely enclosed, and also of embankments made with a view of enclosing portions of invincibly steril and shear sea-mud . . .[5]

And he had this to say about Jack's 'improvements':

Some embankments of this latter description have lately been made, and others are now carrying on, across certain branches of the river Plym, above Catwater. The indisposition of Lord Boringdon, and the absence of his Lordship's steward, deprived the Surveyor of an opportunity of visiting these works; but if he concludes correctly, from the distant view he had of them at Saltram, and a more minute inspection of the work now carrying on under his Lordship's directions, in cutting off a similar arm from the Kingsbridge river, in the Parish of Charlton, these embankments can have no other possible consequence, than, in the first instance, stopping the regular ascent of the tides, the return of which, combined with the land-waters, contribute so essentially to the keeping open, and the preservation of navigation in all such inlets; and, secondly, the procuring a mere site for the incalculable expense of forming a proper soil of land upon, can never for a moment weigh in balance with the injury accruing to navigation, and the mortifying disappointments that must inevitably await the well-meant expectations of the noble proprietor.

*The Cattewater and part of the Citadel from the West Hoe. Here Nanny watched for the French fleet, and, later, Jack was to devote himself to certain public works and improvements.*

Not everyone, however, felt so adversely critical of Jack's work. Other visitors were well pleased with what they saw:

Among the great improvements lately made, and now making, by the noble proprietor of Saltram, may be specified a new approach, which, after passing through a gloomy wood, leads the visitor to a most delightful prospect of the sea, and its promontories, bays, harbours etc. This, though highly ornamental, is exceeded by an improvement truly useful; we mean the construction of a dry dock in Catwater Bay, for the repairing of merchantmen and trading vessels, which has been effected at a great expense by Lord Boringdon, and is sufficiently capacious for ships of seventy-four guns.[6]

The experiences of Theresa and Jack as the eighteenth century ended and the nineteenth century began were to reflect vividly the sweeping tide of social change which had begun to flow during the lives of their parents. Even when Lord Boringdon was nearing his ending, Nanny's letters had been noting the rumours of war which were infecting the country: the 'spectre of war' some called it. Before many years were out, the French invasion scare swept through Plymouth, as other coastal areas. Ships were fearful of being 'pressed' into service. Jack was soon fairly continually with his regiment, the North Devonshire. He gloried in being an officer – and Theresa, too, with this, warmed to an additional admiration of him. Nanny's concern was chiefly with the dangers of naval attack:

I have just heard that the French Fleet is off the Land's End . . . They expect an invasion. I hope you will be in no danger here . . . I cannot say I am much alarmed. – especially as Lord Howe's fleet is so near, and ready in Torbay – They will protect us.[7]

Jack, however – the new Lord Boringdon – did not seem much alarmed. A little later, in the brief interlude given by the Peace of Amiens in 1801, he was still enjoying Paris society. Theresa, from London, kept Nanny informed about all that happened:

My brother is delighted with Paris and its society which I rather believe to be tolerable *because* it is chiefly English. He says it swarms with English. Lord Whitworth has got a splendid hotel there . . .[8]

Young Jack with his Regiment. '... on the brink of those massive events which were to transform European society'.

During his stay there, Jack was to meet a person of no small eminence:

I also could give you an account of my brother's presentation to Buonaparte and his Wife, but you equally well know an Anti-Gallian spirit deters me from it . . .[9]

The aristocratic families of England, the aristocracies of Europe, were still only a small company. A new world was certainly taking shape about the quiet woods and waters of Saltram, and about those who, from that apparently remote corner of Devon, had grown up into the society which ruled the great world. Nanny was watching for the forces of France in Plymouth harbour. Theresa, in London, was watching her brother in the affairs of politics and war. Young Jack – cradled in Saltram, doted on by a charming mother soon to die, having walked at six o'clock in the morning to Plympton school and hunted his hares and foxes on holidays over the Devonshire fields, having been tactfully chastened by Nanny for using perfume in his youth . . . now, for a moment, stood face to face with Napoleon – the man who, with his slight, bent, but powerful figure dominated Europe and the world.

Theresa and Jack – with Nanny still behind them – stood on the brink of those massive events which were to transform European society; the events which were sweeping from Spain, Egypt and the Mediterranean into the very heart of Russia; the momentous events of War and Peace.

All this, however, is another story.

# Notes

\*

# Books
## for Further Reading
*with details of museums and
eighteenth-century houses*

\*

# Index

# NOTES

The letters of the Parker and Robinson families in this book have been selected from unpublished letters and papers which are in the British Museum and the 'Lucas Collection' in the Bedford County Record Office. Considerable use has also been made of the account books belonging to John Parker, later Lord Boringdon, in which were recorded many of the day-to-day expenses of the family during the years 1769–89. These are deposited with the Archives of the Plymouth City Library.

## CHAPTER 1

1 Theresa to Lord Grantham (her father), 26 May 1769

2 Theresa to Thomas, Lord Grantham (her elder brother – her father having died in 1770.) 30 August 1773

3 Sir Joshua Reynolds was a close friend of the Parkers throughout his life. He was born at Plympton on 16 July 1723 and was educated at Plympton Grammar School. There is a story that Lady Catherine – John Parker's mother – presented him with a pencil there, and was one of the first to encourage him in his drawing. The Royal Academy was founded in 1768 and he was its first president, and knighted at the same time. He was already established in his career, and as a friend of the family, when Theresa came to Saltram.

4 Georgiana, Duchess of Devonshire, to her mother: 30 July 1782. The Duke and Duchess of Devonshire and Lady Elizabeth Foster were staying at Plympton House nearby, and visited Saltram.

5 Theresa to Grantham, 3 February 1774

6 Patent Roll 12 Will III p.2 No.8.

7 Indeed, Blackstone gives an excellent and detailed account of the way in which the Feudal system gave way to more complex forms of property and related status in Europe and Britain:

'It is impossible to understand, with any degree of accuracy, either the civil constitution of this kingdom, or the laws which regulate its landed property, without some general acquaintance with the nature and doctrines of the feudal law ... the law of nations in our western world ...'

considered in the light of a civil establishment, rather than as a military plan, the ingenuity of the same ages, which perplexed all theology with the subtilty of scholastic disquisitions, and bewildered philosophy in the mazes of metaphysical jargon, began also to exert its influence on this copious and fruitful subject: in pursuance of which, the most refined and oppressive consequences were drawn from what originally was a plan of simplicity and liberty, equally beneficial to both lord and tenant, and prudently calculated for their mutual protection and defence. From this one foundation, in different countries of Europe, very different superstructures have been raised ...'

Blackstone, strictly speaking, is an excellent social history. Book II of *Commentaries on the Laws of England* – on 'Things', 'Property', and the various kinds of 'Title' and 'Inheritance' is a detailed account of how feudal relationships of property, status and power gradually changed and grew in complexity – as society grew in complexity – from the ancient and medieval world, through important recognitions of changes in Elizabethan times, into the modern world. It is as good an account of these changes as any: giving real detail rather than a simplified picture. It shows, too, how sociology, history, and law must all be combined for any satisfactory knowledge of society.

8 From the Marriage Bond kindly loaned to the BBC by the Sheepscar Archive, Leeds.

9 These descriptions of Dr Johnson are taken from Fanny Burney's Diaries. It was, it seems, Tom Davis a bookseller who said that Dr Johnson's loud laugh reminded him of a rhinoceros. His friends and acquaintances had differing views of the great man. Horace Walpole was very jaundiced: 'With a lumber of learning and some strong parts, Johnson was an odious and mean character. By principle a Jacobite, arrogant, self-sufficient, and overbearing, and of feminine bigotry; he had prostituted his pen to party even in his Dictionary, and had afterwards, for a pension, contradicted his own definition. His manners were sordid, superstitious and brutal; his style ridiculously bombastic and vicious; and, in one word, with all the pedantry he had all the littleness of a country schoolmaster.' (*Memoirs of the Reign of George III*, 2nd Edn. Vol. 1. p.297.)

Dr Johnson also had a great fear of death. Mrs Thrale wrote to Fanny Burney on 18 Feb. 1784: '... Johnson is in a sad way doubtless; yet he may with care last another twelvemonth, and every week's existence is gain to him, who like Hezekiah wearies Heaven with entreaties for life.' He died that December.

10 Letter to a friend in 1763

11 From *Diary of a Tour through Great Britain in 1795* by Rev. William MacRitchie. The Minister of the Parish of Clunie in Perthshire, MacRitchie left Clunie on horseback on the 22nd June and arrived in London through Islington on 20th July. The wicked Pleasure Gardens were one of his first calls – on 22nd July, and he observed their evils at 11.0 o'clock at night having retired to a 'box' with his friend and a bottle of port.

12 The Freeholder No. 22. Monday, 5 March 1716 (1744 volume p.122)

13 A mixture of two letters: Friday 29 Nov 1771, and 8 Nov 1772

14 Theresa to Grantham 20 Oct 1772

15 3 May 1773

16 8 Dec 1771

17 Letter to Fritz 17 March 1772

18 Theresa to Grantham from Sackville Street, March 1774

19 The same – 10 June 1774

20 6 March 1772

21 25 May 1772

## CHAPTER 2

1 William Law (1686–1761) was one of the most able, influential, and controversial theologians of the century. He was a Jacobite, deprived of his fellowship at Cambridge, and tutored the son of Edward Gibbon (see Ch. 8 on the state of the universities.) He contributed to theological controversies ('Three Letters to the Bishop of Bangor,' 1717), but exercised a much wider influence through his books on the more practical aspects of religion. *The Serious Call* . . . influenced the Wesleys, Dr Johnson, George Whitefield, Gibbon, and many others. It could be said, therefore, to have been an influence in the Evangelical revival.

2 This picture of C. of E. parsons is drawn from the *Diary of a Country Parson* The Reverend James Woodforde. (5 vols Oxford University Press, and lovingly edited by John Beresford.) This gives a most pleasurable, leisurely, readable account of day-to-day life in the eighteenth century. There is an abridged 'World Classics' edition. Another excellent book of a similar kind – giving an account of Scotland – is *The Annals of the Parish* by John Galt: a chronicle of Dalmailing during his ministry from 1760–1810. The second edition: T. N. Foulis, 1911 has some beautiful illustrations from watercolours.

3 From Nanny to Fritz, 3 March 1772 – about a large party at Lady Pembroke's.

4 An account of some notorious 'hunting parsons' is to be found in *Old Country Life* by S. Baring Gould (Ch. VI). Some of the parsons in remote country areas had hair-raising reputations – of drunkenness, brutality, and cruelty to their wives. There is also a chapter (Ch. V) on 'Country Parsons', and the book draws on a wide range of historical sources.

5 A remark, in fact, of Parson Woodforde.

6 A letter to the Countess of Huntingdon (friend of George Whitefield and the founder of 'Lady Huntingdon's Connection'), and quoted in *The Church of England in the Eighteenth Century*, Alfred Plummer (1909) p.124.

7 Bishop Butler's sermons – the three famous and excellent sermons 'On Human Nature', which were serious contributions to moral philosophy, and twelve others 'Preached at the Rolls', were published in 1729. This quotation is taken from Sermon XIV 'Upon the Love of God'. He subsequently preached sermons of importance to such bodies as 'The Society for the Propagation of the Gospel in Foreign Parts' (1738), 'The Governors of the Several Hospitals of the City of London' (1740), the House of Lords (1740, 1747), and even to 'The Children Educated in the Charity Schools' (1745).

8 From *A View of Society and Manners in France, Switzerland and Germany* by J. Moore. Vol. 1. 6th Edn. 1786.

9 1765. Quoted in *Chippendale and his School*. J. P. Blake, p.78.

10 Captain Jesse. Quoted in *The Age of Scandal*. T. H. White. Penguin 1962.

11 To a very large extent self-taught, John Coleridge – during the story of John and Theresa Parker at Saltram – was Headmaster of King's School at Ottery St Mary, and taught a wide range of subjects: Latin, Greek, and '. . . any Branch of

Mathematicks'. He had also taught himself the Hebrew language. Samuel Taylor Coleridge was one of his eight sons by his second wife. An interesting story of the family is to be found in *The Story of a Devonshire House* by Lord Coleridge (Fisher Unwin 1906)

12 Actually, this was a story carried by the *Morning Post* on 21 March 1800

13 It was Lady Mary Wortley Montagu who was chiefly responsible for pressing the new methods of inoculation in Britain. There is a remarkable letter from her (when she was the wife of the British Ambassador at Constantinople) to Mrs Sarah Chiswell ('Letters from the East'), written from Adrianople, 1 April 1717, in which she described the local practice of inoculation – called 'ingrafting' – carried on by '. . . a set of old women who make it their business to perform the operation every autumn . . .' She concluded: 'I am patriot enough to take pains to bring this useful invention into fashion in England; and I should not fail to write to some of our doctors very particularly about it, if I knew any one of them that I thought had virtue enough to destroy such a considerable branch of their revenue for the good of mankind . . . Perhaps, if I live to return, I may, however, have courage to war with them.'
Later, she did just this – and very effectively. An account of the struggles she had with both doctors and public opinion, and the relations between her own introduction of inoculation and Dr Jenner's introduction of vaccination, is to be found in *Women, Past and Present* by John Wade, Ch. VII.

14 Quoted in *English Women in Life and Letters*. M. Philips & W. S. Tomkinson. p.308.

15 A letter to J- H- S- Esq (Letter XVII in the published letters) written from Coxwould, 28 July 1761. Sterne was always berating doctors in his letters. The 'errantest charlatans in Europe', he called those in Toulouse, on his continental travels; and he wrote from Montpellier on 1 Feb 1764: 'My physicians have almost poisoned me with what they called *bouillons refraichissants*: 'tis a cock flayed alive, and boiled with poppy-seeds, then pounded in a mortar, afterwards passed through a sieve. – There is to be one crawfish in it; and I was gravely told it must be a male one; – a female would do me more hurt than good.' Laurence Sterne died on 18 March in the year before Theresa came to Saltram.

16 These examples are quoted in Mingay: *English Landed Society in the Eighteenth Century.* Routledge and Kegan Paul, 1963, p.223.

17 The fragrant-sounding recipe for 'Lavender Drops' – which contained 32 ingredients – was given in the diary of Mrs Lybbe Powis, and is quoted in *English Women in Life and Letters*, p.262. An advertisement of 'The Celebrated Codial Balm of Gilead' is given on p.129.

18 Comments from the son of the duc de Liancourt – quoted in *The Age of Scandal*, T. H. White.

19 To Fritz, 1 March 1774.

20 From 'General View of the County of Devon with Observations on the Means of its Improvement' by Robert Fraser (drawn up for the consideration of the Board of Agriculture and Internal Improvement), London 1794. p.345.

21 The same, p.17.

22 This is very much an approximation resulting from the picture presented by Fraser (above), Vancouver: *General View of the Agriculture of Devon* (1808), and – particularly – George Brodrick: *English Land and English Landlords* (1881). The latter gives the detailed picture – county by county – of land ownership in England portrayed by the *New Domesday Book*. This, of course, is much later than the period of our story, but, for want of a better, more contemporary source, I have been chiefly guided by it.

23 This also is Brodrick, p.57.

24 See Fraser and Vancouver.

25 Also from the *Diary of Mrs P. Lybbe Powis* (1756–1808). Ed. Emily J. Climenson. Longmans Green, 1899.

26 A very detailed picture of labourers' dwellings in Devon is given by Charles Vancouver: 'Cob buildings,' he wrote, 'are nearly as numerous as is presumed to have been the case with the Belgae . . . the first who made inroads and established colonies in Devon.' And: '. . . it is utterly impossible, at a distance, to distinguish a village from a beatfield . . . from both of which the stranger perceives smoke issuing.' p.92.

27 This, of course is George Crabbe, and this extract is from *The Village*, 1783. Crabbe had a very realistic eye for the social scene, and wrote on 'The Poor and their Dwellings', 'The Newspaper',

'The Library', etc., and almost every aspect of society. It is interesting to note that Lord Shelburne ignored Crabbe's need for patronage, and that it was Edmund Burke who helped him.

28 From Report of the Poor Law Commission, 1832–34.

29 These details are given in Vancouver, and quoted also in a very pleasant and informative book: *The English Countrywoman: A Farmhouse Social History*. 1500–1900.
This book also has an excellent bibliography.

30 Also Crabbe.

31 Detailed tables of Copper Ore 'Raised and Sold in Cornwall and Devon in Decennial Periods: from 1725–90 and 1794–1855' are given in *Records of Mining and Metallurgy*. J. Arthur Phillips and John Darlington, London 1857. This table, p.30.

32 In 1776 there was a Weavers' Strike in Devonshire, and anxious statements were made in Parliament. Mr John Vowler said, for example: '... the Weavers have many Clubs in several Places in the West of England, particularly at Exeter, where they make Bye-Laws; some of which he has seen; which Bye-Laws are, among other diverse things, to appoint places of meeting, fix their Officers, make Allowances to travelling Workmen and to ascertain their Wages.'

These and other details appear in 'Journal of the House of Commons' Vol. XX, and are quoted in *How They Lived* by Asa Briggs (Basil Blackwell, 1969) Vol. III, p.156–7.

33 The Public Advertiser, 11 Sep. 1760

34 This, really, developed more strongly a little later. This is a quotation given by J. L. and Barbara Hammond in *The Village Labourer* and drawn from the 'Correspondence on the Subject of Secondary Punishments'. The Hammonds comment interestingly on the peculiarity of the culture of the ruling classes at this time and this readiness to countenance the most brutal punishments (p.182).
'... this system was not the invention of some Nero or Caligula; it was the system imposed by men of gentle and refined manners, who talked to each other in Virgil and Lucan of Liberty and justice, who would have died without a murmur to save a French princess from an hour's pain or shame, who put down the abominations of the slave trade ... and it was imposed by them from the belief that as the poor were becoming poorer, only a system of punishment that was becoming more brutal could deter them from crime.'

35 An example of such an execution for conspiracy – the execution of Col. Edward Marcus Despard on 8 Feb. 1802 – is given in *The Dawn of the Nineteenth Century in England* by John Ashton (Fisher Unwin 1906.) Actually, the disembowelling and dismemberment were remitted, and Col. Despard was hung for twenty-five minutes 'until he was quite dead'. An example is also given from the *Morning Post* – as late as 27 April 1810 of the ceremony of driving a stake through the body of a 'suicide' – James Cowling, a deserter from the London Militia who had cut his throat in a public house in Gilbert Street, Clare Market. For decency's sake, the ceremony was 'properly delayed until 12.0 o'clock on Wednesday night'.

# CHAPTER 3

1 These are actual menus described – with much relish – by Parson Woodforde in his Diary.

2 Actually a little later. This was a notice in the *Morning Post* on 26 July 1800 and took place in a village in Cheshire.

3 An interesting example – though a little later than our story – is an account of the provisions which went into the 'public entertainment' of the King, his Family, his Ministers and Members of the Militia given by the Marquis of Salisbury on 18 July 1800: '... 80 hams, and as many rounds of beef; 100 joints of veal; 100 legs of lamb; 100 tongues; 100 meat pies; 25 rumps of beef roasted; 100 joints of mutton; 25 briskets; 25 edge bones of beef; 71 dishes of other roast beef; 100 gooseberry pies; ... For the country people, there were killed at the Salisbury Arms, 3 bullocks, 16 sheep, and 25 lambs. The expense is estimated at £3,000.' (A contemporary account quoted in *The Dawn of the Nineteenth Century in England*.)

4 See: *Travels in England* by Henri Misson – quoted in *Life and Work of the People of England: Eighteenth Century*, Dorothy Hartley and Margaret M. Elliott. (Batsford, 1931) p.28.

5 See Mingay p.218–221.

6 Also Hannah Glasse. Mrs Glasse wrote the *Art of Cookery* (1747), *The Compleat Confectioner* (1770), and *The Servant's Directory* (1760).

7 Theresa to Grantham, 7 Feb 1774

8 This was a well-known farce of the time. Oliver Goldsmith wrote a brief critical note of it which is to be found in many collections of his essays: eg. *The Bee and other Essays* Oxford University Press, 1914, p.61.

9 The Spectator, 11 June 1711

10 Theresa to Fritz, 1 Sept. 1772

11 3 Feb. 1774

12 Theresa to Grantham, 23 August 1771

13 These, and all the following quotations from the 'visiting foreign nobleman', are from Francois de la Rochefoucauld. Quoted by T. H. White in *The Age of Scandal*.

14 These menus are of special high table dinners at Oxford Colleges described by Parson Woodforde.

15 See Arthur Young's *Travels in France*.

16 See 6 above.

17 These are prices quoted about the turn of the century. *The Dawn of the Nineteenth Century in England* p.239.

18 Rochefoucauld: from the same account.

19 During one trip to Newmarket in 1784, Mr Parker sold his horse 'Anvil' to the Prince of Wales for 200 guineas.

20 Mr Parker was, in fact, frequently supplied with turtles for the table by his Naval friends in Plymouth. Several letters from Nanny mention their size, etc.
One particular letter from Nanny – to Fritz on 25 Oct. 1772 – is of interest because of its note of a rather quaint and spicy item: 'Mr Elliot asked whether I would enquire of you if there was such a thing used in the Spanish kitchen as *Congor dust* as there is vast quantity of it sent from a little place near the sea in Cornwall . . . and the people there have a notion that it is used in Spain to give a higher flavour to their dishes. If you have ever eat of it I think I had better not tell you what it is but if you have not it may perhaps prevent your ever being tempted to taste it. It is exactly what the name implies which is the dust of Congor. They get it by hanging up large Congor eels till they can hang no longer and when the maggots feed upon them are dried and turned into powder they send it into Spain. I should not have sent you this nasty account but by particular desire, therefore hope you will excuse it.'

This Mr Elliot must have been something of a collector of local dishes. In Boswell's 'Life' of Johnson is this note:
'Mr Elliot mentioned a curious liquor peculiar to his country, which the Cornish fishermen drink. They call it mahogany; and it is made of two parts gin and one part treacle well beaten together. I begged to have some made; which was done with proper skill by Mr Elliot. I thought it very good liquor; and said it was a counterpart of what is called Athol porridge in the Highlands of Scotland, which is a mixture of whiskey and honey.'

21 A play called *The Clandestine Marriage* includes a similar theme. See *Eighteenth Century Plays* Everyman Edn.

22 Laurence Sterne: *A Sentimental Journey through France and Italy*.

23 A good account of the 'Bluestockings' is to be found in *English Women in Life and Letters* p.246–252, and in *Women, Past and Present* by John Wade, Ch. VII. The latter includes the subject of the relationship – such as it was – between Lady Mary Wortley Montagu and Pope.

24 Joseph Addison: Essays: Sir Roger de Coverley.

25 Defoe wrote a pamphlet in 1725 entitled 'Everybody's Business Nobody's Business' protesting against the new manners of servants.

26 From a letter to *The Times*, 1795.

27 Arthur Young has many such comments on the lives of labouring families in his several 'Tours', his 'Farmer's Calendar', and his 'Annals of Agriculture'. This is quoted in *English Women in Life and Letters* p.286. Cobbett also attacked tea-drinking.

28 Details of these meals of labouring families are given in *The English Countrywoman* Ch's 4 and 5. See also Ivy Pinchbeck: *Women Workers of the Industrial Revolution 1750–1850*, and Sir Frederick Eden: *The State of the Poor* (1797).

29 Vancouver, in *General View of the Agriculture of Devon*, felt it his duty to urge the government against the education of the peasantry. p.468–469.

30 In Smollett's novel, Winifred Jenkins, a very simple country girl, was appalled by the dishonesty of the servants in Bath. This was her letter to Molly – a servant in the house she had just left.

31 This was Charles Edwin Clearwell (possibly of Clearwell Castle). Quoted in Mingay p.231.

32 *The Prose Works of Jonathan Swift*, D.D. Ed. Temple Scott. 1907.

# CHAPTER 4

1 Adam Smith's *Wealth of Nations* was published in 1776 and there is a copy in Saltram library. This book was a tremendous influence on fiscal reform. Pitt and many others acknowledged their indebtedness to Smith – in, for example, greatly simplifying the customs and much reducing the duty on tea.

2 Theresa to Grantham, 5 May 1775

3 Nanny wrote: '.... it is a Keepers Lodge and being a sort of entrance to the Park Mr Parker has bespoke two stags instead of two lions which Mr Adam had intended.'
The extent to which these country houses and gardens were thought of as public show-places may be seen in Mingay, p.211. Theresa and John Parker themselves did some sight-seeing. Theresa wrote to Grantham on 12 July 1772: 'We went to see whilst we were at Holnicote one of the finest Places I ever saw, which is Dunister Castle, belonging to Mr Luttrell. The situation of the House which is a very large old castle is halfway up a prodigiously steep and high hill, the lower part of which falls almost perpendicular from the House is covered with wood, the upper part is almost Bare, excepting very thick shrubs just above the House. It looks over a fine lawn to Hills of the same nature, some wooded and others not.'

4 In *History of a Poet's Garden*, Goldsmith describes William Shenstone's garden and captures all the romanticism of the new 'landscaping'. See *Essay and Essayists* Ed. Henry Newbolt, Nelson, p.83-4.

5 Theresa to Grantham, 3 Feb. 1774

6 *The Gardeners' Notebook*, 1779. See *Life and Work of the People of England: Eighteenth Century*, p.29.

7 From *Journeys of a German in England in 1782*, Carl Philip Moritz. Translated and edited by R. Nettel. Cape, 1965. p.50-1.

8 *The Political Register*, March 1768. See: *How They Lived*, Asa Briggs, Vol. III, p.470.

9 This was the Countess of Cork. Quoted in Mingay, p.124.

10 Moritz: 7 above.

11 Nanny to Grantham, from Saltram 12 Sept. 1780.

12 Theresa to Grantham, Nov. 1774.

13 Again – Parson Woodforde.

14 A useful note of the companies involved in the founding of the colonies is to be found in *Landmarks in English Industrial History*, G. Townsend Warner. Blackie, 1930. p.210.

15 A note of this proposed new colony is to be found in the National Trust booklet on Uppark (Sussex.) Sir Matthew Fetherstonhaugh was the M.P. involved, but the concession was never granted because of the War of Independence in 1775.

16 See 14 above, p.221.

17 The *Edinburgh Advertiser,* 20 Jan. 1769. Quoted in *The Shocking History of Advertising*. E. S. Turner. Michael Joseph, 1953
J. H. Plumb also quotes an example from the Liverpool Chronicle of 15 Dec. 1768:

> To be SOLD
> A FINE NEGROE BOY,
> Of about 4 Feet 5 Inches high.

Of a sober, tractable, humane Disposition, Eleven or Twelve Years of Age, talks English very well, and can Dress Hair in a tollerable way.

See his comments on slavery p.159 *England in the Eighteenth Century* Pelican.

18 These are the words of Sir William Dolben: quoted by J. K. Ingram in *Histroy of Slavery* London, 1895. p.152.

19 Letter from Walpole to Horace Mann, 1750. See G. M. Trevelyan *Illustrated English History*: 3, p.170.

20 On 27 June 1804, this argument was presented during the debate on the third reading of the Bill for the Abolition of the Slave Trade.

21 William Cowper was a poet who came to write against the evils of slavery. He satirised the current attitudes to slavery in a mock-vulgar style: for example:

> I own I am shocked at the purchase of slaves
> And fear those who buy them and sell them are knaves;

What I hear of their hardships, their tortures and groans,
Is almost enough to draw pity from stones.
I pity them greatly, but I must be mum,
For how could we do without sugar or rum?
Especially sugar, so needful we see?
What? Give up our desserts, our coffee and tea?
Besides, if we do, the French, Dutch, and Danes
Will heartily thank us, no doubt, for our pains;
If we do not buy the poor creatures, they will,
And tortures and groans will be multiplied still.'

But he also wrote in a graver manner:

He finds his fellow guilty of a skin
Not coloured like his own; and, having power . . .
Dooms and devotes him as a lawful prey.'

And again:

'But slavery! virtue dreads it as her grave . . .
Canst thou, and honoured with a Christian name,
Buy what is woman born, and feel no shame;
Trade in the blood of innocence, and plead
Expedience as a warrant of the deed?'

# CHAPTER 5

1 I hope it may be seen, here, that my words carry an intended echo of Milton ('dark, dark, dark, amid the blaze of noon') and of Handel's setting of 'The Messiah' ('The people that walked in darkness have seen a great light'). The more one learns about the eighteenth century, the more one sees a vast, complex, consistent growth of society – though fraught with conflict and problems – in thought, feeling, morality, and the re-making of institutions alike; away from the feudal order, through the widening horizons of the Elizabethan period and the splitting up of Christendom, and into a new rational and principled order of re-constituted nation states. A complex re-making of society, with its roots going ever more deeply and confidently into the revived knowledge of the classical world, was afoot. All J. H. Plumb's books are excellent on this, and see also *The Enlightenment* by Norman Hampson, Pelican 1968.

2 To her father, 10 Oct. 1766

3 See the National Trust's booklet on 'The Saltram Collection', p.42.

4 See Blake's *Annotations to Sir Joshua Reynold's Discourses.*

5 An interesting account of Chippendale, placing him in a very colourful way in his social context, is to be found in *Chippendale and his School* by J. P. Blake. Heinemann, 1912.

6 This is a comment of the Scots traveller – Rev. MacRitchie – who made a special note of the Duke of Bridgwater's new canal. 'Curious subterranean works about here . . .' he wrote. (*Diary of a Tour through Great Britain*).

7 Robert Bald, in *Inquiry into the Condition of Women who carry Coals under Ground in Scotland, known by the name of Bearers*. Edinburgh 1812.

8 Richard Ayton: *A Voyage round Great Britain undertaken in the Summer of 1813*. Vol. 2.

9 Children's Employment Commission (Mines) 1842 Vol. XVI.

10 John Wesley, about the people round Huddersfield in 1743. Wesley's 'Journal' is full of social commentary. An abridged version is available (by N. Curnock), published by The Epworth Press.

11 See J. L. and Barbara Hammond *The Skilled Labourer 1760–1832* Ch. 11. This quotation is from an indignant letter to the London newspapers by Richard Atkinson.

12 Written in 1775. From *A Lady of the Last Century* by Dr Doran. Quoted by the Hammonds, as above.

13 These figures were quoted in a discussion on the relative virtues – for work in mines – of candles and lamps. *Records of Mining and Metallurgy*, p.241. This book also contains notes on the improvements of pumping water from mines, and of ventilation. 'The scientific principles of mine ventilation were determined in 1764 by Jars; and in 1760 Spedding of Newcastle first succeeded in carrying air in a single current to any required part of the workings . . . etc.' p.242.

14 This quotation is a mixture of two: one by Cobbett, recalling the method told to him by his grandmother (see *English Women in Life and*

*Letters* p.278) and one by Gilbert White in *The Natural History of Selborne* (also quoted in *The English Countrywoman* p.121).

15 Arthur Young commented on the Witney blanket-weavers in 1767; but see evidence on embroiderers and lace-workers in the Children's Employment Commission. An excellent book on these matters is *England in Transition* by Dorothy George.

16 The steward of the Marquis of Bath, in an 'Address to the Landowners of this Kingdom: with Plans of Cottages'.

17 Near Elphingstone colliery, East Lothian. 1842 Report.

18 There were three chief clubs in London: White's, Brookes', and Boodles'. These are two items (1775 and 1792) drawn from the wager book which was kept when the club was held at Almack's.

19 Nanny herself was pleased to be involved in such lotteries. In a letter to Fritz, 12 Nov. 1780, she wrote: 'I am much obliged to you for the offer of a share of a ticket in the lottery I shall like of very much ... I am in your debt for a ticket last year ...'

20 The case was brought in 1777. See *Georgian Scrapbook*, A. H. Phillips. (Werner Laurie, 1949).

21 Letter from Nanny to Fritz, 13 Nov. 1781

22 Daniel Defoe on Bath and Tunbridge Wells. See also, again, Smollett's novel *Humphrey Clinker*.

23 Quoted in *English Women in Life and Letters* p.116.

24 Orator Henley. Also quoted in *English Women ...* as above.

25 The 'quizzing glasses' which became very fashionable among the 'fops'.

26 1768. Quoted in *Chippendale and his School*, p.79.

27 *The Age of Scandal*, T. H. White. p.35.

28 Nanny to Fritz, 4 April 1775

29 Theresa to Fritz, 17 March 1774

30 Theresa to Grantham, 31 July 1774

31 Theresa to Fritz, 11 Feb. 1774

32 Theresa to Fritz, 3 May 1773

# CHAPTER 6

1 At about the beginning of the eighteenth century, Gregory King estimated that about 22 million acres of Britain were under cultivation – ie. that two fifths of the total area of the country was 'waste'. In 1729, a land agent thought that a half of the country was 'waste'.

2 This was the road from Beverley to Hull. 'At dusk the bells rang from Barton-upon-Humber to guide the traveller ...'

3 This was the Dunstan pillar which guided wayfarers '... across a solitary waste ... from Sleaford to Brigg'.

4 Arthur Young again. In his 'Tours' he was always fulminating against tracks and roads. These conditions of the British landscape before the full development of the industrial revolution are given in a short book by Charles Beard: *The Industrial Revolution* (London, 1901). 'In 1734,' he quotes, 'the forest of Knaresborough was so thick that he was thought a cunning fellow that could readily find those Spaws of Harrowgate'.

5 The Reverend MacRitchie again – on what was clearly a beautiful night on the Thames on Monday, 27 July 1795 (*Diary of a Tour through Great Britain*). He got on shore at Wapping at 10.0. o'clock – then walked back to Oxford Street by way of Tower Hill: a distance, he reckoned, of six miles. Then, he concluded his day's entry: 'Sleep soundly after the numerous and striking adventures of the day'.

6 This was in 1762. See *Old Country Life*, p.213.

7 *Journeys of a German in England 1782* Carl Philip Moritz, Ed. R. Nettel. p.105.

8 Moritz, as 7 above, p.104-5.

9 Vancouver: *General View of the Agriculture of Devon* Ch. XVI p.368. Vancouver argues that it would have been better if the Devonshire road-makers had followed '... the judicious manner practised by the Indians of North America ...' and followed the water-courses!

10 Letter to Fritz, 30 Nov. 1781

11 Details of such travel are given in *The Story of a Devonshire House*, p.153. It is interesting to note that Parson Woodforde travelled to Oxford with William Coleridge of Ottery St Mary – one of Samuel Taylor Coleridge's brothers, and son of John Coleridge who was so forgetful of his wig! See *Diary of a Country Parson*, Vol. I. p.146.

12 Letter to Fritz, 16 Jan. 1784

13 This seems not just to be a personal opinion! In *A Tour to London, 1772*, P. Grosley wrote: '... the English do not seem to have that eagerness

14 Interesting comments on the separateness and great differences of local communities are given in *Old Country Life* Ch. VIII (on Roads) and Ch. X (on the Village Musician.)

15 Extracts from three letters written by Nanny to Fritz: 18 Oct. 1785, 28 Nov. 1785, and 19 Jan. 1786

16 Trevelyan: *Illustrated Social History.* p.55.

17 These were statements made by old labourers to Baring Gould, and are quoted in *Old Country Life* Ch. VIII.

18 Baring Gould gives a very colourful account of the narrowness of the old tracks between the hedge-banks in Devon, and the problems of transport. *Old Country Life.*

19 This statement about the network of canals in the country is taken from *England's Gazeteer: An Accurate Description of all the Cities, Towns, and Villages in the Kingdom,* 1790 (3 vols.) Besides all this, it gives details of the Regiments of Militia of the various counties, the numbers of M.P.s sent up by each county, the *sizes* of the cathedrals and churches in the country, details of the judicial circuits, details of occupations, manufactures, etc.

20 Thomas Pennant, 1782. Quoted by Trevelyan: *Illustrated Social History*: 3, p.166.

21 These extensive plans for canals in the west country were noted by Vancouver *General View of the Agriculture of Devon,* and were much discussed, but little, in fact, came of them.

22 Boswell quoting Johnson, 1773.

23 From *Old Country Life,* p.316.

24 A 'bag' of the Duke of Bedford on a Manor in Norfolk, recorded in 'Field Sports'. There are similar records for Coke of Holkham (See book reference in Note 7, Chapter 7.)

25 This note was written in lead pencil on a blank leaf of Reynolds' pocket-book. See *Life and Times of Sir Joshua Reynolds* C. R. Leslie and T. Taylor. (London, 1865).

26 This was actual evidence given by William Wilberforce in the debate in the House of Commons during the second reading of the Bill to prevent Bull-baiting and Bull-running, on 24 May 1802. The Bill was defeated (64 to 51). Bull-baiting was only made illegal in 1835.

27 Theresa to Grantham, 3 Feb. 1774

28 This, in fact, was a match on 15 July 1802

29 These are items from Mr Parker's account book.

30 Mingay gives details of the extravagances of landowners in maintaining horses for Newmarket. See *English Landed Society in the Eighteenth Century,* p.150–1.

31 On 3 June 1774, Theresa had written to Fritz: 'Mr Parker is returned from Devonshire very well pleased with his Tour and not impatient to go back. His Stud which was the chief thing he went to see, was in high order and what is better, in such high repute, that he actually refused 5000 Gs for Prophet.'

32 Information from the Jockey Club. 'Saltram' was subsequently sold to the Prince of Wales, quartered in the livery stables in Great Portland Street, and let out to stud at 20 guineas a time; and – in 1788 – exported to America for stud purposes. The name of the jockey who rode Saltram to victory was Hindley.

# CHAPTER 7

1 Theresa to Grantham, 5 May 1775

2 This, for example, is how she described certain extravagances of dress in London, in a letter to Fritz from Sackville Street on 11 Feb. 1774: 'There is a ... Mr Hanger and a Mr Corbett who are great Rivals in conceits and fancy in Dress. The former had a different Coat for the morning and evening ... embroidered down the seams, and dances in gold spangled ... stockings at Almack's. But the latter has an *Habit de Caprice* embroidered inside and out, with a particular lappelle, that drove Mr Hanger fairly out of the Opera House. Even Lord Guernsey wears a Silk Muff trimm'd with Blond'.

And here is her account of a Masquerade – also to Fritz, 6 May 1774: 'I must now give you an account of a most Magnificent Masquerade indeed. It is not possible to conceive anything more beautiful than the Illumination. The Room is beautiful in itself, and the Dome very striking, every ornament in which was made out in different Coloured Lamps ... Seeing the people

walking between the Pillars, or leaning over the Balconies & walking up & down stairs, had a most surprising beautifull effect, which I daresay you can easily believe. The Dresses upon the whole were not fine, chiefly Dominoes, Nor were there many characters, or what is called Wits at a Masquerade. Both Nanny and I have been much complimented upon our dresses & indeed I think they were both remarkably well made, & pretty... The only dress that had pretensions to a new thought was a Mile Stone, 45 Miles from Hyde Park Corner writ upon it, but it was a mighty heavy Idea. Vast interest made at last for tickets, 40 or 50 G's offerd over & over...'
This sounds a little like the Rotunda at Ranelagh.

3 Letter to Fritz, 17 March 1774

4 Theresa, 5 August 1774

5 Theresa to Fritz from Sackville Street, 17 March 1774

6 A mixture of comments on the 'Heads' of the time: from Sir Walter Besant, Woolliscroft Rhead (from a book on 'Costume'), and the *Ladies Magazine*, June 1775.

7 This actually happened to Mrs Coke, wife of Coke of Holkham, and it was held that the shock caused her miscarriage. Lady Mary Coke wrote on Sunday, 1 Dec. 1776:
'Did you hear that my cousin Mrs Coke was brought to bed of a dead son, occasioned by a fright; a mouse got into her nightcap and demolished the heir to Holkham'.
See *Coke of Norfolk and his Friends* by A. M. W. Stirling (London, John Lane, 1908. 2 vols.) Vol. I. p.232. This book itself gives an excellent account of eighteenth-century life and society.

8 From the *Morning Post*, 9 March 1776. Quoted in *Georgian Scrapbook*, A. H. Phillips. p.65.

9 From *The London Magazine* of the 1780's. See *English Women in Life and Letters*, p.132–3.

10 See *Perfume, Cosmetics and Soaps*, W. A. Poucher. Vol. 2. Chapman and Hall, 1959. p.17.

11 From Fanny Burney's Diaries.

12 *The Age of Scandal*, T. H. White, p.148.

13 Quoted in *English Women in Life and Letters*, p.113, 116.

14 Hannah More: *Strictures on the Modern System of Female Education*, 1799, Ch. XVI p.140. Hannah More's views on education were sound and excellent in many ways, and also remarkably relevant to our own time.

15 Daniel Defoe: *Tour through the Southern Counties of England,* 1722.

16 Theresa to Grantham, 5 August 1774. She also wrote on 3 June: 'You see some of my little Boys Drawing or Writing whichever you please to call it. It was with difficulty I prevented his scribbling all over the sheet'.

17 Theresa to Fritz, 24 August 1775

18 Theresa to her brothers in Spain, 6 May 1774

19 Theresa to Grantham, 24 August 1775

20 Theresa to Fritz, 9 April 1772

21 Theresa to Grantham, 2 April 1772

22 From 'B. Angeloni, Letters on the English Nation', 1755. J. Shebbeare. Vol. II. Quoted in *How They Lived*, Asa Briggs, Vol. III.

23 Lord Chesterfield's Letters to his son.

24 These are comments on the use of a powder-stand, commonly taken to be a wig-stand, by J. P. Blake in *Chippendale and his School*.

25 Quoted in *English Women in Life and Letters*, p.168.

26 This terrible account can be found in *The Noels and the Milbankes,* Malcolm Elwin (Macdonald, 1967), p.187–8, 192.

27 From the *Torrington Diaries 1781–94.* Ed. C. Bruyn Andrews, Vol. 1. p.190.

28 This was the account of John Yeoman, a country bumpkin: quoted in *The Age of Scandal*, T. H. White. But it was not only country bumpkins who were 'electrified'. On 20 Oct 1784, Nanny wrote to Grantham: '.... Lady Chatham is certainly better for being Electrified, but still very weak...'

29 *The Dawn of the Nineteenth Century in England*, p.389–90.

30 The Duke of Chandos' first wife. See Mingay *English Landed Society in the Eighteenth Century*, p.225.

31 Theresa to Grantham, May 1775.

32 *Life and Work of the People of England : Eighteenth Century*, p.26.

33 19 Sept. 1775

34 Theresa to Grantham, 31 July 1774

35 Theresa to Grantham, 2 Sept. 1775

36 Theresa's last letter: to Fritz, 20 Oct. 1775

# CHAPTER 8

1 Theresa to Grantham, June 1775
2 From *A Plan of Education for the Young Nobility and Gentry of Great Britain* by Thomas Sheridan, 1769. Thomas Sheridan was the father of Richard Brinsley Sheridan, the playwright. It was through his efforts that Dr Johnson was given a pension, and he himself was granted a pension (£200 a year) by Lord Bute in connection with his scheme for a 'Pronouncing Dictionary'. He studied the educational system in France between 1764 and 1766, and wrote his *Plan of Education*... on his return to England. It is an excellent book, outlining and advocating an education which fitted the young for responsible life in society.
3 Theresa to Fritz, 6 May 1774
4 Grantham (in Madrid) to John Parker, 29 Jan. 1776
5 Nanny to Grantham, 1 Nov. 1776
6 Nanny to Fritz, 1 March 1774
7 This and all the following letters of Jack's education are from Nanny to either Fritz or Grantham.
8 From *The Times*, 2 Nov. 1797. See *How They Lived* Vol. III, p.239.
9 Hannah More attacked the whole idea of a girl's education as being an 'acquisition of accomplishments'. This quotation is from her story of Farmer and Mrs Bragwell of Somerset who sent their daughter to a fashionable boarding-school. See *English Women in Life and Letters*, p.214.
10 Hannah More in *On Female Education*.
11 Mary Astell: quoted in *The English Countrywoman*, p.106. Even as early as 1694 Mary Astell proposed a college for the higher education of women.
12 Hannah More: *On Female Education*.
13 *The Rivals*, Act 1, Scene II.
14 Hannah More: *On Female Education*, p.106–7. Vol. I.
15 This word seems like Fitchey in the letter. Fitches are polecats, but it seems questionable whether young Jack would be hunting polecats in the Hall at night. I have left the word 'Fitchey' thinking that it might *possibly* have been some pet.
16 A very rare letter from Mr Parker (actually, by then Lord Boringdon), Tuesday, 8 Feb. 1785.
17 Autobiographical notes of Charles Bosanquet, quoted in *The Creevey Papers* Ed. John Gore (Batsford, 1963) p.269.
18 Accidents happened at these schools then, as now. Theresa wrote to Fritz on 3 June 1774:
'Poor Dr Warren has been in a dreadful situation, his Eldest Boy tore his hand with some Iron Spikes at Westminster which I understand are put upon little Doors in the Boarding Houses, there to guard the Bread and Butter. The wound was healing well when he showed some Symptoms of that frightful disorder a Locked Jaw'.

Indeed, accidents to children had a familiar ring about them. Nanny told Fritz of the tragedy of Capt. Pole who frequently visited Saltram (29 Nov. 1786):
'Capt. Pole has had a sad accident in his family, his third daughter, between three and four years old was standing near the fire her frock caught fire and tho' it was soon put out and no great appearance of her being dangerously burned, she died two days after'.
19 From *The Young Gentleman and Lady's Private Tutor*, Mathew Towle, 1770.
20 From *A Tour to London*, 1772. Grosley.
21 *Journeys of a German in England*, 1782. Carl Philip Moritz.
22 Moritz: as above.
23 From *The Poor Girl's Primer* used in the Sheffield Girls' Charity School in 1789. Quoted in *How They Live*, Briggs.
24 Isaac Watts: 'An Essay Towards the Encouragement of Charity Schools', 1728.
25 Rev. MacRitchie: *Diary of a Tour through Great Britain*, p.5.
26 Vancouver: *General View of the Agriculture of Devon*, p.469.
27 The story of Betty Broom told by Dr Johnson. See *English Women in Life and Letters*, p.201–2.
28 From *The Principles of Sound Policy*, J. Fawel, 1785.
29 See *Tour through the South of England*, 1791, E. D. Clarke, p.397. The author wrote, for example:
'... It is a kind of anarchy in stone and mortar... architecture in a high fever... There is a *Mausoleum* for a *library*, and a *cock-pit* for *public disputants*. There is a *sepulchre* of *manuscripts*, and a long gallery, where heroes with ugly faces, and

learned graduates in full bottomed wigs, are copiously displayed upon canvass. What shall be said of CHRIST-CHURCH? where neat little PECK-WATER cements the dirty puddle and the leaden mercury that disgraces its neighbouring quadrangle...'
These views, however, were not shared by everyone. See also: *The Ancient and Present State of the City of Oxford* by Anthony Wood, 1773. This author thought Oxford: '... the Delight and Ornament of the Kingdom, not to say of the World'.

30 1752. See Trevelyan *Illustrated Social History*: 3, p.126.

31 William Cowper also came to attack the formal provisions of education almost as vehemently as slavery:

> 'Oh barbarous! wouldest thou with a Gothic hand
> Pull down the schools – what! – all the schools i' th' land;
> Or throw them up to livery-nags and grooms,
> Or turn them into shops and auction rooms?
> A captious question, sir, (and your's is one)
> Deserves an answer similar, or none.
> Wouldest thou, possessor of a flock, employ
> (Apprized that he is such) a careless boy,
> And feed him well, and give him handsome pay,
> Merely to sleep, and let them run astray?
> Survey our schools and colleges, and see
> A sight not much unlike my simile.
> From education, as the leading cause,
> The public character its colour draws;
> Thence the prevailing manners take their cast,
> Extravagant or sober, loose or chaste.
> And, though I would not advertise them yet,
> Nor write on each – *This Building to be Let*,
> Unless the world were all prepared to embrace
> A plan well worthy to supply their place;
> Yet, backward as they are, and long have been,
> To cultivate and keep the MORALS clean,
> (Forgive the crime) I wish them, I confess,
> Or better managed, or encouraged less.'

32 This again is Parson Woodforde. He frequently spoke of 'being in beer', and it was he who took his BA degree and had his glass doors broken at three o'clock in the morning. See *Diary of a Country Parson*, Vol. I. p.17, 26.

33 *Diary of a Country Parson*, Vol. I, p.158–60.

34 Francois de la Rochefoucauld *A Frenchman in England*, 1784. Ed. J. Marchand (1933) p.122.

35 Jack to his father, 23 Feb. 1787

36 From letters from Nanny to Fritz during December 1786.

37 One of these was George Canning, later to be Foreign Secretary.

38 *Torrington Diaries, 1781–94.* Vol. I. p.294.

39 See Mingay, p.140.

40 A letter of Theresa's – to Grantham, 10 July 1775

41 Lord Chesterfield.

# CHAPTER 9

1 Nanny to Fritz, 19 July 1786

2 Very interesting comments, details, and quotations on this is given in *Old Country Life*, Ch. X. For example:
'In 1648 the Provost-marshal was given power to arrest all ballad-singers. Organs were everywhere destroyed, and probably a great many viols, lutes, and other instruments. One gentleman, when he adopted Puritanism, had a deep hole dug in his garden, and buried in it: '£200 worth of music-books six feet underground, being, as he said, love-songs and vanity...' Oliver Cromwell's third Parliament passed an Act ordering the arrest and punishment of all minstrels and musicians who performed in taverns.' etc. p.252.

3 The novels of Thomas Hardy, of course, still describe this country music and these country musicians.

4 Nanny to Fritz, 16 Jan. 1787

5 Theresa had once written to Fritz about his friend Dick Thompson whom she 'did not quite give up' because he had once been a favourite of his (17 March 1774). She wrote: '... if you can raise his Ideas above the nosegay Women in St James Park, you will do him great service'.

6 Letters from Nanny to Fritz on 19 Dec. 1783, and 8 Oct. 1784. She added: 'I ought to beg your pardon for taking up your time talking of such nonsense...'

7 Letter from Walpole to Hon. H. S. Conway, 1784. Quoted in *Georgian Scrapbook*, Phillips. p.85.

8 This, actually, was an earlier letter of Theresa's. A little afterwards – on 5 August 1774 – she wrote to Fritz telling him more of the story: 'The chief talk of Plymouth is about Mr Blake's Vessell which a man from London has undertaken to raise his name is Falk & is I understand a Quack Doctor. I doubt his schemes, especially as I find he is silly enough to suppose it possible that the poor Man that went down in her may be alive. He has a very clever Fisherman with him who has so simple a plan for raising it & so reasonable that I am convinced if anything will succeed it is his method. There is a vast concourse of people upon the Spot, in expectation of seeing it come up, they have been at work two days upon it.'

9 For example, Nanny wrote to Fritz on 23 July 1782:
'If you have time in your walks of a morning to call at the Bookbinders Mr Parker would be much obliged to you if you would ask when Sir Wil<sup>m</sup> Hamilton's books will be finished and desire him to send them down.'

10 Good accounts of the 'Bluestockings' are given in *English Women in Life and Letters*, p.246, and in *Women, Past and Present*, John Wade, Ch. VII. On Benjamin Stillingfleet, Boswell wrote: 'His dress was remarkably grave and in particular it was observed that he wore blue stockings. Such was the excellence of his conversation, that his absence was felt a loss, that it used to be said "We can do nothing without the *blue stockings*," and thus by degrees the title was established.'

11 Hannah More wrote *Tales for the Common People* as well as very influential books on education, and she and her sisters opened private schools.

12 From her letters to her daughter (the Countess of Bute) See *English Women in Life and Letters*, p.184.

13 1773, when she was 21 years old. From Fanny Burney's 'Diaries'.

14 Nanny to Fritz, 24 July 1786

15 Nanny to Fritz, 20 Dec. 1784

16 Not dated but approximately 20 July 1786 (preceded and followed immediately by other dated letters). Grantham's death was a great blow.

17 In July 1787, Fritz was, in fact, granted a pension of £900 by the Crown, and vacated his seat in Parliament (which he held for Ripon from 1780.) He himself lived only five years longer.

18 Theresa to Fritz from Sackville Street, 24 March 1775

19 Nanny to Grantham, 12 Sept. 1780

20 12 Sept. 1781. Nanny's letter also says: 'He won a good sweepstakes today and is in hopes of winning the cup tomorrow.' Betting was obviously like breathing to Mr Parker – and just as difficult to stop!

21 From young Jack at Hammersmith: Wed. 22 Nov. 1786

22 In a letter about a month earlier – 25 Oct. – Jack had also written: 'I have seen Sir L. Copley in London. I am sorry he has won all your money.' Jack's youthful letters seemed nicely – whether in artless or masterly fashion – to be able to carry a sting in the tail!

23 An interesting account of Mrs Delaney's life, and marriage to her 'fat, snuffy' old Cornishman is given in *Social England*, Vol. V. p.200. It was Lord and Lady Lansdowne – just released from two years imprisonment in the Tower – who arranged the marriage, evidently for political reasons. Alexander Pendarves was the Cornishman, and before she knew she was to marry him, Mary Granville called him 'Gromio'. She was subsequently very friendly with 'Fidget' Elizabeth Montagu. They stayed with the Duchess of Portland, about whom Lord Chesterfield wrote: 'She knows more than is necessary for any woman, for she understands Latin perfectly well, tho' she wisely conceals it.' See also *Old Country Life*.

24 Hannah More: *On Female Education*.

25 *Diary of a Country Parson*, Vol. I. p.69. See also: *The English Church in the Eighteenth Century*, Abbey and Overton, and *English Church Life*, Wickham Legg.

26 Parson Woodforde actually officiated at this wedding on 22 Nov. 1768. *Diary of a Country Parson*, p.82.

27 Examples of wife-selling are given in *The Dawn of the Nineteenth Century in England*, p.282–3.

28 From Fanny Burney's Diaries – on a Wednesday in July.

29 Nanny to Fritz, 31 August 1784

30 Francis Grose, *The Olio*, 1793. Quoted in *The English Countrywoman*, p.112.

207

31 Theresa to Grantham, 10 July 1775
32 Nanny to Fritz from Sackville Street, 5 Nov. 1784
33 From *The Noels and the Milbankes*, Malcolm Elwin. p.221.

## CHAPTER 10

1 Actually, Nanny wrote a brief one-line letter on the Sunday, and this longer letter on the following day.
2 From *Life and Times of Sir Joshua Reynolds*, Vol. II, p.40.
3 From the estate account book.
4 To Fritz, 8 Oct. 1784
5 16 Jan. 1787
6 21 Jan. 1787
7 26 Oct. 1787
8 Nanny to Fritz, 20 June 1788
9 12 Aug. 1788
10 25 Aug. 1788
11 4 Sept. 1788
12 The poster was dated 7 June 1788. It was thought that those who committed the robbery must have been intimately acquainted with the house.
13 Nanny to Fritz, 19 Oct. 1788
14 All the financial details given are derived from Lord Morley's (unpublished) *History of the Parker Family*, and the account books at Lord Boringdon's death, in the Plymouth City Library: Archives Department.
15 Saltram was so described by the Rev. S. Shaw in *A Tour to the West of England*, 1788. Quoted in *Early Tours in Devon and Cornwall*, Ed. R. Pearse Chope. (David and Charles, Newton Abbot, 1967).
16 From *Diary and Letters of Madame D'Arblay*, Vol. 5. 1789-93, (London, 1854). The visit was in August, 1789. In fact, Fanny Burney disliked being Mistress of the Robes. Evidently Queen Charlotte '. . . used to complain to Mrs Delaney that Miss Burney could not learn to tie the bow of her necklace on Court days without giving her pain by getting the hair at the back of the neck tied in with it.' She retired after five years.
Even Fanny Burney, incidentally, had to have her fling at the Duchess of Devonshire. Walking in the Park one Sunday morning, she wrote, '. . . we saw the young and handsome Duchess of Devonshire walking in such an undressed and slatternly manner . . . Two of her curls came quite unpinned, and fell lank on one of her shoulders; one shoe was down at heel, the trimming of her jacket and petticoat was in some places unsown; her cap was awry, and her cloak which was rusty and powdered, was flung half on and half off. Had she not had a servant in superb livery behind her she would certainly have been affronted. Every creature turned back to stare at her.'
17 A man by the name of Murdoch, a metal founder at Redruth, lit his house and offices up with gas in 1792. He also had a 'steam-carriage', and '. . . in this uncanny conveyance he would take bladders of this new inflammable air, and actually burn a light without a wick.'
18 For some reason, I have W. B. Yeats' image closely in mind here:
'. . . a vast image out of *Spiritus Mundi*
Troubles my sight . . .
A shape with lion body and the head of a man,
A gaze blank and pitiless as the sun,
Is moving its slow thighs . . .
The darkness drops again; but now I know
That twenty centuries of stony sleep
Were vexed to nightmare by a rocking cradle,
And what rough beast, its hour come round at last,
Slouches towards Bethlehem to be born?'
19 Hannah More: *On Female Education*.
20 'Advertisement' of Theresa Parker's death written by Sir Joshua Reynolds in 1775.
21 Hannah More: *On Female Education*.
22 When Mr Parker – Lord Boringdon – died, William Blake was preparing his 'Songs of Innocence', for publication in 1789, and William Wordsworth was a young man of 18 at St John's College, Cambridge, busy with his first poem of consequence – 'The Evening Walk' – which he was to finish in 1789.

## EPILOGUE

1 Nanny to Fritz, 26 May 1788. Concerning 'Either of the Places', Nanny also said:

'... I should rather think Mrs Chetwynds the most creditable. I will answer for Lady Sydneys readiness to apply for me, as she once offer'd to do so, or to second any application that might be made on my account if a vacancy should have happened by the Death of Mrs Brudenel, the Bed Chamber woman who was at that time very ill. I would write to Lady Sidney myself about this post, but not knowing exactly what you may determine upon, it may make a jumble. I can only say that, whatever will satisfy you best and you think properest for me, I will most readily agree to.' But again, she had made her preference plain: '... tho' the very beauties of this place are melancholy to me, I must own I feel easier here than I think I could anywhere else.'

2 Nanny to a friend, 5 and 9 Sept. 1797

3 Theresa Villiers to Nanny from Upper Grosvenor St, 8 Nov. 1805

4 Theresa to Nanny, 26 May 1798

5 Vancouver: *General View of the Agriculture of Devon,* p.301.

6 *The Beauties of England and Wales,* John Britton and E. W. Brayley. Vol. IV. p.142–5. (London, 1803).

7 13 Oct. 1793

8 Nov. 1802

9 19 Dec. 1802

# BOOKS FOR FURTHER READING
*with details of museums and eighteenth-century houses*

The following is a selected list of books on many of the topics touched upon, and is intended for those who would like to read more about the various aspects of eighteenth-century life. Where possible, cheap editions have been suggested and most of the books should be easily obtainable. The more expensive or specialised books can usually be obtained from the Public Library. There are numerous novels and biographies which give a good account of country life in the eighteenth century, but these have not been included, though one or two have been mentioned in the Notes on the chapters. Local libraries are usually very helpful in giving advice on books in this category.

Some of these books deserve special note in that they themselves are useful and often well illustrated collections of sources on eighteenth-century life, and are eminently readable and entertaining whilst covering a wide range of reliable information. A few which can be warmly recommended are:

WHITE, T. H. *The age of scandal* 1950. Penguin Books, 5s.

TREVELYAN, G. M. *Illustrated English social history Vol. 3: The eighteenth century* 1964. Penguin Books, 10s.

FUSSELL, G. E. and K. R. *The English countrywoman: a farmhouse social history 1500–1900* 1953. A. Melrose, o.p.

PHILLIPS, M. and TOMKINSON, W. S. *English women in life and letters* 1927. O.U.P., o.p.

BRIGGS, A. *How they lived Vol. 3: 1700–1815* 1969. Oxford: B. Blackwell, 45s.

*Social England Vol. V* 1903. Cassell, o.p.

One book which must be specially recommended because of the rich detail and flavour of eighteenth-century life which it presents, and also for its sheer delight, is:

WOODFORDE, Rev. J. *The diary of a country parson*; ed. by J. Beresford. 5 vols. 1931. O.U.P., 10 gns. set; 1949. O.U.P., World Classics, 18s.

More serious histories of the period, but still enjoyable reading, are all the books by J. H. Plumb, and perhaps especially:

PLUMB, J. H. *England in the eighteenth century* 1950. Penguin Books, 8s. 6d.

And also:

MINGAY, G. E. *English landed society in the eighteenth century* 1963. Routledge, 56s.

A less detailed book which has the merit of bringing the history of the landed aristocracy up to date is:

SUTHERLAND, D. *The landowners* 1968. Blond, 50s.

Some readers may be especially interested in the conditions of Devon and its agricultural changes at the time of our story. An excellent source of this is:

VANCOUVER, C. *General view of the agriculture of the county of Devon* 1969. David & Charles, 84s.

A few other books are worth mentioning because they are little known. One which gives an account of life in country houses from the time of Chaucer to the end of the nineteenth century is:

ESCOTT, T. H. S. *Society in the country house* 1907. Unwin. o.p.

There is one very charming set of books which not only offers much information about furniture, but also places the styles of furniture and the great designers themselves in the social background of their time. This is:

HOPKINS, A. E. Reviers and BLAKE, J. P. *Little books about old furniture* 4 vols. 1912. Heinemann. o.p.
Vol. 3 *Chippendale and his school*
Vol. 4 *The Sheraton period: post-Chippendale designers 1760–1820*

Also much to be recommended is:

MORE, H. *Strictures on the modern system of female education* 2 vols. London, 1799. o.p.

Readers specially interested in education will be fascinated by the extent to which the views of Hannah More (as of other Bluestockings) appear strikingly up-to-date and relevant to the problems of our own time.

The rest of the books have been listed as conveniently as possible under particular subject-headings.

## General background reading

WILLIAMS, E. N. *Life in Georgian England* 1962. Batsford, 25s.

MARSHALL, D. *English people in the eighteenth century* 1956. Longmans, 50s.

PLUMB, J. H. *The first four Georges* 1966. Fontana, reprinting, n.d.

WATSON, J. S. *The reign of George III, 1760–1815* (Oxford history of England, Vol. 12) 1960. O.U.P., 42s.

HAMPSON, N. *The enlightenment* (Pelican history of European thought, Vol. 4) 1968. Penguin Books, 7s. 6d.
BURNEY, F. (Madame D'Arblay) *The diary and letters of Madame D'Arblay* 7 vols. 1854. Hurst, o.p.
*Diary of Fanny Burney* (Everyman series) 1940. Dent, 16s.

## Rural life

GEORGE, M. D. *England in transition* 1931. Routledge, o.p. 1967. Penguin Books, 5s.
CHAMBERS, J. D. and MINGAY, G. E. *The agricultural revolution 1750–1880* 1966. Batsford, 45s.
BOVILL, E. W. *English country life, 1780–1830* 1962. O.U.P., 30s.
FUSSELL, G. E. *The farmer's tools 1500–1900: the history of British farm implements, tools and machinery before the tractor came* 1952. A. Melrose, o.p.
LASLETT, P. *The world we have lost* 1965. Methuen, 35s.; University Paperbacks, 16s.
HAMMOND, J. L. and B. *The village labourer, 1760–1832* 4th edn. 1966. Longmans, paperback 18s.
BRODRICK, G. C. *English land and English landlords* 1881. Cassell, Petter, Galpin & Co., o.p.; 1968. David & Charles, 75s.

## The Industrial Revolution

ASHTON, T. S. *An economic history of England: the eighteenth century* 1955. Methuen, 30s.
ASHTON, T. S. *The Industrial Revolution 1760–1830* (Opus books) 2nd edn. 1968. O.U.P., 7s. 6d.
HAMMOND, J. L. and B. *The town labourer, 1760–1832*. 1966. Longmans, paperback 18s.
HAMMOND, J. L. and B. *The skilled labourer, 1760–1832*. 1919. Longmans, o.p.
HAYEK, F. A., ed. *Capitalism and the historians* 1954. Routledge, o.p.

## Coal

ASHTON, T. S. and SYKES, J. *The coal industry of the eighteenth century* 2nd rev. edn. 1964. Manchester U.P., 35s.
TOMALIN, M. *Coal mines and miners* 1960. Methuen, 15s.

## Horses and transport

LIVINGSTONE-LEARMONTH, D. *The horse in art* 1958. Studio Publications, o.p.
COPELAND, J. *Roads and their traffic, 1750–1850* 1968. David & Charles, 45s.

VALE, E. *The mail-coach men of the late eighteenth century* 1967. David & Charles, 45s.
CHOPE, R. P., ed. *Early tours in Devon and Cornwall* 1967. David & Charles, 45s.

## Canals

HADFIELD, C. *British canals: an illustrated history* 4th edn. 1969. David & Charles, 50s.

## Domestic life

QUENNELL, M. and C. H. B. *A history of everyday things in England* Vol. III: The rise of industrialism 1733–1851 6th edn. 1961. Batsford, 25s.
BURTON, E. *The Georgians at home 1714–1830* 1967. Longmans, 55s.
HECHT, J. J. *The domestic servant class in eighteenth-century England* 1956. Routledge, 25s.
WHATMAN, S. *The housekeeping book of Susannah Whatman 1776–1800;* ed. by T. Balston. 1956. Bles, o.p.

## Food

General reading on food and serving of meals, not restricted to the eighteenth century.

HUTCHINS, S. *English recipes and others* 1967. Methuen, 63s.
HARTLEY, D. *Food in England* 1955. Macdonald, 65s.
BRETT, G. *Dinner is served* 1968. Hart-Davis, 84s.
GLASSE, Mrs. H. *The art of cookery made plain and easy* London, 1747. o.p.; 2nd edn. with new recipes appendixed 1770. o.p.
TRUSLER, J. *The honours of the table for the use of young people, or rules of behaviour during meals with the whole art of carving* Bath, 1788. o.p.

## Sanitation

WRIGHT, L. *Clean and decent* 1960. Routledge, 40s.; 1966. paperback 12s. 6d.

## Cosmetics and make-up

BINDER, P. *Muffs and morals* 1953. Harrap, o.p.
WYKES-JOYCE, M. *Cosmetics and adornment* 1961. P. Owen, 30s.
WILLIAMS, N. *Powder and paint* 1957. Longmans, o.p.

## Costume

CUNNINGTON, C. W. and P. *Handbook of English costume in the eighteenth century* 2nd edn. 1965. Faber, 70s.

## Health
BUER, M. C. *Health, wealth and population in the early days of the Industrial Revolution* 2nd edn. 1968. Routledge, 45s.
GUTHRIE, D. *A history of medicine* 2nd edn. 1958. Nelson, 63s.
FISK, D. *Doctor Jenner of Berkeley* 1959. Heinemann, o.p.

## The Church
CRAGG, G. R. *The Church and the Age of Reason, 1648–1789* 1960. Penguin Books, o.p.; 1962. Hodder, 25s.
EDWARDS, M. L. *John Wesley and the eighteenth century* rev. edn. 1955. Epworth Pr., o.p.
SYKES, N. *Church and State in England in the eighteenth century* (Birbeck lectures in ecclesiastical history) 1934. C.U.P., o.p.
WEARMOUTH, R. F. *Methodism and the common people of the eighteenth century* 1945. Epworth Pr., o.p.
WESLEY, J. *John Wesley's journal*; ed. by N. Curnock. 1909. Epworth Pr., 8 vols. 10 gns. set; 1950. o.p.; abbr. edn. 1952. 17s. 6d.

## Education
JONES, M. G. *The Charity School Movement: a study of eighteenth-century Puritanism in action* 1938. C.U.P., o.p.
MCLACHAN, H. *English education under the Test Acts: the history of the non conformist academics, 1662–1820* 1931. Manchester U.P., o.p.
WINSTANLEY, D. A. *The University of Cambridge in the eighteenth century* 1922. C.U.P., 30s.
GODLEY, A. D. *Oxford in the eighteenth century* 1908. Methuen, o.p.

## The Grand Tour
BURGESS, A. and HASKELL, F., eds. *The age of the Grand Tour* 1967. Elek, 10 gns.
CHESTERFIELD, P. D. S., Lord. *Letters of Lord Chesterfield to his son* (Everyman) 1929. Dent, 14s.

## Art and craftsmanship: Architecture
HUSSEY, C. *English country houses: Vol. 2 Mid-Georgian 1760–1800* 1956. Country Life, o.p.
SUMMERSON, J. *Architecture in Britain, 1530–1830* (Pelican history of art) Penguin Books, 13os.
LEES-MILNE, J. *The age of Adam* 1948. Batsford, o.p.
FLEMING, J. *Robert Adam and his circle* 1962. J. Murray, 55s.

## Furniture and Furnishings
EDWARDS, R. and RAMSEY, L. G. G., eds. *The Connoisseur period guide to the houses, decoration, furnishings and chattels of the classic periods: The late Georgian period 1760–1810* 1956. Connoisseur, o.p.
JOURDAIN, M. *English interior decoration, 1500–1830* 1950. Batsford, o.p.

## Painting
WATERHOUSE, E. K. *Painting in Britain 1530–1790* (Pelican history of art) 1953. Penguin Books, 110s.
REYNOLDS, Sir J. *Discourses on art (1769–90)*; ed. by R. R. Wark. 1960. O.U.P., o.p.; 1961. Collier-Macmillan, 6s.

## Landscape gardening
CLARK, H. F. *The English landscape garden* 1948. Pleiades Books, o.p.

## Politics
NAMIER, L. *The structure of politics at the accession of George III* 2nd edn. 1957. Macmillan, 75s.; Papermac 30s.
NAMIER, L. *England in the age of the American Revolution* 2nd edn. 1961. Macmillan, 70s.; 1962. Papermac 30s.
PARES, R. *King George III and the politicians* (Ford lectures 1951–2) 1953. O.U.P., 30s.; 1968. paperback 7s. 6d.
BUTTERFIELD, H. *George III: Lord North and the people 1779–80* 1949. G. Bell, o.p.
RUDÉ, G. *Wilkes and liberty: social study of 1763–1774* 1965. O.U.P., 30s.; paperback 8s. 6d.
WILLIAMS, E. N. *The eighteenth-century constitution 1688–1815* 1961. C.U.P., 63s.; students edn. 27s. 6d.

## Cook and exploration
WILLIAMSON, J. A. *Cook and the opening of the Pacific* (Teach yourself history) 1946. English U.P., o.p.
COOK, J. *Captain Cook's voyages of Cook round the world*; ed. by C. Lloyd. 1950. Cresset Pr., o.p.
VILLIERS, A. *Captain Cook, the seamen's seaman* 1967. Hodder, 42s.; 1969. Penguin Books, 6s.

## America
MILLER, J. C. *Origins of the American Revolution* 1945. Faber, o.p.; 1960. O.U.P., 81s.; 1966. paperback 36s.

ANDREWS, C. M. *The Colonial background of the American Revolution* 1924. Milford, o.p.; rev. edn. 1931. O.U.P., o.p.; 1961. Yale U.P., $6 or $1.75 paperback.

ALDEN, J. R. *The American Revolution 1775–1783* 1954. Harper & Row (New American nation series), 74s.; paperback 21s.; 1954. H. Hamilton, o.p.

## Slavery

COUPLAND, R. *Wilberforce: a narrative* 1923. Milford, o.p.

WILLIAMS, E. *Capitalism and slavery* 1945. O.U.P., o.p.; 1964. Deutsch, 30s.; paperback 15s.

INGRAM, J K. *A history of slavery and serfdom* 1895. A. & C. Black, o.p.

## The Bluestockings

SCOTT, W. *The Bluestocking ladies* 1947. J. Green, o.p.

WADE, J. *Women, past and present* London, 1859. o.p.

## Eighteenth-century furniture and décor

Victoria & Albert Museum
Geffrye Museum, Kingsland Road, London, E2
Sir John Soane Museum, 13 Lincoln's Inn Fields, London, WC 2

## Costume

Museum of Costume, Assembly Rooms, Bath
Victoria & Albert Museum
London Museum, Kensington Palace, London W 8

## Medical implements

Wellcome Museum, Euston Road, London, NW 1

## Toys

Birmingham Museum and Art Gallery
Museum of Childhood, Hyndford's Close, 34 High Street, Edinburgh

## Sport

Marylebone Cricket Club, Lord's Ground, St John's Wood, London, NW 8

## Embroidery

Victoria & Albert Museum

## MUSEUMS

The following museums have interesting exhibits of eighteenth-century life.
These are grouped under subject headings.

### Carts, carriages and agriculture

(Mainly nineteenth century, but some eighteenth century)
Bicton Countryside Museum, East Budleigh, Devon
Science Museum, South Kensington, London, SW 7
Arlington Court Museum, nr. Barnstaple, Devon
Maidstone Museum of Carriages, Mill Street, Maidstone, Kent
The Museum of Staffordshire Life, Shugborough, Great Haywood, Stafford
Reading Museum of Rural Life, White Knights Park, Reading

### Everyday objects, china and glass

Birmingham Museum and Art Gallery (including Pinto Collection), Congreve Street, Birmingham
Victoria & Albert Museum, South Kensington, London, SW7

## HOUSES

The following National Trust properties are of particular interest for their eighteenth-century architecture, furnishings and *objets d'art*.

BUSCOT *Berkshire*
(Between Lechlade and Faringdon on A417)

An eighteen-century house in the Adam style containing the Faringdon collection of paintings – including some Rembrandts – and fine furniture. In the 55-acre park are delightful water gardens. The National Trust also owns most of Buscot village.

CLAYDON HOUSE *Buckinghamshire*
(In Middle Clayton, 13m NW of Aylesbury)

Claydon House contains probably the most celebrated rococo suite of rooms in the country and the Saloon, great staircase and Chinese room are outstanding. Florence Nightingale used to stay at Claydon: her bedroom is on view.

CLANDON PARK *Surrey*

One of the most outstanding Palladian houses in the country currently being restored by the Trust to its original magnificence before being opened to the public. The house dates from 1735 and will contain the important furniture, paintings and porcelain known as the Gubbay Collection, as well as other contemporary furniture.

WEST WYCOMBE PARK *Buckinghamshire*
(At the W end of West Wycombe, S of A40)

During the eighteenth century the house was rebuilt in the Palladian style when the double colonnades and porticos were added and the grounds laid out with temples and an artificial lake. The Trust also owns most of West Wycombe village.

OSTERLEY PARK *Middlesex*
(Just N of Osterley station between A4 and M4)

Originally Elizabethan, the house was remodelled by Robert Adam in the eighteenth century – his hand can be seen in the imposing portico, the furniture made for the house and even down to details such as the doorhandles. The stables in the grounds are Elizabethan.

HATCHLANDS *Surrey*
(Just E of East Clandon, N of A426)

A red brick eighteenth-century house in a large park. Part of the interior was decorated in 1759 by Robert Adam – his first commission.

ICKWORTH *Suffolk*
(3m SW of Bury St Edmunds on W side of A143)

One of the country's most individual houses: a lofty rotunda forms the central portion from which curved flanking corridors form the wings. The builder was the eccentric Earl of Bristol, Bishop of Derry, who did not live to see the house completed (building continued from 1794 to 1830). The contents include late Regency and eighteenth-century French furniture, a magnificent collection of silver, and family portraits by Reynolds, Gainsborough, Angelica Kauffmann and other famous artists. Ickworth stands in a setting of magnificent beeches, cypresses and cedars.

BERRINGTON HALL *Herefordshire*
(3m N of Leominster on W side of A49)

Built about 1780 by Henry Holland, the house has hardly been altered at all. There are beautifully decorated ceilings and interesting battle paintings of Admiral Rodney's naval engagements. The grounds were laid out by 'Capability' Brown with fine trees. Beyond the park are panoramic views over the Welsh hills.

WALLINGTON *Northumberland*
(At Cambo, 12m W of Morpeth, B6342)

Built on the site of earlier houses (the cellars are medieval) in 1688, the interior was greatly altered in the eighteenth century when rococo plasterwork was introduced. The Saloon is one of the most beautiful rooms in the North of England. Fine portraits, porcelain, needlework and furniture. The conservatory in the walled garden contains magnificent fuchsias.

BENINGBOROUGH HALL
(8m NW of York, 3m W of Shipton A19)

Dating from about 1716, this important house stands in a wooded park. There is some excellent wood carving in the house, notably on the staircase and in the Drawing Room, Saloon and State Bedroom.

# INDEX

Adam, Robert 20, 22, 46–7, 72, 73–9, 83
Addison, Joseph 21, 55
Agriculture (and agricultural improvements) 11–12, 35–6, 93, 179
American Colonies 63, 69
American Revolution 11
Armorial Bearings 168
Art (amateur) 59, 76, 114
Australia 69–70

Balloons 48–9
Bickersteth 86
Bishop Butler 29, 194
Blackstone, William 17, 193
Blake, William 11, 76, 186, 199, 206
Bleeding 31, 117
Bluestockings 54, 112, 149–50, 181, 197
Boarding Schools (girls) 128, (boys) 133
Boodles 24, 85, 200
Books 59, (of voyages) 69, 72, 126
Boulton, Matthew 74, 79
Breakfast 34–5
Buckinghamshire, Duchess of 28, 83
Bull-baiting 103
Burney, Fanny (Madame d'Arblay) 84, 148, 150, 176–8, 187, 193, 206

Canals 79, 94, 100–1, 179, 201
Candles 80, 82–3
Card-playing 24, 84–9
Carter, Thomas 16, 75
Catherine, Lady 15, 106
Chamber-pots 53, 57
Charity Schools 135–7
Chatham, Lord and Lady, 48, 202
Chevalier d'Eon 84
Child-birth, children, and attitudes towards 25, 119–22, 163
Child-labour 38–9, 80–2
Chimney-sweepers 82
Chinese (style) 115
Chippendale, Thomas 74, 77, 83, 89

Church of England 27–9, 43, 135
Classics 133
Clergy 27–9, 43, 86
Clubs (London) 24, 84–5, 200
Coaches (waggons, etc) 94–100
Coal 80–2
Cock-fighting 103
Coleridge, Rev. John (and family, including Samuel Taylor Coleridge, the poet) 30, 97, 194 200
Communications (and community) 98
Companies and colonies 68–70
Company – and attitudes towards 23, 46, 183
Congor Dust 197
Continental Cookery 50
Continental visitors (their observations on English manners and customs) 34–5, 48–50, 52–3, 63–6, 134–5
Cook, Captain 69–70
Cosmetic poisoning 111
Cottages 37, 83, 100, 195
County Families 23, 46–8, 85, 153
Cowper, William 198–9, 204
Crabbe, George 38–9, 195–6
Cricket 104

Damp 79
Debts 174–5
Defoe, Daniel 55, 112
Delaney, Mrs 158–9, 205
Dinner 48–54
Dinner-table conversation 53–4
Docks 178, 189

Education (and television) 8, (of peasants) 56, (of servants) 56, 123–44, (of girls) 128–31, 146, 159, (of boys) 133–5, 137–43, 183, 204
Elections 64–7
Embroidery 146, 162
Enclosures 12, 37, (of Saltram park) 14
English view on continentals 50
Enlightenment, The 75, 107–8
Exploration 69–70

Fashion 85–9, 108–112
Fielding, Henry 40, 148
Food 43–4, 49–51, (of the poor) 56, 196–7
Foppishness 30, 54
Fox-hunting 101–3
Franking (letters) 67
French Revolution 11, 179, 190–2
Funerals 170, 175–6

Gambling 84–9, 103–5
Games 156–7
Game Laws 41
Gardens and gardening 61–3, 198
George III 54, 63–4, 158, 164, 168, 176–8
Georgiana, Duchess of Devonshire 9, 13, 46, 53, 85, 86, 107, 150–1, 206
Glasse, Mrs Hannah 43, 50–1, 196
Grand Tour 22, 139, 141–3

Hair Styles 85, 109–10
Hanging 41
Heppelwhite 77
Highwaymen 96
Holidays (of the children at Saltram) 131–3
Horses 53, 90–105 (pack-horses) 99–100, 169
Horse-Racing 104–5, 169
Humphrey Clinker 56, 79, 197
Hunting 101–3, 132
Hunting Parsons 28, 194

Illness 31, 117–9, 147, 152, 169
Improvements 188–90
Inheritance 17–20
Inns 96
Inoculation 32
Invasion scare 190

Jenner, Dr 33
Johnson, Dr 20, 71, 77, 101, 117, 193

Kauffmann, Angelica 49, 75
Kettle, Henry 74, 79

Land-ownership 36–7
Law, William (Theologian) 27, 194

215

Letters Patent 168
Lotteries 84

Macaroni (style) 86, 148
Magistrates 40
Mahogany 77
Manners 50, 134
Mansfield, Lord 71, 84
Manufacturers 39, 179
Marriage (arrangements, settlements, attitudes towards, etc) 13–4, 16–9, 150, 159–62, (clandestine and irregular) 159, (forced) 160, (Public Marriage Act) 161, 174
Mechanization (machine age) 179
Medicine 31–4, 117–9, (for horses) 93
Menus 43–4, 48–9, 51
Methodism 28
Mines and miners 39, 80–2, 185, 199
Montagu, Mrs Elizabeth 81–2, 95, 129, 150, 158
Montagu, Lady Mary Wortley 33, 54, 129, 150, 195
Montague Parker 23, 87, 89, 155
More, Hannah 54, 56, 129, 150, 184–5, 202, 205
Morley, Earl of (present) 8, (1st) 188
Music 145–7, 204

Napoleon 11, 192
Newspapers 34, 43, 55, 59, 136, 147
New Zealand 69–70
Nollekens, Joseph 62, 76

Parish Workhouse 38
Peerage 168
Physicians 31–4, 117–22, 147, 152
Pitt, William 77, 154–5
Pleasure Gardens (Vauxhall, Ranelagh) 21, 24
Politics and Parliament 20, 24, 40, 63–8, 154–5, 173
Poor, The (paupers, beggars, vagrants, etc) 12, 36–9, (education of) 135–7

Poor Law Commission 38
Pope, Alexander 54, 71
Porcelain 114
Post Office 67, 98
Preparatory School 127
Prescriptions 33
Prize-fighting 103–4
Property 17, 36–7
Public Marriage Act 161
Public Penance 160
Punishments 40–2, 196

Queen Charlotte 79, 109, 158, 164, 176–8

Religion 27–9
Reynolds, Sir Joshua 9, 13, 20, 22, 59–61, 76, 77, 87, 102–3, 114, 137, 158, 184, 186
Rioting 40
Roads 94–100
Robbery 172–3
Romantic Movement 108
Royal Academy 59, 76, 168
Royal Mail 98
Royal Marriage Bill 24
Royal Society 69
Royal Society of Arts 20, 77, 188
Rushlights 82–3

Sanitation 29, 53, 115–7
Scots clergyman (Rev. Wm. MacRitchie) 21, 94, 194, 200
Sculpture 62
Sea-bathing 151–2
Servants 44–6, 54–8 (Rules and Directions for) 57
Shelburne, Lord 20, 22, 133
Sheraton 77
Sheridan, Richard Brinsley 129
Sheridan, Thomas 124, 203
Shopping 164–5
Siddons, Mrs 187–8
Slavery 70–2, 198–9
Smallpox 31–2
Smith, Adam 59, 68, 198
Smollett 56, 79, 148, 197
Smuggling 67
Social Classes 17
Spa-towns 89

Spectator, The 46, 85, 112
Spillikins 156–8
Spinsters 162–4
Stables 90–3
Sterne, Laurence 33, 53, 59, 148, 195
Swift, Jonathan 57, 158

Tea 55, 165–6
Teeth and toothache 33
Trade Unions 40, 179, 196
Transport 93–101
Transportation (as punishment) 40
Trees (planting and felling) 61, 167, 173
Truckamucks 99

Undergraduates 138–9
Universities 137, (examinations) 139

Vaccination 33
Victorian Reformers 182

Wages (children's) 39, (servants) 55, 166, (blanket-weavers, embroiderers) 83, (grooms) 93
Walpole, Horace 20, 56, 71, 77, 111, 148
Watts, Isaac 135
Weavers 40
Wedgwood, Josiah 71, 79
Wesley, John 28, 71, 81, 89
Wife-selling 160
Wigs 30, 108–110
Wilkes, John 54, 63, 147
Wine 51, 68, (prices of) 52
Witty, Thomas 75
Woodforde, Parson 43, 49, 68, 194, 200, 205
Wordsworth, William 186, 206

Young, Arthur 36, 55, 81, 94, 197, 200
Youth 54

Zucchi, Antonio 75, 76, 83